The Practice of Programming

Addison-Wesley Professional Computing Series

Brian W. Kernighan, Consulting Editor

Matthew H. Austern, *Generic Programming and the STL: Using and Extending the C++ Standard Template Library*

David R. Butenhof, *Programming with POSIX® Threads*

Brent Callaghan, *NFS Illustrated*

Tom Cargill, *C++ Programming Style*

William R. Cheswick/Steven M. Bellovin/Aviel D. Rubin, *Firewalls and Internet Security, Second Edition: Repelling the Wily Hacker*

David A. Curry, *UNIX® System Security: A Guide for Users and System Administrators*

Stephen C. Dewhurst, *C++ Gotchas: Avoiding Common Problems in Coding and Design*

Dan Farmer/Wietse Venema, *Forensic Discovery*

Erich Gamma/Richard Helm/Ralph Johnson/John Vlissides, *Design Patterns: Elements of Reusable Object-Oriented Software*

Erich Gamma/Richard Helm/Ralph Johnson/John Vlissides, *Design Patterns CD: Elements of Reusable Object-Oriented Software*

Peter Haggar, *Practical Java™ Programming Language Guide*

David R. Hanson, *C Interfaces and Implementations: Techniques for Creating Reusable Software*

Mark Harrison/Michael McLennan, *Effective Tcl/Tk Programming: Writing Better Programs with Tcl and Tk*

Michi Henning/Steve Vinoski, *Advanced CORBA® Programming with C++*

Brian W. Kernighan/Rob Pike, *The Practice of Programming*

S. Keshav, *An Engineering Approach to Computer Networking: ATM Networks, the Internet, and the Telephone Network*

John Lakos, *Large-Scale C++ Software Design*

Scott Meyers, *Effective C++ CD: 85 Specific Ways to Improve Your Programs and Designs*

Scott Meyers, *Effective C++, Third Edition: 55 Specific Ways to Improve Your Programs and Designs*

Scott Meyers, *More Effective C++: 35 New Ways to Improve Your Programs and Designs*

Scott Meyers, *Effective STL: 50 Specific Ways to Improve Your Use of the Standard Template Library*

Robert B. Murray, *C++ Strategies and Tactics*

David R. Musser/Gillmer J. Derge/Atul Saini, *STL Tutorial and Reference Guide, Second Edition: C++ Programming with the Standard Template Library*

John K. Ousterhout, *Tcl and the Tk Toolkit*

Craig Partridge, *Gigabit Networking*

Radia Perlman, *Interconnections, Second Edition: Bridges, Routers, Switches, and Internetworking Protocols*

Stephen A. Rago, *UNIX® System V Network Programming*

Eric S. Raymond, *The Art of UNIX Programming*

Marc J. Rochkind, *Advanced UNIX Programming, Second Edition*

Curt Schimmel, *UNIX® Systems for Modern Architectures: Symmetric Multiprocessing and Caching for Kernel Programmers*

W. Richard Stevens, *TCP/IP Illustrated, Volume 1: The Protocols*

W. Richard Stevens, *TCP/IP Illustrated, Volume 3: TCP for Transactions, HTTP, NNTP, and the UNIX® Domain Protocols*

W. Richard Stevens/Bill Fenner/Andrew M. Rudoff, *UNIX Network Programming Volume 1, Third Edition: The Sockets Networking API*

W. Richard Stevens/Stephen A. Rago, *Advanced Programming in the UNIX® Environment, Second Edition*

W. Richard Stevens/Gary R. Wright, *TCP/IP Illustrated Volumes 1-3 Boxed Set*

John Viega/Gary McGraw, *Building Secure Software: How to Avoid Security Problems the Right Way*

Gary R. Wright/W. Richard Stevens, *TCP/IP Illustrated, Volume 2: The Implementation*

Ruixi Yuan/W. Timothy Strayer, *Virtual Private Networks: Technologies and Solutions*

Visit www.awprofessional.com/series/professionalcomputing for more information about these titles.

The Practice of Programming

Brian W. Kernighan
Rob Pike

ADDISON–WESLEY

Boston • San Francisco • New York • Toronto • Montreal
London • Munich • Paris • Madrid
Capetown • Sydney • Tokyo • Singapore • Mexico City

The publisher offers discounts on this book when ordered in quantity for special sales. For more information, please contact:

Pearson Education Corporate Sales Division
201 W. 103rd Street
Indianapolis, IN 46290
(800) 428-5331
corpsales@pearsoned.com

Visit AW on the Web: www.awprofessional.com

This book was typeset (grap|pic|tbl|eqn|troff - mpm) in Times and Lucida Sans Typewriter by the authors.

Library of Congress Cataloging-in-Publication Data

Kernighan, Brian W.
    The practice of programming / Brian W. Kernighan, Rob Pike.
    p. cm. --(Addison-Wesley professional computing series)
  Includes bibliographical references.
  ISBN 0-201-61586-X
  1. Computer programming. I. Pike, Rob. II. Title. III. Series.
  QA76.6 .K48 1999
  005.1--dc21   99-10131
                                                              CIP

ISBN 0-201-61586-X

Text printed in the United States at RR Donnelley Harrisonburg in Harrisonburg, Virginia.

18th Printing   June 2009

Contents

Preface

Have you ever...

> wasted a lot of time coding the wrong algorithm?
> used a data structure that was much too complicated?
> tested a program but missed an obvious problem?
> spent a day looking for a bug you should have found in five minutes?
> needed to make a program run three times faster and use less memory?
> struggled to move a program from a workstation to a PC or vice versa?
> tried to make a modest change in someone else's program?
> rewritten a program because you couldn't understand it?

Was it fun?

These things happen to programmers all the time. But dealing with such problems is often harder than it should be because topics like testing, debugging, portability, performance, design alternatives, and style—the *practice* of programming—are not usually the focus of computer science or programming courses. Most programmers learn them haphazardly as their experience grows, and a few never learn them at all.

In a world of enormous and intricate interfaces, constantly changing tools and languages and systems, and relentless pressure for more of everything, one can lose sight of the basic principles—simplicity, clarity, generality—that form the bedrock of good software. One can also overlook the value of tools and notations that mechanize some of software creation and thus enlist the computer in its own programming.

Our approach in this book is based on these underlying, interrelated principles, which apply at all levels of computing. These include *simplicity*, which keeps programs short and manageable; *clarity*, which makes sure they are easy to understand, for people as well as machines; *generality*, which means they work well in a broad range of situations and adapt well as new situations arise; and *automation*, which lets the machine do the work for us, freeing us from mundane tasks. By looking at computer programming in a variety of languages, from algorithms and data structures through design, debugging, testing, and performance improvement, we can illustrate universal engineering concepts that are independent of language, operating system, or programming paradigm.

This book comes from many years of experience writing and maintaining a lot of software, teaching programming courses, and working with a wide variety of programmers. We want to share lessons about practical issues, to pass on insights from our experience, and to suggest ways for programmers of all levels to be more proficient and productive.

We are writing for several kinds of readers. If you are a student who has taken a programming course or two and would like to be a better programmer, this book will expand on some of the topics for which there wasn't enough time in school. If you write programs as part of your work, but in support of other activities rather than as the goal in itself, the information will help you to program more effectively. If you are a professional programmer who didn't get enough exposure to such topics in school or who would like a refresher, or if you are a software manager who wants to guide your staff in the right direction, the material here should be of value.

We hope that the advice will help you to write better programs. The only prerequisite is that you have done some programming, preferably in C, C++ or Java. Of course the more experience you have, the easier it will be; nothing can take you from neophyte to expert in 21 days. Unix and Linux programmers will find some of the examples more familiar than will those who have used only Windows and Macintosh systems, but programmers from any environment should discover things to make their lives easier.

The presentation is organized into nine chapters, each focusing on one major aspect of programming practice.

Chapter 1 discusses programming style. Good style is so important to good programming that we have chosen to cover it first. Well-written programs are better than badly-written ones—they have fewer errors and are easier to debug and to modify—so it is important to think about style from the beginning. This chapter also introduces an important theme in good programming, the use of idioms appropriate to the language being used.

Algorithms and data structures, the topics of Chapter 2, are the core of the computer science curriculum and a major part of programming courses. Since most readers will already be familiar with this material, our treatment is intended as a brief review of the handful of algorithms and data structures that show up in almost every program. More complex algorithms and data structures usually evolve from these building blocks, so one should master the basics.

Chapter 3 describes the design and implementation of a small program that illustrates algorithm and data structure issues in a realistic setting. The program is implemented in five languages; comparing the versions shows how the same data structures are handled in each, and how expressiveness and performance vary across a spectrum of languages.

Interfaces between users, programs, and parts of programs are fundamental in programming and much of the success of software is determined by how well interfaces are designed and implemented. Chapter 4 shows the evolution of a small library for parsing a widely used data format. Even though the example is small, it illustrates many of the concerns of interface design: abstraction, information hiding, resource management, and error handling.

Much as we try to write programs correctly the first time, bugs, and therefore debugging, are inevitable. Chapter 5 gives strategies and tactics for systematic and effective debugging. Among the topics are the signatures of common bugs and the importance of ''numerology,'' where patterns in debugging output often indicate where a problem lies.

Testing is an attempt to develop a reasonable assurance that a program is working correctly and that it stays correct as it evolves. The emphasis in Chapter 6 is on systematic testing by hand and machine. Boundary condition tests probe at potential weak spots. Mechanization and test scaffolds make it easy to do extensive testing with modest effort. Stress tests provide a different kind of testing than typical users do and ferret out a different class of bugs.

Computers are so fast and compilers are so good that many programs are fast enough the day they are written. But others are too slow, or they use too much memory, or both. Chapter 7 presents an orderly way to approach the task of making a program use resources efficiently, so that the program remains correct and sound as it is made more efficient.

Chapter 8 covers portability. Successful programs live long enough that their environment changes, or they must be moved to new systems or new hardware or new countries. The goal of portability is to reduce the maintenance of a program by minimizing the amount of change necessary to adapt it to a new environment.

Computing is rich in languages, not just the general-purpose ones that we use for the bulk of programming, but also many specialized languages that focus on narrow domains. Chapter 9 presents several examples of the importance of notation in computing, and shows how we can use it to simplify programs, to guide implementations, and even to help us write programs that write programs.

To talk about programming, we have to show a lot of code. Most of the examples were written expressly for the book, although some small ones were adapted from other sources. We've tried hard to write our own code well, and have tested it on half a dozen systems directly from the machine-readable text. More information is available at the web site for *The Practice of Programming*:

```
http://tpop.awl.com
```

The majority of the programs are in C, with a number of examples in C++ and Java and some brief excursions into scripting languages. At the lowest level, C and C++ are almost identical and our C programs are valid C++ programs as well. C++ and Java are lineal descendants of C, sharing more than a little of its syntax and much of its efficiency and expressiveness, while adding richer type systems and libraries.

In our own work, we routinely use all three of these languages, and many others. The choice of language depends on the problem: operating systems are best written in an efficient and unrestrictive language like C or C++; quick prototypes are often easiest in a command interpreter or a scripting language like Awk or Perl; for user interfaces, Visual Basic and Tcl/Tk are strong contenders, along with Java.

There is an important pedagogical issue in choosing a language for our examples. Just as no language solves all problems equally well, no single language is best for presenting all topics. Higher-level languages preempt some design decisions. If we use a lower-level language, we get to consider alternative answers to the questions; by exposing more of the details, we can talk about them better. Experience shows that even when we use the facilities of high-level languages, it's invaluable to know how they relate to lower-level issues; without that insight, it's easy to run into performance problems and mysterious behavior. So we will often use C for our examples, even though in practice we might choose something else.

For the most part, however, the lessons are independent of any particular programming language. The choice of data structure is affected by the language at hand; there may be few options in some languages while others might support a variety of alternatives. But the way to approach making the choice will be the same. The details of how to test and debug are different in different languages, but strategies and tactics are similar in all. Most of the techniques for making a program efficient can be applied in any language.

Whatever language you write in, your task as a programmer is to do the best you can with the tools at hand. A good programmer can overcome a poor language or a clumsy operating system, but even a great programming environment will not rescue a bad programmer. We hope that, no matter what your current experience and skill, this book will help you to program better and enjoy it more.

We are deeply grateful to friends and colleagues who read drafts of the manuscript and gave us many helpful comments. Jon Bentley, Russ Cox, John Lakos, John Linderman, Peter Memishian, Ian Lance Taylor, Howard Trickey, and Chris Van Wyk read the manuscript, some more than once, with exceptional care and thoroughness. We are indebted to Tom Cargill, Chris Cleeland, Steve Dewhurst, Eric Grosse, Andrew Herron, Gerard Holzmann, Doug McIlroy, Paul McNamee, Peter Nelson, Dennis Ritchie, Rich Stevens, Tom Szymanski, Kentaro Toyama, John Wait, Daniel C. Wang, Peter Weinberger, Margaret Wright, and Cliff Young for invaluable comments on drafts at various stages. We also appreciate good advice and thoughtful suggestions from Al Aho, Ken Arnold, Chuck Bigelow, Joshua Bloch, Bill Coughran, Bob Flandrena, Renée French, Mark Kernighan, Andy Koenig, Sape Mullender, Evi Nemeth, Marty Rabinowitz, Mark V. Shaney, Bjarne Stroustrup, Ken Thompson, and Phil Wadler. Thank you all.

Brian W. Kernighan

Rob Pike

Style

It is an old observation that the best writers sometimes disregard the rules of rhetoric. When they do so, however, the reader will usually find in the sentence some compensating merit, attained at the cost of the violation. Unless he is certain of doing as well, he will probably do best to follow the rules.

William Strunk and E. B. White, *The Elements of Style*

This fragment of code comes from a large program written many years ago:

```
if ( (country == SING) || (country == BRNI) ||
     (country == POL) || (country == ITALY) )
{
    /*
     * If the country is Singapore, Brunei or Poland
     * then the current time is the answer time
     * rather than the off hook time.
     * Reset answer time and set day of week.
     */
    ...
```

It's carefully written, formatted, and commented, and the program it comes from works extremely well; the programmers who created this system are rightly proud of what they built. But this excerpt is puzzling to the casual reader. What relationship links Singapore, Brunei, Poland and Italy? Why isn't Italy mentioned in the comment? Since the comment and the code differ, one of them must be wrong. Maybe both are. The code is what gets executed and tested, so it's more likely to be right; probably the comment didn't get updated when the code did. The comment doesn't say enough about the relationship among the three countries it does mention; if you had to maintain this code, you would need to know more.

The few lines above are typical of much real code: mostly well done, but with some things that could be improved.

This book is about the practice of programming—how to write programs for real. Our purpose is to help you to write software that works at least as well as the program this example was taken from, while avoiding trouble spots and weaknesses. We will talk about writing better code from the beginning and improving it as it evolves.

We are going to start in an unusual place, however, by discussing programming style. The purpose of style is to make the code easy to read for yourself and others, and good style is crucial to good programming. We want to talk about it first so you will be sensitive to it as you read the code in the rest of the book.

There is more to writing a program than getting the syntax right, fixing the bugs, and making it run fast enough. Programs are read not only by computers but also by programmers. A well-written program is easier to understand and to modify than a poorly-written one. The discipline of writing well leads to code that is more likely to be correct. Fortunately, this discipline is not hard.

The principles of programming style are based on common sense guided by experience, not on arbitrary rules and prescriptions. Code should be clear and simple—straightforward logic, natural expression, conventional language use, meaningful names, neat formatting, helpful comments—and it should avoid clever tricks and unusual constructions. Consistency is important because others will find it easier to read your code, and you theirs, if you all stick to the same style. Details may be imposed by local conventions, management edict, or a program, but even if not, it is best to obey a set of widely shared conventions. We follow the style used in the book *The C Programming Language*, with minor adjustments for C++ and Java.

We will often illustrate rules of style by small examples of bad and good programming, since the contrast between two ways of saying the same thing is instructive. These examples are not artificial. The ''bad'' ones are all adapted from real code, written by ordinary programmers (occasionally ourselves) working under the common pressures of too much work and too little time. Some will be distilled for brevity, but they will not be misrepresented. Then we will rewrite the bad excerpts to show how they could be improved. Since they are real code, however, they may exhibit multiple problems. Addressing every shortcoming would take us too far off topic, so some of the good examples will still harbor other, unremarked flaws.

To distinguish bad examples from good, throughout the book we will place question marks in the margins of questionable code, as in this real excerpt:

```
?       #define ONE 1
?       #define TEN 10
?       #define TWENTY 20
```

Why are these #defines questionable? Consider the modifications that will be necessary if an array of TWENTY elements must be made larger. At the very least, each name should be replaced by one that indicates the role of the specific value in the program:

```
#define INPUT_MODE 1
#define INPUT_BUFSIZE 10
#define OUTPUT_BUFSIZE 20
```

1.1 Names

What's in a name? A variable or function name labels an object and conveys information about its purpose. A name should be informative, concise, memorable, and pronounceable if possible. Much information comes from context and scope; the broader the scope of a variable, the more information should be conveyed by its name.

Use descriptive names for globals, short names for locals. Global variables, by definition, can crop up anywhere in a program, so they need names long enough and descriptive enough to remind the reader of their meaning. It's also helpful to include a brief comment with the declaration of each global:

```
int npending = 0;  // current length of input queue
```

Global functions, classes, and structures should also have descriptive names that suggest their role in a program.

By contrast, shorter names suffice for local variables; within a function, n may be sufficient, npoints is fine, and numberOfPoints is overkill.

Local variables used in conventional ways can have very short names. The use of i and j for loop indices, p and q for pointers, and s and t for strings is so frequent that there is little profit and perhaps some loss in longer names. Compare

```
?       for (theElementIndex = 0; theElementIndex < numberOfElements;
?               theElementIndex++)
?           elementArray[theElementIndex] = theElementIndex;
```

to

```
        for (i = 0; i < nelems; i++)
            elem[i] = i;
```

Programmers are often encouraged to use long variable names regardless of context. That is a mistake: clarity is often achieved through brevity.

There are many naming conventions and local customs. Common ones include using names that begin or end with p, such as nodep, for pointers; initial capital letters for Globals; and all capitals for CONSTANTS. Some programming shops use more sweeping rules, such as notation to encode type and usage information in the variable, perhaps pch to mean a pointer to a character and strTo and strFrom to mean strings that will be written to and read from. As for the spelling of the names themselves, whether to use npending or numPending or num_pending is a matter of taste; specific rules are much less important than consistent adherence to a sensible convention.

Naming conventions make it easier to understand your own code, as well as code written by others. They also make it easier to invent new names as the code is being written. The longer the program, the more important is the choice of good, descriptive, systematic names.

Namespaces in C++ and packages in Java provide ways to manage the scope of names and help to keep meanings clear without unduly long names.

Be consistent. Give related things related names that show their relationship and high-light their difference.

Besides being much too long, the member names in this Java class are wildly inconsistent:

```
?        class UserQueue {
?             int noOfItemsInQ, frontOfTheQueue, queueCapacity;
?             public int noOfUsersInQueue() {...}
?        }
```

The word "queue" appears as Q, Queue and queue. But since queues can only be accessed from a variable of type UserQueue, member names do not need to mention "queue" at all; context suffices, so

```
?        queue.queueCapacity
```

is redundant. This version is better:

```
        class UserQueue {
             int nitems, front, capacity;
             public int nusers() {...}
        }
```

since it leads to statements like

```
        queue.capacity++;
        n = queue.nusers();
```

No clarity is lost. This example still needs work, however: "items" and "users" are the same thing, so only one term should be used for a single concept.

Use active names for functions. Function names should be based on active verbs, perhaps followed by nouns:

```
        now = date.getTime();
        putchar('\n');
```

Functions that return a boolean (true or false) value should be named so that the return value is unambiguous. Thus

```
?        if (checkoctal(c)) ...
```

does not indicate which value is true and which is false, while

```
        if (isoctal(c)) ...
```

makes it clear that the function returns true if the argument is octal and false if not.

Be accurate. A name not only labels, it conveys information to the reader. A mis-leading name can result in mystifying bugs.

One of us wrote and distributed for years a macro called isoctal with this incor-rect implementation:

```
?       #define isoctal(c) ((c) >= '0' && (c) <= '8')
```

instead of the proper

```
#define isoctal(c) ((c) >= '0' && (c) <= '7')
```

In this case, the name conveyed the correct intent but the implementation was wrong; it's easy for a sensible name to disguise a broken implementation.

Here's an example in which the name and the code are in complete contradiction:

```
?       public boolean inTable(Object obj) {
?           int j = this.getIndex(obj);
?           return (j == nTable);
?       }
```

The function getIndex returns a value between zero and nTable-1 if it finds the object, and returns nTable if not. The boolean value returned by inTable is thus the opposite of what the name implies. At the time the code is written, this might not cause trouble, but if the program is modified later, perhaps by a different programmer, the name is sure to confuse.

Exercise 1-1. Comment on the choice of names and values in the following code.

```
?       #define TRUE 0
?       #define FALSE 1
?
?       if ((ch = getchar()) == EOF)
?           not_eof = FALSE;
```

□

Exercise 1-2. Improve this function:

```
?       int smaller(char *s, char *t) {
?           if (strcmp(s, t) < 1)
?               return 1;
?           else
?               return 0;
?       }
```

□

Exercise 1-3. Read this code aloud:

```
?       if ((falloc(SMRHSHSCRTCH, S_IFEXT|0644, MAXRODDHSH)) < 0)
?           ...
```

□

1.2 Expressions and Statements

By analogy with choosing names to aid the reader's understanding, write expressions and statements in a way that makes their meaning as transparent as possible. Write the clearest code that does the job. Use spaces around operators to suggest grouping; more generally, format to help readability. This is trivial but valuable, like keeping a neat desk so you can find things. Unlike your desk, your programs are likely to be examined by others.

Indent to show structure. A consistent indentation style is the lowest-energy way to make a program's structure self-evident. This example is badly formatted:

```
?       for(n++;n<100;field[n++]='\0');
?       *i = '\0'; return('\n');
```

Reformatting improves it somewhat:

```
?       for (n++; n < 100; field[n++] = '\0')
?           ;
?       *i = '\0';
?       return('\n');
```

Even better is to put the assignment in the body and separate the increment, so the loop takes a more conventional form and is thus easier to grasp:

```
    for (n++; n < 100; n++)
        field[n] = '\0';
    *i = '\0';
    return '\n';
```

Use the natural form for expressions. Write expressions as you might speak them aloud. Conditional expressions that include negations are always hard to understand:

```
?       if (!(block_id < actblks) || !(block_id >= unblocks))
?           ...
```

Each test is stated negatively, though there is no need for either to be. Turning the relations around lets us state the tests positively:

```
    if ((block_id >= actblks) || (block_id < unblocks))
        ...
```

Now the code reads naturally.

Parenthesize to resolve ambiguity. Parentheses specify grouping and can be used to make the intent clear even when they are not required. The inner parentheses in the previous example are not necessary, but they don't hurt, either. Seasoned programmers might omit them, because the relational operators (< <= == != >= >) have higher precedence than the logical operators (&& and ||).

When mixing unrelated operators, though, it's a good idea to parenthesize. C and its friends present pernicious precedence problems, and it's easy to make a mistake.

Because the logical operators bind tighter than assignment, parentheses are mandatory for most expressions that combine them:

```
    while ((c = getchar()) != EOF)
        ...
```

The bitwise operators & and | have lower precedence than relational operators like ==, so despite its appearance,

```
?       if (x&MASK == BITS)
?           ...
```

actually means

```
?       if (x & (MASK==BITS))
?           ...
```

which is certainly not the programmer's intent. Because it combines bitwise and relational operators, the expression needs parentheses:

```
    if ((x&MASK) == BITS)
        ...
```

Even if parentheses aren't necessary, they can help if the grouping is hard to grasp at first glance. This code doesn't need parentheses:

```
?   leap_year = y % 4 == 0 && y % 100 != 0 || y % 400 == 0;
```

but they make it easier to understand:

```
    leap_year = ((y%4 == 0) && (y%100 != 0)) || (y%400 == 0);
```

We also removed some of the blanks: grouping the operands of higher-precedence operators helps the reader to see the structure more quickly.

Break up complex expressions. C, C++, and Java have rich expression syntax and operators, and it's easy to get carried away by cramming everything into one construction. An expression like the following is compact but it packs too many operations into a single statement:

```
?   *x += (*xp=(2*k < (n-m) ? c[k+1] : d[k--]));
```

It's easier to grasp when broken into several pieces:

```
    if (2*k < n-m)
        *xp = c[k+1];
    else
        *xp = d[k--];
    *x += *xp;
```

Be clear. Programmers' endless creative energy is sometimes used to write the most concise code possible, or to find clever ways to achieve a result. Sometimes these skills are misapplied, though, since the goal is to write clear code, not clever code.

What does this intricate calculation do?

```
?        subkey = subkey >> (bitoff - ((bitoff >> 3) << 3));
```

The innermost expression shifts bitoff three bits to the right. The result is shifted left again, thus replacing the three shifted bits by zeros. This result in turn is subtracted from the original value, yielding the bottom three bits of bitoff. These three bits are used to shift subkey to the right.

Thus the original expression is equivalent to

```
        subkey = subkey >> (bitoff & 0x7);
```

It takes a while to puzzle out what the first version is doing; the second is shorter and clearer. Experienced programmers make it even shorter by using an assignment operator:

```
        subkey >>= bitoff & 0x7;
```

Some constructs seem to invite abuse. The ?: operator can lead to mysterious code:

```
?        child=(!LC&&!RC)?0:(!LC?RC:LC);
```

It's almost impossible to figure out what this does without following all the possible paths through the expression. This form is longer, but much easier to follow because it makes the paths explicit:

```
        if (LC == 0 && RC == 0)
            child = 0;
        else if (LC == 0)
            child = RC;
        else
            child = LC;
```

The ?: operator is fine for short expressions where it can replace four lines of if-else with one, as in

```
        max = (a > b) ? a : b;
```

or perhaps

```
        printf("The list has %d item%s\n", n, n==1 ? "" : "s");
```

but it is not a general replacement for conditional statements.

Clarity is not the same as brevity. Often the clearer code will be shorter, as in the bit-shifting example, but it can also be longer, as in the conditional expression recast as an if-else. The proper criterion is ease of understanding.

Be careful with side effects. Operators like ++ have *side effects*: besides returning a value, they also modify an underlying variable. Side effects can be extremely convenient, but they can also cause trouble because the actions of retrieving the value and updating the variable might not happen at the same time. In C and C++, the order of execution of side effects is undefined, so this multiple assignment is likely to produce the wrong answer:

```
?    str[i++] = str[i++] = ' ';
```

The intent is to store blanks at the next two positions in str. But depending on when i is updated, a position in str could be skipped and i might end up increased only by 1. Break it into two statements:

```
    str[i++] = ' ';
    str[i++] = ' ';
```

Even though it contains only one increment, this assignment can also give varying results:

```
?    array[i++] = i;
```

If i is initially 3, the array element might be set to 3 or 4.

It's not just increments and decrements that have side effects; I/O is another source of behind-the-scenes action. This example is an attempt to read two related numbers from standard input:

```
?    scanf("%d %d", &yr, &profit[yr]);
```

It is broken because part of the expression modifies yr and another part uses it. The value of profit[yr] can never be right unless the new value of yr is the same as the old one. You might think that the answer depends on the order in which the arguments are evaluated, but the real issue is that *all* the arguments to scanf are evaluated before the routine is called, so &profit[yr] will always be evaluated using the old value of yr. This sort of problem can occur in almost any language. The fix is, as usual, to break up the expression:

```
    scanf("%d", &yr);
    scanf("%d", &profit[yr]);
```

Exercise caution in any expression with side effects.

Exercise 1-4. Improve each of these fragments:

```
?    if ( !(c == 'y' || c == 'Y') )
?        return;


?    length = (length < BUFSIZE) ? length : BUFSIZE;


?    flag = flag ? 0 : 1;


?    quote = (*line == '"') ? 1 : 0;
```

```
?      if (val & 1)
?          bit = 1;
?      else
?          bit = 0;
```

□

Exercise 1-5. What is wrong with this excerpt?

```
?      int read(int *ip) {
?          scanf("%d", ip);
?          return *ip;
?      }
?          ...
?      insert(&graph[vert], read(&val), read(&ch));
```

□

Exercise 1-6. List all the different outputs this could produce with various orders of evaluation:

```
?      n = 1;
?      printf("%d %d\n", n++, n++);
```

Try it on as many compilers as you can, to see what happens in practice. □

1.3 Consistency and Idioms

Consistency leads to better programs. If formatting varies unpredictably, or a loop over an array runs uphill this time and downhill the next, or strings are copied with strcpy here and a for loop there, the variations make it harder to see what's really going on. But if the same computation is done the same way every time it appears, any variation suggests a genuine difference, one worth noting.

Use a consistent indentation and brace style. Indentation shows structure, but which indentation style is best? Should the opening brace go on the same line as the if or on the next? Programmers have always argued about the layout of programs, but the specific style is much less important than its consistent application. Pick one style, preferably ours, use it consistently, and don't waste time arguing.

Should you include braces even when they are not needed? Like parentheses, braces can resolve ambiguity and occasionally make the code clearer. For consistency, many experienced programmers always put braces around loop or if bodies. But if the body is a single statement they are unnecessary, so we tend to omit them. If you also choose to leave them out, make sure you don't drop them when they are needed to resolve the "dangling else" ambiguity exemplified by this excerpt:

```
?      if (month == FEB) {
?          if (year%4 == 0)
?              if (day > 29)
?                  legal = FALSE;
?          else
?              if (day > 28)
?                  legal = FALSE;
?      }
```

The indentation is misleading, since the else is actually attached to the line

```
?                  if (day > 29)
```

and the code is wrong. When one if immediately follows another, always use braces:

```
?      if (month == FEB) {
?          if (year%4 == 0) {
?              if (day > 29)
?                  legal = FALSE;
?          } else {
?              if (day > 28)
?                  legal = FALSE;
?          }
?      }
```

Syntax-driven editing tools make this sort of mistake less likely.

Even with the bug fixed, though, the code is hard to follow. The computation is easier to grasp if we use a variable to hold the number of days in February:

```
?      if (month == FEB) {
?          int nday;
?
?          nday = 28;
?          if (year%4 == 0)
?              nday = 29;
?          if (day > nday)
?              legal = FALSE;
?      }
```

The code is still wrong—2000 is a leap year, while 1900 and 2100 are not—but this structure is much easier to adapt to make it absolutely right.

By the way, if you work on a program you didn't write, preserve the style you find there. When you make a change, don't use your own style even though you prefer it. The program's consistency is more important than your own, because it makes life easier for those who follow.

Use idioms for consistency. Like natural languages, programming languages have idioms, conventional ways that experienced programmers write common pieces of code. A central part of learning any language is developing a familiarity with its idioms.

One of the most common idioms is the form of a loop. Consider the C, C++, or Java code for stepping through the n elements of an array, for example to initialize them. Someone might write the loop like this:

```
?       i = 0;
?       while (i <= n-1)
?           array[i++] = 1.0;
```

or perhaps like this:

```
?       for (i = 0; i < n; )
?           array[i++] = 1.0;
```

or even:

```
?       for (i = n; --i >= 0; )
?           array[i] = 1.0;
```

All of these are correct, but the idiomatic form is like this:

```
        for (i = 0; i < n; i++)
            array[i] = 1.0;
```

This is not an arbitrary choice. It visits each member of an n-element array indexed from 0 to n-1. It places all the loop control in the for itself, runs in increasing order, and uses the very idiomatic ++ operator to update the loop variable. It leaves the index variable at a known value just beyond the last array element. Native speakers recognize it without study and write it correctly without a moment's thought.

In C++ or Java, a common variant includes the declaration of the loop variable:

```
        for (int i = 0; i < n; i++)
            array[i] = 1.0;
```

Here is the standard loop for walking along a list in C:

```
        for (p = list; p != NULL; p = p->next)
            ...
```

Again, all the loop control is in the for.

For an infinite loop, we prefer

```
        for (;;)
            ...
```

but

```
        while (1)
            ...
```

is also popular. Don't use anything other than these forms.

Indentation should be idiomatic, too. This unusual vertical layout detracts from readability; it looks like three statements, not a loop:

```
?      for (
?          ap = arr;
?          ap < arr + 128;
?          *ap++ = 0
?          )
?      {
?          ;
?      }
```

A standard loop is much easier to read:

```
for (ap = arr; ap < arr+128; ap++)
    *ap = 0;
```

Sprawling layouts also force code onto multiple screens or pages, and thus detract from readability.

Another common idiom is to nest an assignment inside a loop condition, as in

```
while ((c = getchar()) != EOF)
    putchar(c);
```

The `do-while` statement is used much less often than `for` and `while`, because it always executes at least once, testing at the bottom of the loop instead of the top. In many cases, that behavior is a bug waiting to bite, as in this rewrite of the `getchar` loop:

```
?      do {
?          c = getchar();
?          putchar(c);
?      } while (c != EOF);
```

It writes a spurious output character because the test occurs after the call to `putchar`. The do-while loop is the right one only when the body of the loop must always be executed at least once; we'll see some examples later.

One advantage of the consistent use of idioms is that it draws attention to non-standard loops, a frequent sign of trouble:

```
?      int i, *iArray, nmemb;
?
?      iArray = malloc(nmemb * sizeof(int));
?      for (i = 0; i <= nmemb; i++)
?          iArray[i] = i;
```

Space is allocated for nmemb items, `iArray[0]` through `iArray[nmemb-1]`, but since the loop test is `<=` the loop walks off the end of the array and overwrites whatever is stored next in memory. Unfortunately, errors like this are often not detected until long after the damage has been done.

C and C++ also have idioms for allocating space for strings and then manipulating it, and code that doesn't use them often harbors a bug:

```
?      char *p, buf[256];
?
?      gets(buf);
?      p = malloc(strlen(buf));
?      strcpy(p, buf);
```

One should never use `gets`, since there is no way to limit the amount of input it will read. This leads to security problems that we'll return to in Chapter 6, where we will show that `fgets` is always a better choice. But there is another problem as well: `strlen` does not count the `'\0'` that terminates a string, while `strcpy` copies it. So not enough space is allocated, and `strcpy` writes past the end of the allocated space. The idiom is

```
p = malloc(strlen(buf)+1);
strcpy(p, buf);
```

or

```
p = new char[strlen(buf)+1];
strcpy(p, buf);
```

in C++. If you don't see the +1, beware.

Java doesn't suffer from this specific problem, since strings are not represented as null-terminated arrays. Array subscripts are checked as well, so it is not possible to access outside the bounds of an array in Java.

Most C and C++ environments provide a library function, `strdup`, that creates a copy of a string using `malloc` and `strcpy`, making it easy to avoid this bug. Unfortunately, `strdup` is not part of the ANSI C standard.

By the way, neither the original code nor the corrected version check the value returned by `malloc`. We omitted this improvement to focus on the main point, but in a real program the return value from `malloc`, `realloc`, `strdup`, or any other allocation routine should always be checked.

Use else-ifs for multi-way decisions. Multi-way decisions are idiomatically expressed as a chain of if ... else if ... else, like this:

```
if (condition₁)
    statement₁
else if (condition₂)
    statement₂
...
else if (conditionₙ)
    statementₙ
else
    default-statement
```

The *conditions* are read from top to bottom; at the first *condition* that is satisfied, the *statement* that follows is executed, and then the rest of the construct is skipped. The *statement* part may be a single statement or a group of statements enclosed in braces.

The last else handles the "default" situation, where none of the other alternatives was chosen. This trailing else part may be omitted if there is no action for the default, although leaving it in with an error message may help to catch conditions that "can't happen."

Align all of the else clauses vertically rather than lining up each else with the corresponding if. Vertical alignment emphasizes that the tests are done in sequence and keeps them from marching off the right side of the page.

A sequence of nested if statements is often a warning of awkward code, if not outright errors:

```
?       if (argc == 3)
?           if ((fin = fopen(argv[1], "r")) != NULL)
?               if ((fout = fopen(argv[2], "w")) != NULL) {
?                   while ((c = getc(fin)) != EOF)
?                       putc(c, fout);
?                   fclose(fin); fclose(fout);
?               } else
?                   printf("Can't open output file %s\n", argv[2]);
?           else
?               printf("Can't open input file %s\n", argv[1]);
?       else
?           printf("Usage: cp inputfile outputfile\n");
```

The sequence of ifs requires us to maintain a mental pushdown stack of what tests were made, so that at the appropriate point we can pop them until we determine the corresponding action (if we can still remember). Since at most one action will be performed, we really want an else if. Changing the order in which the decisions are made leads to a clearer version, in which we have also corrected the resource leak in the original:

```
if (argc != 3)
    printf("Usage: cp inputfile outputfile\n");
else if ((fin = fopen(argv[1], "r")) == NULL)
    printf("Can't open input file %s\n", argv[1]);
else if ((fout = fopen(argv[2], "w")) == NULL) {
    printf("Can't open output file %s\n", argv[2]);
    fclose(fin);
} else {
    while ((c = getc(fin)) != EOF)
        putc(c, fout);
    fclose(fin);
    fclose(fout);
}
```

We read down the tests until the first one that is true, do the corresponding action, and continue after the last else. The rule is to follow each decision as closely as possible by its associated action. Or, to put it another way, each time you make a test, do something.

Attempts to re-use pieces of code often lead to tightly knotted programs:

```
?      switch (c) {
?      case '-':  sign = -1;
?      case '+':  c = getchar();
?      case '.':  break;
?      default:   if (!isdigit(c))
?                         return 0;
?      }
```

This uses a tricky sequence of fall-throughs in the switch statement to avoid duplicating one line of code. It's also not idiomatic; cases should almost always end with a
break, with the rare exceptions commented. A more traditional layout and structure
is easier to read, though longer:

```
?      switch (c) {
?      case '-':
?          sign = -1;
?          /* fall through */
?      case '+':
?          c = getchar();
?          break;
?      case '.':
?          break;
?      default:
?          if (!isdigit(c))
?              return 0;
?          break;
?      }
```

The increase in size is more than offset by the increase in clarity. However, for such
an unusual structure a sequence of else-if statements is even clearer:

```
if (c == '-') {
    sign = -1;
    c = getchar();
} else if (c == '+') {
    c = getchar();
} else if (c != '.' && !isdigit(c)) {
    return 0;
}
```

The braces around the one-line blocks highlight the parallel structure.
    An acceptable use of a fall-through occurs when several cases have identical code;
the conventional layout is like this:

```
case '0':
case '1':
case '2':
    ...
    break;
```

and no comment is required.

Exercise 1-7. Rewrite these C/C++ excerpts more clearly:

```
?      if (istty(stdin))  ;
?      else if (istty(stdout))  ;
?           else if (istty(stderr))  ;
?               else return(0);


?      if (retval != SUCCESS)
?      {
?          return (retval);
?      }
?      /* All went well! */
?      return SUCCESS;


?      for (k = 0; k++ < 5; x += dx)
?          scanf("%lf", &dx);
```

☐

Exercise 1-8. Identify the errors in this Java fragment and repair it by rewriting with an idiomatic loop:

```
?      int count = 0;
?      while (count < total) {
?          count++;
?          if (this.getName(count) == nametable.userName()) {
?              return (true);
?          }
?      }
```

☐

1.4 Function Macros

There is a tendency among older C programmers to write macros instead of functions for very short computations that will be executed frequently; I/O operations such as getchar and character tests like isdigit are officially sanctioned examples. The reason is performance: a macro avoids the overhead of a function call. This argument was weak even when C was first defined, a time of slow machines and expensive function calls; today it is irrelevant. With modern machines and compilers, the drawbacks of function macros outweigh their benefits.

Avoid function macros. In C++, inline functions render function macros unnecessary; in Java, there are no macros. In C, they cause more problems than they solve.

One of the most serious problems with function macros is that a parameter that appears more than once in the definition might be evaluated more than once; if the argument in the call includes an expression with side effects, the result is a subtle bug. This code attempts to implement one of the character tests from <ctype.h>:

```
?       #define isupper(c) ((c) >= 'A' && (c) <= 'Z')
```

Note that the parameter c occurs twice in the body of the macro. If isupper is called in a context like this,

```
?       while (isupper(c = getchar()))
?           ...
```

then each time an input character is greater than or equal to A, it will be discarded and another character read to be tested against Z. The C standard is carefully written to permit isupper and analogous functions to be macros, but only if they guarantee to evaluate the argument only once, so this implementation is broken.

It's always better to use the ctype functions than to implement them yourself, and it's safer not to nest routines like getchar that have side effects. Rewriting the test to use two expressions rather than one makes it clearer and also gives an opportunity to catch end-of-file explicitly:

```
        while ((c = getchar()) != EOF && isupper(c))
            ...
```

Sometimes multiple evaluation causes a performance problem rather than an outright error. Consider this example:

```
?       #define ROUND_TO_INT(x) ((int) ((x)+(((x)>0)?0.5:-0.5)))
?           ...
?       size = ROUND_TO_INT(sqrt(dx*dx + dy*dy));
```

This will perform the square root computation twice as often as necessary. Even given simple arguments, a complex expression like the body of ROUND_TO_INT translates into many instructions, which should be housed in a single function to be called when needed. Instantiating a macro at every occurrence makes the compiled program larger. (C++ inline functions have this drawback, too.)

Parenthesize the macro body and arguments. If you insist on using function macros, be careful. Macros work by textual substitution: the parameters in the definition are replaced by the arguments of the call and the result replaces the original call, as text. This is a troublesome difference from functions. The expression

```
        1 / square(x)
```

works fine if square is a function, but if it's a macro like this,

```
?       #define square(x)    (x) * (x)
```

the expression will be expanded to the erroneous

```
?     1 / (x) * (x)
```

The macro should be rewritten as

```
#define square(x)    ((x) * (x))
```

All those parentheses are necessary. Even parenthesizing the macro properly does not address the multiple evaluation problem. If an operation is expensive or common enough to be wrapped up, use a function.

In C++, inline functions avoid the syntactic trouble while offering whatever performance advantage macros might provide. They are appropriate for short functions that set or retrieve a single value.

Exercise 1-9. Identify the problems with this macro definition:

```
?     #define ISDIGIT(c) ((c >= '0') && (c <= '9')) ? 1 : 0
```

☐

1.5 Magic Numbers

Magic numbers are the constants, array sizes, character positions, conversion factors, and other literal numeric values that appear in programs.

Give names to magic numbers. As a guideline, any number other than 0 or 1 is likely to be magic and should have a name of its own. A raw number in program source gives no indication of its importance or derivation, making the program harder to understand and modify. This excerpt from a program to print a histogram of letter frequencies on a 24 by 80 cursor-addressed terminal is needlessly opaque because of a host of magic numbers:

```
?        fac = lim / 20;      /* set scale factor */
?        if (fac < 1)
?            fac = 1;
?                             /* generate histogram */
?        for (i = 0, col = 0; i < 27; i++, j++) {
?            col += 3;
?            k = 21 - (let[i] / fac);
?            star = (let[i] == 0) ? ' ' : '*';
?            for (j = k; j < 22; j++)
?                draw(j, col, star);
?        }
?        draw(23, 2, ' '); /* label x axis */
?        for (i = 'A'; i <= 'Z'; i++)
?            printf("%c  ", i);
```

The code includes, among others, the numbers 20, 21, 22, 23, and 27. They're clearly related... or are they? In fact, there are only three numbers critical to this program: 24, the number of rows on the screen; 80, the number of columns; and 26, the number of letters in the alphabet. But none of these appears in the code, which makes the numbers that do even more magical.

By giving names to the principal numbers in the calculation, we can make the code easier to follow. We discover, for instance, that the number 3 comes from $(80-1)/26$ and that let should have 26 entries, not 27 (an off-by-one error perhaps caused by 1-indexed screen coordinates). Making a couple of other simplifications, this is the result:

```
enum {
    MINROW   = 1,                    /* top edge */
    MINCOL   = 1,                    /* left edge */
    MAXROW   = 24,                   /* bottom edge (<=) */
    MAXCOL   = 80,                   /* right edge (<=) */
    LABELROW = 1,                    /* position of labels */
    NLET     = 26,                   /* size of alphabet */
    HEIGHT   = MAXROW - 4,           /* height of bars */
    WIDTH    = (MAXCOL-1)/NLET       /* width of bars */
};
    ...
    fac = (lim + HEIGHT-1) / HEIGHT;     /* set scale factor */
    if (fac < 1)
        fac = 1;
    for (i = 0; i < NLET; i++) {     /* generate histogram */
        if (let[i] == 0)
            continue;
        for (j = HEIGHT - let[i]/fac; j < HEIGHT; j++)
            draw(j+1 + LABELROW, (i+1)*WIDTH, '*');
    }
    draw(MAXROW-1, MINCOL+1, ' ');   /* label x axis */
    for (i = 'A'; i <= 'Z'; i++)
        printf("%c  ", i);
```

Now it's clearer what the main loop does: it's an idiomatic loop from 0 to NLET, indicating that the loop is over the elements of the data. Also the calls to draw are easier to understand because words like MAXROW and MINCOL remind us of the order of arguments. Most important, it's now feasible to adapt the program to another size of display or different data. The numbers are demystified and so is the code.

Define numbers as constants, not macros. C programmers have traditionally used #define to manage magic number values. The C preprocessor is a powerful but blunt tool, however, and macros are a dangerous way to program because they change the lexical structure of the program underfoot. Let the language proper do the work. In C and C++, integer constants can be defined with an enum statement, as we saw in the previous example. Constants of any type can be declared with const in C++:

```
const int MAXROW = 24, MAXCOL = 80;
```

or `final` in Java:

```
static final int MAXROW = 24, MAXCOL = 80;
```

C also has `const` values but they cannot be used as array bounds, so the `enum` statement remains the method of choice in C.

Use character constants, not integers. The functions in `<ctype.h>` or their equivalent should be used to test the properties of characters. A test like this:

```
?       if (c >= 65 && c <= 90)
?           ...
```

depends completely on a particular character representation. It's better to use

```
?       if (c >= 'A' && c <= 'Z')
?           ...
```

but that may not have the desired effect if the letters are not contiguous in the character set encoding or if the alphabet includes other letters. Best is to use the library:

```
        if (isupper(c))
            ...
```

in C or C++, or

```
        if (Character.isUpperCase(c))
            ...
```

in Java.

A related issue is that the number 0 appears often in programs, in many contexts. The compiler will convert the number into the appropriate type, but it helps the reader to understand the role of each 0 if the type is explicit. For example, use `(void*)0` or `NULL` to represent a zero pointer in C, and `'\0'` instead of 0 to represent the null byte at the end of a string. In other words, don't write

```
?       str = 0;
?       name[i] = 0;
?       x = 0;
```

but rather:

```
        str = NULL;
        name[i] = '\0';
        x = 0.0;
```

We prefer to use different explicit constants, reserving 0 for a literal integer zero, because they indicate the use of the value and thus provide a bit of documentation. In C++, however, 0 rather than `NULL` is the accepted notation for a null pointer. Java solves the problem best by defining the keyword `null` for an object reference that doesn't refer to anything.

Use the language to calculate the size of an object. Don't use an explicit size for any data type; use `sizeof(int)` instead of 2 or 4, for instance. For similar reasons, `sizeof(array[0])` may be better than `sizeof(int)` because it's one less thing to change if the type of the array changes.

The `sizeof` operator is sometimes a convenient way to avoid inventing names for the numbers that determine array sizes. For example, if we write

```
char buf[1024];

fgets(buf, sizeof(buf), stdin);
```

the buffer size is still a magic number, but it occurs only once, in the declaration. It may not be worth inventing a name for the size of a local array, but it is definitely worth writing code that does not have to change if the size or type changes.

Java arrays have a `length` field that gives the number of elements:

```
char buf[] = new char[1024];

for (int i = 0; i < buf.length; i++)
    ...
```

There is no equivalent of `.length` in C and C++, but for an array (not a pointer) whose declaration is visible, this macro computes the number of elements in the array:

```
#define NELEMS(array) (sizeof(array) / sizeof(array[0]))

double dbuf[100];

for (i = 0; i < NELEMS(dbuf); i++)
    ...
```

The array size is set in only one place; the rest of the code does not change if the size does. There is no problem with multiple evaluation of the macro argument here, since there can be no side effects, and in fact the computation is done as the program is being compiled. This is an appropriate use for a macro because it does something that a function cannot: compute the size of an array from its declaration.

Exercise 1-10. How would you rewrite these definitions to minimize potential errors?

```
?    #define FT2METER    0.3048
?    #define METER2FT    3.28084
?    #define MI2FT       5280.0
?    #define MI2KM       1.609344
?    #define SQMI2SQKM   2.589988
```

□

1.6 Comments

Comments are meant to help the reader of a program. They do not help by saying things the code already plainly says, or by contradicting the code, or by distracting the reader with elaborate typographical displays. The best comments aid the understanding of a program by briefly pointing out salient details or by providing a larger-scale view of the proceedings.

Don't belabor the obvious. Comments shouldn't report self-evident information, such as the fact that i++ has incremented i. Here are some of our favorite worthless comments:

```
?       /*
?        * default
?        */
?       default:
?           break;


?       /* return SUCCESS */
?       return SUCCESS;


?       zerocount++;    /* Increment zero entry counter */


?       /* Initialize "total" to "number_received" */
?       node->total = node->number_received;
```

All of these comments should be deleted; they're just clutter.

Comments should add something that is not immediately evident from the code, or collect into one place information that is spread through the source. When something subtle is happening, a comment may clarify, but if the actions are obvious already, restating them in words is pointless:

```
?       while ((c = getchar()) != EOF && isspace(c))
?           ;                         /* skip white space */
?       if (c == EOF)                 /* end of file */
?           type = endoffile;
?       else if (c == '(')            /* left paren */
?           type = leftparen;
?       else if (c == ')')            /* right paren */
?           type = rightparen;
?       else if (c == ';')            /* semicolon */
?           type = semicolon;
?       else if (is_op(c))            /* operator */
?           type = operator;
?       else if (isdigit(c))          /* number */
?           ...
```

These comments should also be deleted, since the well-chosen names already convey the information.

Comment functions and global data. Comments *can* be useful, of course. We comment functions, global variables, constant definitions, fields in structures and classes, and anything else where a brief summary can aid understanding.

Global variables have a tendency to crop up intermittently throughout a program; a comment serves as a reminder to be referred to as needed. Here's an example from a program in Chapter 3 of this book:

```
struct State {  /* prefix + suffix list */
    char    *pref[NPREF];   /* prefix words */
    Suffix  *suf;           /* list of suffixes */
    State   *next;          /* next in hash table */
};
```

A comment that introduces each function sets the stage for reading the code itself. If the code isn't too long or technical, a single line is enough:

```
// random: return an integer in the range [0..r-1].
int random(int r)
{
    return (int)(Math.floor(Math.random()*r));
}
```

Sometimes code is genuinely difficult, perhaps because the algorithm is complicated or the data structures are intricate. In that case, a comment that points to a source of understanding can aid the reader. It may also be valuable to suggest why particular decisions were made. This comment introduces an extremely efficient implementation of an inverse discrete cosine transform (DCT) used in a JPEG image decoder.

```
/*
 * idct: Scaled integer implementation of
 * Inverse two dimensional 8x8 Discrete Cosine Transform,
 * Chen-Wang algorithm (IEEE ASSP-32, pp 803-816, Aug 1984)
 *
 * 32-bit integer arithmetic (8-bit coefficients)
 * 11 multiplies, 29 adds per DCT
 *
 * Coefficients extended to 12 bits for
 * IEEE 1180-1990 compliance
 */

static void idct(int b[8*8])
{
    ...
}
```

This helpful comment cites the reference, briefly describes the data used, indicates the performance of the algorithm, and tells how and why the original algorithm has been modified.

Don't comment bad code, rewrite it. Comment anything unusual or potentially confusing, but when the comment outweighs the code, the code probably needs fixing. This example uses a long, muddled comment and a conditionally-compiled debugging print statement to explain a single statement:

```
?       /* If "result" is 0 a match was found so return true (non-zero).
?          Otherwise, "result" is non-zero so return false (zero). */
?
?       #ifdef DEBUG
?       printf("*** isword returns !result = %d\n", !result);
?       fflush(stdout);
?       #endif
?
?       return(!result);
```

Negations are hard to understand and should be avoided. Part of the problem is the uninformative variable name, `result`. A more descriptive name, `matchfound`, makes the comment unnecessary and cleans up the print statement, too.

```
        #ifdef DEBUG
        printf("*** isword returns matchfound = %d\n", matchfound);
        fflush(stdout);
        #endif

        return matchfound;
```

Don't contradict the code. Most comments agree with the code when they are written, but as bugs are fixed and the program evolves, the comments are often left in their original form, resulting in disagreement with the code. This is the likely explanation for the inconsistency in the example that opens this chapter.

Whatever the source of the disagreement, a comment that contradicts the code is confusing, and many a debugging session has been needlessly protracted because a mistaken comment was taken as truth. When you change code, make sure the comments are still accurate.

Comments should not only agree with code, they should support it. The comment in this example is correct—it explains the purpose of the next two lines—but it appears to contradict the code; the comment talks about newline and the code talks about blanks:

```
?       time(&now);
?       strcpy(date, ctime(&now));
?       /* get rid of trailing newline character copied from ctime */
?       i = 0;
?       while(date[i] >= ' ') i++;
?       date[i] = 0;
```

One improvement is to rewrite the code more idiomatically:

```
?     time(&now);
?     strcpy(date, ctime(&now));
?     /* get rid of trailing newline character copied from ctime */
?     for (i = 0; date[i] != '\n'; i++)
?         ;
?     date[i] = '\0';
```

Code and comment now agree, but both can be improved by being made more direct.
The problem is to delete the newline that ctime puts on the end of the string it
returns. The comment should say so, and the code should do so:

```
time(&now);
strcpy(date, ctime(&now));
/* ctime() puts newline at end of string; delete it */
date[strlen(date)-1] = '\0';
```

This last expression is the C idiom for removing the last character from a string. The
code is now short, idiomatic, and clear, and the comment supports it by explaining
why it needs to be there.

Clarify, don't confuse. Comments are supposed to help readers over the hard parts,
not create more obstacles. This example follows our guidelines of commenting the
function and explaining unusual properties; on the other hand, the function is strcmp
and the unusual properties are peripheral to the job at hand, which is the implementation of a standard and familiar interface:

```
?     int strcmp(char *s1, char *s2)
?     /* string comparison routine returns -1 if s1 is */
?     /* above s2 in an ascending order list, 0 if equal */
?     /* 1 if s1 below s2 */
?     {
?         while(*s1==*s2)  {
?             if(*s1=='\0')  return(0);
?             s1++;
?             s2++;
?         }
?         if(*s1>*s2) return(1);
?         return(-1);
?     }
```

When it takes more than a few words to explain what's happening, it's often an indication that the code should be rewritten. Here, the code could perhaps be improved
but the real problem is the comment, which is nearly as long as the implementation
and confusing, too (which way is "above"?). We're stretching the point to say this
routine is hard to understand, but since it implements a standard function, its comment
can help by summarizing the behavior and telling us where the definition originates;
that's all that's needed:

```
/* strcmp: return < 0 if s1<s2, > 0 if s1>s2, 0 if equal */
/*         ANSI C, section 4.11.4.2 */
int strcmp(const char *s1, const char *s2)
{
    ...
}
```

Students are taught that it's important to comment everything. Professional programmers are often required to comment all their code. But the purpose of commenting can be lost in blindly following rules. Comments are meant to help a reader understand parts of the program that are not readily understood from the code itself. As much as possible, write code that is easy to understand; the better you do this, the fewer comments you need. Good code needs fewer comments than bad code.

Exercise 1-11. Comment on these comments.

```
?    void dict::insert(string& w)
?    // returns 1 if w in dictionary, otherwise returns 0


?    if (n > MAX || n % 2 > 0) // test for even number


?    // Write a message
?    // Add to line counter for each line written
?
?    void write_message()
?    {
?        // increment line counter
?        line_number = line_number + 1;
?        fprintf(fout, "%d  %s\n%d  %s\n%d  %s\n",
?            line_number, HEADER,
?            line_number + 1, BODY,
?            line_number + 2, TRAILER);
?        // increment line counter
?        line_number = line_number + 2;
?    }
```

□

1.7 Why Bother?

In this chapter, we've talked about the main concerns of programming style: descriptive names, clarity in expressions, straightforward control flow, readability of code and comments, and the importance of consistent use of conventions and idioms in achieving all of these. It's hard to argue that these are bad things.

But why worry about style? Who cares what a program looks like if it works? Doesn't it take too much time to make it look pretty? Aren't the rules arbitrary anyway?

The answer is that well-written code is easier to read and to understand, almost surely has fewer errors, and is likely to be smaller than code that has been carelessly tossed together and never polished. In the rush to get programs out the door to meet some deadline, it's easy to push style aside, to worry about it later. This can be a costly decision. Some of the examples in this chapter show what can go wrong if there isn't enough attention to good style. Sloppy code is bad code—not just awkward and hard to read, but often broken.

The key observation is that good style should be a matter of habit. If you think about style as you write code originally, and if you take the time to revise and improve it, you will develop good habits. Once they become automatic, your subconscious will take care of many of the details for you, and even the code you produce under pressure will be better.

Supplementary Reading

As we said at the beginning of the chapter, writing good code has much in common with writing good English. Strunk and White's *The Elements of Style* (Allyn & Bacon) is still the best short book on how to write English well.

This chapter draws on the approach of *The Elements of Programming Style* by Brian Kernighan and P. J. Plauger (McGraw-Hill, 1978). Steve Maguire's *Writing Solid Code* (Microsoft Press, 1993) is an excellent source of programming advice. There are also helpful discussions of style in Steve McConnell's *Code Complete* (Microsoft Press, 1993) and Peter van der Linden's *Expert C Programming: Deep C Secrets* (Prentice Hall, 1994).

2

Algorithms and
Data Structures

In the end, only familiarity with the tools and techniques of the field will provide the right solution for a particular problem, and only a certain amount of experience will provide consistently professional results.

Raymond Fielding, *The Technique of Special Effects Cinematography*

The study of algorithms and data structures is one of the foundations of computer science, a rich field of elegant techniques and sophisticated mathematical analyses. And it's more than just fun and games for the theoretically inclined: a good algorithm or data structure might make it possible to solve a problem in seconds that could otherwise take years.

In specialized areas like graphics, databases, parsing, numerical analysis, and simulation, the ability to solve problems depends critically on state-of-the-art algorithms and data structures. If you are developing programs in a field that's new to you, you *must* find out what is already known, lest you waste your time doing poorly what others have already done well.

Every program depends on algorithms and data structures, but few programs depend on the invention of brand new ones. Even within an intricate program like a compiler or a web browser, most of the data structures are arrays, lists, trees, and hash tables. When a program needs something more elaborate, it will likely be based on these simpler ones. Accordingly, for most programmers, the task is to know what appropriate algorithms and data structures are available and to understand how to choose among alternatives.

Here is the story in a nutshell. There are only a handful of basic algorithms that show up in almost every program—primarily searching and sorting—and even those are often included in libraries. Similarly, almost every data structure is derived from a few fundamental ones. Thus the material covered in this chapter will be familiar to almost all programmers. We have written working versions to make the discussion concrete, and you can lift code verbatim if necessary, but do so only after you have investigated what the programming language and its libraries have to offer.

2.1 Searching

Nothing beats an array for storing static tabular data. Compile-time initialization makes it cheap and easy to construct such arrays. (In Java, the initialization occurs at run-time, but this is an unimportant implementation detail unless the arrays are large.) In a program to detect words that are used rather too much in bad prose, we can write

```
char *flab[] = {
    "actually",
    "just",
    "quite",
    "really",
    NULL
};
```

The search routine needs to know how many elements are in the array. One way to tell it is to pass the length as an argument; another, used here, is to place a NULL marker at the end of the array:

```
/* lookup: sequential search for word in array */
int lookup(char *word, char *array[])
{
    int i;

    for (i = 0; array[i] != NULL; i++)
        if (strcmp(word, array[i]) == 0)
            return i;
    return -1;
}
```

In C and C++, a parameter that is an array of strings can be declared as char *array[] or char **array. Although these forms are equivalent, the first makes it clearer how the parameter will be used.

This search algorithm is called *sequential search* because it looks at each element in turn to see if it's the desired one. When the amount of data is small, sequential search is fast enough. There are standard library routines to do sequential search for specific data types; for example, functions like strchr and strstr search for the first instance of a given character or substring in a C or C++ string, the Java String class has an indexOf method, and the generic C++ find algorithms apply to most data types. If such a function exists for the data type you've got, use it.

Sequential search is easy but the amount of work is directly proportional to the amount of data to be searched; doubling the number of elements will double the time to search if the desired item is not present. This is a linear relationship—run-time is a linear function of data size—so this method is also known as *linear search*.

Here's an excerpt from an array of more realistic size from a program that parses HTML, which defines textual names for well over a hundred individual characters:

```
typedef struct Nameval Nameval;
struct Nameval {
    char    *name;
    int      value;
};

/* HTML characters, e.g. AElig is ligature of A and E. */
/* Values are Unicode/ISO10646 encoding. */

Nameval htmlchars[] = {
    "AElig",    0x00c6,
    "Aacute",   0x00c1,
    "Acirc",    0x00c2,
    /* ... */
    "zeta",     0x03b6,
};
```

For a larger array like this, it's more efficient to use *binary search*. The binary search algorithm is an orderly version of the way we look up words in a dictionary. Check the middle element. If that value is bigger than what we are looking for, look in the first half; otherwise, look in the second half. Repeat until the desired item is found or determined not to be present.

For binary search, the table must be sorted, as it is here (that's good style anyway; people find things faster in sorted tables too), and we must know how long the table is. The NELEMS macro from Chapter 1 can help:

```
printf("The HTML table has %d words\n", NELEMS(htmlchars));
```

A binary search function for this table might look like this:

```
/* lookup: binary search for name in tab; return index */
int lookup(char *name, Nameval tab[], int ntab)
{
    int low, high, mid, cmp;

    low = 0;
    high = ntab - 1;
    while (low <= high) {
        mid = (low + high) / 2;
        cmp = strcmp(name, tab[mid].name);
        if (cmp < 0)
            high = mid - 1;
        else if (cmp > 0)
            low = mid + 1;
        else    /* found match */
            return mid;
    }
    return -1;  /* no match */
}
```

Putting all this together, to search `htmlchars` we write

```
half = lookup("frac12", htmlchars, NELEMS(htmlchars));
```

to find the array index of the character ½.

Binary search eliminates half the data at each step. The number of steps is therefore proportional to the number of times we can divide n by 2 before we're left with a single element. Ignoring roundoff, this is $\log_2 n$. If we have 1000 items to search, linear search takes up to 1000 steps, while binary search takes about 10; if we have a million items, linear takes a million steps and binary takes 20. The more items, the greater the advantage of binary search. Beyond some size of input (which varies with the implementation), binary search is faster than linear search.

2.2 Sorting

Binary search works only if the elements are sorted. If repeated searches are going to be made in some data set, it will be profitable to sort once and then use binary search. If the data set is known in advance, it can be sorted when the program is written and built using compile-time initialization. If not, it must be sorted when the program is run.

One of the best all-round sorting algorithms is *quicksort*, which was invented in 1960 by C. A. R. Hoare. Quicksort is a fine example of how to avoid extra computing. It works by partitioning an array into little and big elements:

> pick one element of the array (the "pivot").
> partition the other elements into two groups:
>> "little ones" that are less than the pivot value, and
>> "big ones" that are greater than or equal to the pivot value.
> recursively sort each group.

When this process is finished, the array is in order. Quicksort is fast because once an element is known to be less than the pivot value, we don't have to compare it to any of the big ones; similarly, big ones are not compared to little ones. This makes it much faster than the simple sorting methods such as insertion sort and bubble sort that compare each element directly to all the others.

Quicksort is practical and efficient; it has been extensively studied and myriad variations exist. The version that we present here is just about the simplest implementation but it is certainly not the quickest.

This `quicksort` function sorts an array of integers:

```
/* quicksort: sort v[0]..v[n-1] into increasing order */
void quicksort(int v[], int n)
{
    int i, last;

    if (n <= 1)   /* nothing to do */
        return;
    swap(v, 0, rand() % n);    /* move pivot elem to v[0] */
    last = 0;
    for (i = 1; i < n; i++)    /* partition */
        if (v[i] < v[0])
            swap(v, ++last, i);
    swap(v, 0, last);           /* restore pivot */
    quicksort(v, last);         /* recursively sort */
    quicksort(v+last+1, n-last-1); /*   each part */
}
```

The swap operation, which interchanges two elements, appears three times in quicksort, so it is best made into a separate function:

```
/* swap:  interchange v[i] and v[j] */
void swap(int v[], int i, int j)
{
    int temp;

    temp = v[i];
    v[i] = v[j];
    v[j] = temp;
}
```

Partitioning selects a random element as the pivot, swaps it temporarily to the front, then sweeps through the remaining elements, exchanging those smaller than the pivot ("little ones") towards the beginning (at location last) and big ones towards the end (at location i). At the beginning of the process, just after the pivot has been swapped to the front, last = 0 and elements i = 1 through n-1 are unexamined:

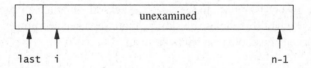

At the top of the for loop, elements 1 through last are strictly less than the pivot, elements last+1 through i-1 are greater than or equal to the pivot, and elements i through n-1 have not been examined yet. Until v[i] >= v[0], the algorithm may swap v[i] with itself; this wastes some time but not enough to worry about.

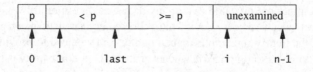

After all elements have been partitioned, element 0 is swapped with the `last` element to put the pivot element in its final position; this maintains the correct ordering. Now the array looks like this:

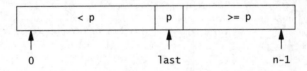

The same process is applied to the left and right sub-arrays; when this has finished, the whole array has been sorted.

How fast is quicksort? In the best possible case,

- the first pass partitions n elements into two groups of about $n/2$ each.
- the second level partitions two groups, each of about $n/2$ elements, into four groups each of about $n/4$.
- the next level partitions four groups of about $n/4$ into eight of about $n/8$.
- and so on.

This goes on for about $\log_2 n$ levels, so the total amount of work in the best case is proportional to $n + 2{\times}n/2 + 4{\times}n/4 + 8{\times}n/8$ ... ($\log_2 n$ terms), which is $n\log_2 n$. On the average, it does only a little more work. It is customary to use base 2 logarithms; thus we say that quicksort takes time proportional to $n\log n$.

This implementation of quicksort is the clearest for exposition, but it has a weakness. If each choice of pivot splits the element values into two nearly equal groups, our analysis is correct, but if the split is uneven too often, the run-time can grow more like n^2. Our implementation uses a random element as the pivot to reduce the chance that unusual input data will cause too many uneven splits. But if all the input values are the same, our implementation splits off only one element each time and will thus run in time proportional to n^2.

The behavior of some algorithms depends strongly on the input data. Perverse or unlucky inputs may cause an otherwise well-behaved algorithm to run extremely slowly or use a lot of memory. In the case of quicksort, although a simple implementation like ours might sometimes run slowly, more sophisticated implementations can reduce the chance of pathological behavior to almost zero.

2.3 Libraries

The standard libraries for C and C++ include sort functions that should be robust against adverse inputs, and tuned to run as fast as possible.

Library routines are prepared to sort any data type, but in return we must adapt to their interface, which may be somewhat more complicated than what we showed above. In C, the library function is named `qsort`, and we need to provide a comparison function to be called by `qsort` whenever it needs to compare two values. Since the values might be of any type, the comparison function is handed two void* pointers to the data items to be compared. The function casts the pointers to the proper type, extracts the data values, compares them, and returns the result (negative, zero, or positive according to whether the first value is less than, equal to, or greater than the second).

Here's an implementation for sorting an array of strings, which is a common case. We define a function scmp to cast the arguments and call strcmp to do the comparison.

```
/* scmp: string compare of *p1 and *p2 */
int scmp(const void *p1, const void *p2)
{
    char *v1, *v2;

    v1 = *(char **) p1;
    v2 = *(char **) p2;
    return strcmp(v1, v2);
}
```

We could write this as a one-line function, but the temporary variables make the code easier to read.

We can't use strcmp directly as the comparison function because qsort passes the address of each entry in the array, &str[i] (of type char**), not str[i] (of type char*), as shown in this figure:

array of N pointers:

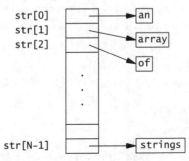

To sort elements str[0] through str[N-1] of an array of strings, qsort must be called with the array, its length, the size of the items being sorted, and the comparison function:

```
char *str[N];

qsort(str, N, sizeof(str[0]), scmp);
```

Here's a similar function icmp for comparing integers:

```
/* icmp: integer compare of *p1 and *p2 */
int icmp(const void *p1, const void *p2)
{
    int v1, v2;

    v1 = *(int *) p1;
    v2 = *(int *) p2;
    if (v1 < v2)
        return -1;
    else if (v1 == v2)
        return 0;
    else
        return 1;
}
```

We could write

```
?    return v1-v2;
```

but if v2 is large and positive and v1 is large and negative or vice versa, the resulting overflow would produce an incorrect answer. Direct comparison is longer but safe.

Again, the call to qsort requires the array, its length, the size of the items being sorted, and the comparison function:

```
int arr[N];

qsort(arr, N, sizeof(arr[0]), icmp);
```

ANSI C also defines a binary search routine, bsearch. Like qsort, bsearch requires a pointer to a comparison function (often the same one used for qsort); it returns a pointer to the matching element or NULL if not found. Here is our HTML lookup routine, rewritten to use bsearch:

```
/* lookup: use bsearch to find name in tab, return index */
int lookup(char *name, Nameval tab[], int ntab)
{
    Nameval key, *np;

    key.name = name;
    key.value = 0;  /* unused; anything will do */
    np = (Nameval *) bsearch(&key, tab, ntab,
                             sizeof(tab[0]), nvcmp);
    if (np == NULL)
        return -1;
    else
        return np-tab;
}
```

As with qsort, the comparison routine receives the address of the items to be compared, so the key must have that type; in this example, we need to construct a fake Nameval entry that is passed to the comparison routine. The comparison routine itself is a function `nvcmp` that compares two `Nameval` items by calling `strcmp` on their string components, ignoring their values:

```
/* nvcmp: compare two Nameval names */
int nvcmp(const void *va, const void *vb)
{
    const Nameval *a, *b;

    a = (Nameval *) va;
    b = (Nameval *) vb;
    return strcmp(a->name, b->name);
}
```

This is analogous to `scmp` but differs because the strings are stored as members of a structure.

The clumsiness of providing the key means that `bsearch` provides less leverage than `qsort`. A good general-purpose sort routine takes a page or two of code, while binary search is not much longer than the code it takes to interface to `bsearch`. Nevertheless, it's a good idea to use `bsearch` instead of writing your own. Over the years, binary search has proven surprisingly hard for programmers to get right.

The standard C++ library has a generic algorithm called `sort` that guarantees $O(n\log n)$ behavior. The code is easier because it needs no casts or element sizes, and it does not require an explicit comparison function for types that have an order relation.

```
int arr[N];

sort(arr, arr+N);
```

The C++ library also has generic binary search routines, with similar notational advantages.

Exercise 2-1. Quicksort is most naturally expressed recursively. Write it iteratively and compare the two versions. (Hoare describes how hard it was to work out quicksort iteratively, and how neatly it fell into place when he did it recursively.) □

2.4 A Java Quicksort

The situation in Java is different. Early releases had no standard sort function, so we needed to write our own. More recent versions do provide a `sort` function, however, which operates on classes that implement the `Comparable` interface, so we can now ask the library to sort for us. But since the techniques are useful in other situations, in this section we will work through the details of implementing quicksort in Java.

It's easy to adapt a quicksort for each type we might want to sort, but it is more instructive to write a generic sort that can be called for any kind of object, more in the style of the qsort interface.

One big difference from C or C++ is that in Java it is not possible to pass a comparison function to another function; there are no function pointers. Instead we create an *interface* whose sole content is a function that compares two Objects. For each data type to be sorted, we then create a class with a member function that implements the interface for that data type. We pass an instance of that class to the sort function, which in turn uses the comparison function within the class to compare elements.

We begin by defining an interface named Cmp that declares a single member, a comparison function cmp that compares two Objects:

```
interface Cmp {
    int cmp(Object x, Object y);
}
```

Then we can write comparison functions that implement this interface; for example, this class defines a function that compares Integers:

```
// Icmp: Integer comparison
class Icmp implements Cmp {
    public int cmp(Object o1, Object o2)
    {
        int i1 = ((Integer) o1).intValue();
        int i2 = ((Integer) o2).intValue();
        if (i1 < i2)
            return -1;
        else if (i1 == i2)
            return 0;
        else
            return 1;
    }
}
```

and this compares Strings:

```
// Scmp: String comparison
class Scmp implements Cmp {
    public int cmp(Object o1, Object o2)
    {
        String s1 = (String) o1;
        String s2 = (String) o2;
        return s1.compareTo(s2);
    }
}
```

We can sort only types that are derived from Object with this mechanism; it cannot be applied to the basic types like int or double. This is why we sort Integers rather than ints.

With these components, we can now translate the C `quicksort` function into Java and have it call the comparison function from a `Cmp` object passed in as an argument. The most significant change is the use of indices `left` and `right`, since Java does not have pointers into arrays.

```
// Quicksort.sort: quicksort v[left]..v[right]
static void sort(Object[] v, int left, int right, Cmp cmp)
{
    int i, last;

    if (left >= right)  // nothing to do
        return;
    swap(v, left, rand(left,right));   // move pivot elem
    last = left;                       //    to v[left]
    for (i = left+1; i <= right; i++)  // partition
        if (cmp.cmp(v[i], v[left]) < 0)
            swap(v, ++last, i);
    swap(v, left, last);               // restore pivot elem
    sort(v, left, last-1, cmp);        // recursively sort
    sort(v, last+1, right, cmp);       //    each part
}
```

`Quicksort.sort` uses `cmp` to compare a pair of objects, and calls `swap` as before to interchange them.

```
// Quicksort.swap: swap v[i] and v[j]
static void swap(Object[] v, int i, int j)
{
    Object temp;

    temp = v[i];
    v[i] = v[j];
    v[j] = temp;
}
```

Random number generation is done by a function that produces a random integer in the range `left` to `right` inclusive:

```
static Random rgen = new Random();

// Quicksort.rand: return random integer in [left,right]
static int rand(int left, int right)
{
    return left + Math.abs(rgen.nextInt())%(right-left+1);
}
```

We compute the absolute value, using `Math.abs`, because Java's random number generator returns negative integers as well as positive.

The functions `sort`, `swap`, and `rand`, and the generator object `rgen` are the members of a class `Quicksort`.

Finally, to call `Quicksort.sort` to sort a `String` array, we would say

```
String[] sarr = new String[n];

// fill n elements of sarr...

Quicksort.sort(sarr, 0, sarr.length-1, new Scmp());
```

This calls `sort` with a string-comparison object created for the occasion.

Exercise 2-2. Our Java quicksort does a fair amount of type conversion as items are cast from their original type (like `Integer`) to `Object` and back again. Experiment with a version of `Quicksort.sort` that uses the specific type being sorted, to estimate what performance penalty is incurred by type conversions. □

2.5 O-Notation

We've described the amount of work to be done by a particular algorithm in terms of n, the number of elements in the input. Searching unsorted data can take time proportional to n; if we use binary search on sorted data, the time will be proportional to $\log n$. Sorting times might be proportional to n^2 or $n \log n$.

We need a way to make such statements more precise, while at the same time abstracting away details like the CPU speed and the quality of the compiler (and the programmer). We want to compare running times and space requirements of algorithms independently of programming language, compiler, machine architecture, processor speed, system load, and other complicating factors.

There is a standard notation for this idea, called ''O-notation.'' Its basic parameter is n, the size of a problem instance, and the *complexity* or running time is expressed as a function of n. The ''O'' is for *order*, as in ''Binary search is $O(\log n)$; it takes on the order of $\log n$ steps to search an array of n items.'' The notation $O(f(n))$ means that, once n gets large, the running time is proportional to at most $f(n)$, for example, $O(n^2)$ or $O(n \log n)$. Asymptotic estimates like this are valuable for theoretical analyses and very helpful for gross comparisons of algorithms, but details may make a difference in practice. For example, a low-overhead $O(n^2)$ algorithm may run faster than a high-overhead $O(n \log n)$ algorithm for small values of n, but inevitably, if n gets large enough, the algorithm with the slower-growing functional behavior will be faster.

We must also distinguish between *worst-case* and *expected* behavior. It's hard to define ''expected,'' since it depends on assumptions about what kinds of inputs will be given. We can usually be precise about the worst case, although that may be misleading. Quicksort's worst-case run-time is $O(n^2)$ but the expected time is $O(n \log n)$. By choosing the pivot element carefully each time, we can reduce the probability of quadratic or $O(n^2)$ behavior to essentially zero; in practice, a well-implemented quicksort usually runs in $O(n \log n)$ time.

These are the most important cases:

Notation	Name	Example
$O(1)$	constant	array index
$O(\log n)$	logarithmic	binary search
$O(n)$	linear	string comparison
$O(n \log n)$	$n \log n$	quicksort
$O(n^2)$	quadratic	simple sorting methods
$O(n^3)$	cubic	matrix multiplication
$O(2^n)$	exponential	set partitioning

Accessing an item in an array is a constant-time or $O(1)$ operation. An algorithm that eliminates half the input at each stage, like binary search, will generally take $O(\log n)$. Comparing two n-character strings with `strcmp` is $O(n)$. The traditional matrix multiplication algorithm takes $O(n^3)$, since each element of the output is the result of multiplying n pairs and adding them up, and there are n^2 elements in each matrix.

Exponential-time algorithms are often the result of evaluating all possibilities: there are 2^n subsets of a set of n items, so an algorithm that requires looking at all subsets will be exponential or $O(2^n)$. Exponential algorithms are generally too expensive unless n is very small, since adding one item to the problem doubles the running time. Unfortunately there are many problems, such as the famous "Traveling Salesman Problem," for which only exponential algorithms are known. When that is the case, algorithms that find approximations to the best answer are often substituted.

Exercise 2-3. What are some input sequences that might cause a quicksort implementation to display worst-case behavior? Try to find some that provoke your library version into running slowly. Automate the process so that you can specify and perform a large number of experiments easily. □

Exercise 2-4. Design and implement an algorithm that will sort an array of n integers as slowly as possible. You have to play fair: the algorithm must make progress and eventually terminate, and the implementation must not cheat with tricks like time-wasting loops. What is the complexity of your algorithm as a function of n? □

2.6 Growing Arrays

The arrays used in the past few sections have been static, with their size and contents fixed at compile time. If the flabby word or HTML character tables were to be modified at run-time, a hash table would be a more appropriate data structure. Growing a sorted array by inserting n elements one at a time is an $O(n^2)$ operation that should be avoided if n is large.

Often, though, we need to keep track of a variable but small number of things, and arrays can still be the method of choice. To minimize the cost of allocation, the array should be resized in chunks, and for cleanliness the array should be gathered together with the information necessary to maintain it. In C++ or Java, this would be done with classes from standard libraries; in C, we can achieve a similar result with a `struct`.

The following code defines a growable array of `Nameval` items; new items are added at the end of the array, which is grown as necessary to make room. Any element can be accessed through its subscript in constant time. This is analogous to the vector classes in the Java and C++ libraries.

```
typedef struct Nameval Nameval;
struct Nameval {
    char    *name;
    int     value;
};

struct NVtab {
    int     nval;       /* current number of values */
    int     max;        /* allocated number of values */
    Nameval *nameval;   /* array of name-value pairs */
} nvtab;

enum { NVINIT = 1, NVGROW = 2 };

/* addname: add new name and value to nvtab */
int addname(Nameval newname)
{
    Nameval *nvp;

    if (nvtab.nameval == NULL) { /* first time */
        nvtab.nameval =
            (Nameval *) malloc(NVINIT * sizeof(Nameval));
        if (nvtab.nameval == NULL)
            return -1;
        nvtab.max = NVINIT;
        nvtab.nval = 0;
    } else if (nvtab.nval >= nvtab.max) { /* grow */
        nvp = (Nameval *) realloc(nvtab.nameval,
                (NVGROW*nvtab.max) * sizeof(Nameval));
        if (nvp == NULL)
            return -1;
        nvtab.max *= NVGROW;
        nvtab.nameval = nvp;
    }
    nvtab.nameval[nvtab.nval] = newname;
    return nvtab.nval++;
}
```

The function addname returns the index of the item just added, or -1 if some error occurred.

The call to realloc grows the array to the new size, preserving the existing elements, and returns a pointer to it or NULL if there isn't enough memory. Doubling the size in each realloc keeps the expected cost of copying each element constant; if the array grew by just one element on each call, the performance could be $O(n^2)$. Since the address of the array may change when it is reallocated, the rest of the program must refer to elements of the array by subscripts, not pointers. Note that the code doesn't say

```
?       nvtab.nameval = (Nameval *) realloc(nvtab.nameval,
?               (NVGROW*nvtab.max) * sizeof(Nameval));
```

In this form, if the reallocation were to fail, the original array would be lost.

We start with a very small initial value (NVINIT = 1) for the array size. This forces the program to grow its arrays right away and thus ensures that this part of the program is exercised. The initial size can be increased once the code goes into production use, though the cost of starting small is negligible.

The return value of realloc does not need to be cast to its final type because C promotes the void* automatically. But C++ does not; there the cast is required. One can argue about whether it is safer to cast (cleanliness, honesty) or not to cast (the cast can hide genuine errors). We chose to cast because it makes the program legal in both C and C++; the price is less error-checking from the C compiler, but that is offset by the extra checking available from using two compilers.

Deleting a name can be tricky, because we must decide what to do with the resulting gap in the array. If the order of elements does not matter, it is easiest to swap the last element into the hole. If order is to be preserved, however, we must move the elements beyond the hole down by one position:

```
/* delname: remove first matching nameval from nvtab */
int delname(char *name)
{
    int i;

    for (i = 0; i < nvtab.nval; i++)
        if (strcmp(nvtab.nameval[i].name, name) == 0) {
            memmove(nvtab.nameval+i, nvtab.nameval+i+1,
                (nvtab.nval-(i+1)) * sizeof(Nameval));
            nvtab.nval--;
            return 1;
        }
    return 0;
}
```

The call to memmove squeezes the array by moving the elements down one position; memmove is a standard library routine for copying arbitrary-sized blocks of memory.

The ANSI C standard defines two functions: memcpy, which is fast but might overwrite memory if source and destination overlap; and memmove, which might be slower but will always be correct. The burden of choosing correctness over speed should not be placed upon the programmer; there should be only one function. Pretend there is, and always use memmove.

We could replace the memmove call with the following loop:

```
int j;
for (j = i; j < nvtab.nval-1; j++)
    nvtab.nameval[j] = nvtab.nameval[j+1];
```

We prefer to use memmove because it avoids the easy-to-make mistake of copying the elements in the wrong order. If we were inserting instead of deleting, the loop would need to count down, not up, to avoid overwriting elements. By calling memmove we don't need to think it through each time.

An alternative to moving the elements of the array is to mark deleted elements as unused. Then to add a new item, first search for an unused slot and grow the vector only if none is found. In this example, an element can be marked as unused by setting its name field to NULL.

Arrays are the simplest way to group data; it's no accident that most languages provide efficient and convenient indexed arrays and represent strings as arrays of characters. Arrays are easy to use, provide $O(1)$ access to any item, work well with binary search and quicksort, and have little space overhead. For fixed-size data sets, which can even be constructed at compile time, or for guaranteed small collections of data, arrays are unbeatable. But maintaining a changing set of values in an array can be expensive, so if the number of elements is unpredictable and potentially large, it may be better to use another data structure.

Exercise 2-5. In the code above, delname doesn't call realloc to return the memory freed by the deletion. Is this worthwhile? How would you decide whether to do so? □

Exercise 2-6. Implement the necessary changes to addname and delname to delete items by marking deleted items as unused. How isolated is the rest of the program from this change? □

2.7 Lists

Next to arrays, lists are the most common data structure in typical programs. Many languages have built-in list types—some, such as Lisp, are based on them—but in C we must build them ourselves. In C++ and Java, lists are implemented by a library, but we still need to know how and when to use it. In this section we're going to discuss lists in C but the lessons apply more broadly.

A *singly-linked list* is a set of items, each with data and a pointer to the next item. The head of the list is a pointer to the first item and the end of the list is marked by a null pointer. This shows a list with four elements:

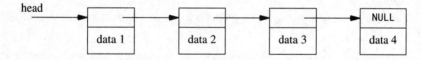

There are several important differences between arrays and lists. First, arrays have fixed size but a list is always exactly the size it needs to be to hold its contents, plus some per-item storage overhead to hold the pointers. Second, lists can be rearranged by exchanging a few pointers, which is cheaper than the block move necessary in an array. Finally, when items are inserted or deleted the other items aren't moved; if we store pointers to the elements in some other data structure, they won't be invalidated by changes to the list.

These differences suggest that if the set of items will change frequently, particularly if the number of items is unpredictable, a list is the way to store them; by comparison, an array is better for relatively static data.

There are a handful of fundamental list operations: add a new item to the front or back, find a specific item, add a new item before or after a specific item, and perhaps delete an item. The simplicity of lists makes it easy to add other operations as appropriate.

Rather than defining an explicit List type, the usual way lists are used in C is to start with a type for the elements, such as our HTML Nameval, and add a pointer that links to the next element:

```
typedef struct Nameval Nameval;
struct Nameval {
    char    *name;
    int     value;
    Nameval *next;  /* in list */
};
```

It's difficult to initialize a non-empty list at compile time, so, unlike arrays, lists are constructed dynamically. First, we need a way to construct an item. The most direct approach is to allocate one with a suitable function, which we call newitem:

```
/* newitem: create new item from name and value */
Nameval *newitem(char *name, int value)
{
    Nameval *newp;

    newp = (Nameval *) emalloc(sizeof(Nameval));
    newp->name = name;
    newp->value = value;
    newp->next = NULL;
    return newp;
}
```

The routine emalloc is one we'll use throughout the book; it calls malloc, and if the allocation fails, it reports the error and exits the program. We'll show the code in Chapter 4; for now, it's sufficient to regard emalloc as a memory allocator that never returns failure.

The simplest and fastest way to assemble a list is to add each new element to the front:

```
/* addfront: add newp to front of listp */
Nameval *addfront(Nameval *listp, Nameval *newp)
{
    newp->next = listp;
    return newp;
}
```

When a list is modified, it may acquire a different first element, as it does when addfront is called. Functions that update a list must return a pointer to the new first element, which is stored in the variable that holds the list. The function addfront and other functions in this group all return the pointer to the first element as their function value; a typical use is

```
nvlist = addfront(nvlist, newitem("smiley", 0x263A));
```

This design works even if the existing list is empty (null) and makes it easy to combine the functions in expressions. It seems more natural than the alternative of passing in a pointer to the pointer holding the head of the list.

Adding an item to the end of a list is an $O(n)$ procedure, since we must walk the list to find the end:

```
/* addend: add newp to end of listp */
Nameval *addend(Nameval *listp, Nameval *newp)
{
    Nameval *p;

    if (listp == NULL)
        return newp;
    for (p = listp; p->next != NULL; p = p->next)
        ;
    p->next = newp;
    return listp;
}
```

If we want to make addend an $O(1)$ operation, we can keep a separate pointer to the end of the list. The drawback to this approach, besides the bother of maintaining the end pointer, is that a list is no longer represented by a single pointer variable. We'll stick with the simple style.

To search for an item with a specific name, follow the next pointers:

```
/* lookup: sequential search for name in listp */
Nameval *lookup(Nameval *listp, char *name)
{
    for ( ; listp != NULL; listp = listp->next)
        if (strcmp(name, listp->name) == 0)
            return listp;
    return NULL;     /* no match */
}
```

This takes $O(n)$ time and there's no way to improve that bound in general. Even if the list is sorted, we need to walk along the list to get to a particular element. Binary search does not apply to lists.

To print the elements of a list, we can write a function to walk the list and print each element; to compute the length of a list, we can write a function to walk the list and increment a counter; and so on. An alternative is to write one function, apply, that walks a list and calls another function for each list element. We can make apply more flexible by providing it with an argument to be passed each time it calls the function. So apply has three arguments: the list, a function to be applied to each element of the list, and an argument for that function:

```
/* apply: execute fn for each element of listp */
void apply(Nameval *listp,
        void (*fn)(Nameval*, void*), void *arg)
{
    for ( ; listp != NULL; listp = listp->next)
        (*fn)(listp, arg);  /* call the function */
}
```

The second argument of apply is a pointer to a function that takes two arguments and returns void. The standard but awkward syntax,

```
void (*fn)(Nameval*, void*)
```

declares fn to be a pointer to a void-valued function, that is, a variable that holds the address of a function that returns void. The function takes two arguments, a Nameval*, which is the list element, and a void*, which is a generic pointer to an argument for the function.

To use apply, for example to print the elements of a list, we could write a trivial function whose argument is a format string:

```
/* printnv: print name and value using format in arg */
void printnv(Nameval *p, void *arg)
{
    char *fmt;

    fmt = (char *) arg;
    printf(fmt, p->name, p->value);
}
```

which we call like this:

```
        apply(nvlist, printnv, "%s: %x\n");
```

To count the elements, we define a function whose argument is a pointer to an integer
to be incremented:

```
/* inccounter: increment counter *arg */
void inccounter(Nameval *p, void *arg)
{
    int *ip;

    /* p is unused */
    ip = (int *) arg;
    (*ip)++;
}
```

and call it like this:

```
int n;

n = 0;
apply(nvlist, inccounter, &n);
printf("%d elements in nvlist\n", n);
```

Not every list operation is best done this way. For instance, to destroy a list we
must use more care:

```
/* freeall: free all elements of listp */
void freeall(Nameval *listp)
{
    Nameval *next;

    for ( ; listp != NULL; listp = next) {
        next = listp->next;
        /* assumes name is freed elsewhere */
        free(listp);
    }
}
```

Memory cannot be used after it has been freed, so we must save listp->next in a
local variable, called next, before freeing the element pointed to by listp. If the
loop read, like the others,

```
?    for ( ; listp != NULL; listp = listp->next)
?        free(listp);
```

the value of listp->next could be overwritten by free and the code would fail.

Notice that freeall does not free listp->name. It assumes that the name field of
each Nameval will be freed somewhere else, or was never allocated. Making sure
items are allocated and freed consistently requires agreement between newitem and
freeall; there is a tradeoff between guaranteeing that memory gets freed and making
sure things aren't freed that shouldn't be. Bugs are frequent when this is done wrong.

In other languages, including Java, garbage collection solves this problem for you. We will return to the topic of resource management in Chapter 4.

Deleting a single element from a list is more work than adding one:

```
/* delitem: delete first "name" from listp */
Nameval *delitem(Nameval *listp, char *name)
{
    Nameval *p, *prev;

    prev = NULL;
    for (p = listp; p != NULL; p = p->next) {
        if (strcmp(name, p->name) == 0) {
            if (prev == NULL)
                listp = p->next;
            else
                prev->next = p->next;
            free(p);
            return listp;
        }
        prev = p;
    }
    eprintf("delitem: %s not in list", name);
    return NULL;    /* can't get here */
}
```

As in `freeall`, `delitem` does not free the `name` field.

The function `eprintf` displays an error message and exits the program, which is clumsy at best. Recovering gracefully from errors can be difficult and requires a longer discussion that we defer to Chapter 4, where we will also show the implementation of `eprintf`.

These basic list structures and operations account for the vast majority of applications that you are likely to write in ordinary programs. But there are many alternatives. Some libraries, including the C++ Standard Template Library, support doubly-linked lists, in which each element has two pointers, one to its successor and one to its predecessor. Doubly-linked lists require more overhead, but finding the last element and deleting the current element are $O(1)$ operations. Some allocate the list pointers separately from the data they link together; these are a little harder to use but permit items to appear on more than one list at the same time.

Besides being suitable for situations where there are insertions and deletions in the middle, lists are good for managing unordered data of fluctuating size, especially when access tends to be last-in-first-out (LIFO), as in a stack. They make more effective use of memory than arrays do when there are multiple stacks that grow and shrink independently. They also behave well when the information is ordered intrinsically as a chain of unknown *a priori* size, such as the successive words of a document. If you must combine frequent update with random access, however, it would be wiser to use a less insistently linear data structure, such as a tree or hash table.

Exercise 2-7. Implement some of the other list operators: copy, merge, split, insert before or after a specific item. How do the two insertion operations differ in difficulty? How much can you use the routines we've written, and how much must you create yourself? □

Exercise 2-8. Write recursive and iterative versions of reverse, which reverses a list. Do not create new list items; re-use the existing ones. □

Exercise 2-9. Write a generic List type for C. The easiest way is to have each list item hold a void* that points to the data. Do the same for C++ by defining a template and for Java by defining a class that holds lists of type Object. What are the strengths and weaknesses of the various languages for this job? □

Exercise 2-10. Devise and implement a set of tests for verifying that the list routines you write are correct. Chapter 6 discusses strategies for testing. □

2.8 Trees

A tree is a hierarchical data structure that stores a set of items in which each item has a value, may point to zero or more others, and is pointed to by exactly one other. The *root* of the tree is the sole exception; no item points to it.

There are many types of trees that reflect complex structures, such as parse trees that capture the syntax of a sentence or a program, or family trees that describe relationships among people. We will illustrate the principles with binary search trees, which have two links at each node. They're the easiest to implement, and demonstrate the essential properties of trees. A node in a binary search tree has a value and two pointers, left and right, that point to its children. The child pointers may be null if the node has fewer than two children. In a binary search tree, the values at the nodes define the tree: all children to the left of a particular node have lower values, and all children to the right have higher values. Because of this property, we can use a variant of binary search to search the tree quickly for a specific value or determine that it is not present.

The tree version of Nameval is straightforward:

```
typedef struct Nameval Nameval;
struct Nameval {
    char    *name;
    int     value;
    Nameval *left;  /* lesser */
    Nameval *right; /* greater */
};
```

The *lesser* and *greater* comments refer to the properties of the links: left children store lesser values, right children store greater values.

As a concrete example, this figure shows a subset of a character name table stored as a binary search tree of Namevals, sorted by ASCII character values in the names:

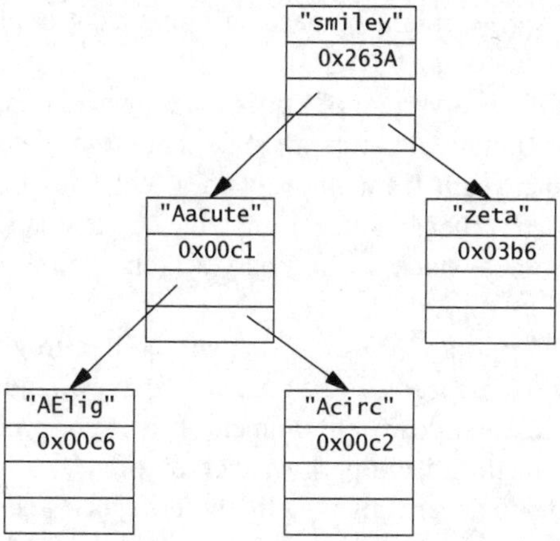

With multiple pointers to other elements in each node of a tree, many operations that take time $O(n)$ in lists or arrays require only $O(\log n)$ time in trees. The multiple pointers at each node reduce the time complexity of operations by reducing the number of nodes one must visit to find an item.

A binary search tree (which we'll call just "tree" in this section) is constructed by descending into the tree recursively, branching left or right as appropriate, until we find the right place to link in the new node, which must be a properly initialized object of type Nameval: a name, a value, and two null pointers. The new node is added as a *leaf*, that is, it has no children yet.

```
/* insert: insert newp in treep, return treep */
Nameval *insert(Nameval *treep, Nameval *newp)
{
    int cmp;

    if (treep == NULL)
        return newp;
    cmp = strcmp(newp->name, treep->name);
    if (cmp == 0)
        weprintf("insert: duplicate entry %s ignored",
            newp->name);
    else if (cmp < 0)
        treep->left = insert(treep->left, newp);
    else
        treep->right = insert(treep->right, newp);
    return treep;
}
```

We haven't said anything before about duplicate entries. This version of insert complains about attempts to insert duplicate entries (cmp == 0) in the tree. The list insert routine didn't complain because that would require searching the list, making insertion $O(n)$ rather than $O(1)$. With trees, however, the test is essentially free and the properties of the data structure are not as clearly defined if there are duplicates. In other applications, though, it might be necessary to accept duplicates, or it might be reasonable to ignore them completely.

The weprintf routine is a variant of eprintf; it prints an error message, prefixed with the word warning, but unlike eprintf it does not terminate the program.

A tree in which each path from the root to a leaf has approximately the same length is called *balanced*. The advantage of a balanced tree is that searching it for an item is an $O(\log n)$ process, since, as in binary search, the number of possibilities is halved at each step.

If items are inserted into a tree as they arrive, the tree might not be balanced; in fact, it might be badly unbalanced. If the elements arrive already sorted, for instance, the code will always descend down one branch of the tree, producing in effect a list down the right links, with all the performance problems of a list. If the elements arrive in random order, however, this is unlikely to happen and the tree will be more or less balanced.

It is complicated to implement trees that are guaranteed to be balanced; this is one reason there are many kinds of trees. For our purposes, we'll just sidestep the issue and assume that incoming data is sufficiently random to keep the tree balanced enough.

The code for lookup is similar to insert:

```
/* lookup: look up name in tree treep */
Nameval *lookup(Nameval *treep, char *name)
{
    int cmp;

    if (treep == NULL)
        return NULL;
    cmp = strcmp(name, treep->name);
    if (cmp == 0)
        return treep;
    else if (cmp < 0)
        return lookup(treep->left, name);
    else
        return lookup(treep->right, name);
}
```

There are a couple of things to notice about lookup and insert. First, they look remarkably like the binary search algorithm at the beginning of the chapter. This is no accident, since they share an idea with binary search: divide and conquer, the origin of logarithmic-time performance.

Second, these routines are recursive. If they are rewritten as iterative algorithms they will be even more similar to binary search. In fact, the iterative version of lookup can be constructed by applying an elegant transformation to the recursive version. Unless we have found the item, lookup's last action is to return the result of a call to itself, a situation called *tail recursion*. This can be converted to iteration by patching up the arguments and restarting the routine. The most direct method is to use a goto statement, but a while loop is cleaner:

```
/* nrlookup: non-recursively look up name in tree treep */
Nameval *nrlookup(Nameval *treep, char *name)
{
    int cmp;

    while (treep != NULL) {
        cmp = strcmp(name, treep->name);
        if (cmp == 0)
            return treep;
        else if (cmp < 0)
            treep = treep->left;
        else
            treep = treep->right;
    }
    return NULL;
}
```

Once we can walk the tree, the other common operations follow naturally. We can use some of the techniques from list management, such as writing a general tree-traverser that calls a function at each node. This time, however, there is a choice to make: when do we perform the operation on this item and when do we process the rest of the tree? The answer depends on what the tree is representing; if it's storing data in order, such as a binary search tree, we visit the left half before the right. Sometimes the tree structure reflects some intrinsic ordering of the data, such as in a family tree, and the order in which we visit the leaves will depend on the relationships the tree represents.

An *in-order* traversal executes the operation after visiting the left subtree and before visiting the right subtree:

```
/* applyinorder: inorder application of fn to treep */
void applyinorder(Nameval *treep,
        void (*fn)(Nameval*, void*), void *arg)
{
    if (treep == NULL)
        return;
    applyinorder(treep->left, fn, arg);
    (*fn)(treep, arg);
    applyinorder(treep->right, fn, arg);
}
```

This sequence is used when nodes are to be processed in sorted order, for example to print them all in order, which would be done as

```
applyinorder(treep, printnv, "%s: %x\n");
```

It also suggests a reasonable way to sort: insert items into a tree, allocate an array of the right size, then use in-order traversal to store them in the array in sequence.

A *post-order* traversal invokes the operation on the current node after visiting the children:

```
/* applypostorder: postorder application of fn to treep */
void applypostorder(Nameval *treep,
        void (*fn)(Nameval*, void*), void *arg)
{
    if (treep == NULL)
        return;
    applypostorder(treep->left, fn, arg);
    applypostorder(treep->right, fn, arg);
    (*fn)(treep, arg);
}
```

Post-order traversal is used when the operation on the node depends on the subtrees below it. Examples include computing the height of a tree (take the maximum of the height of each of the two subtrees and add one), laying out a tree in a graphics drawing package (allocate space on the page for each subtree and combine them for this node's space), and measuring total storage.

A third choice, *pre-order*, is rarely used so we'll omit it.

Realistically, binary search trees are infrequently used, though B-trees, which have very high branching, are used to maintain information on secondary storage. In day-to-day programming, one common use of a tree is to represent the structure of a statement or expression. For example, the statement

```
mid = (low + high) / 2;
```

can be represented by the *parse tree* shown in the figure below. To evaluate the tree, do a post-order traversal and perform the appropriate operation at each node.

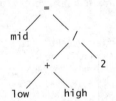

We'll take a longer look at parse trees in Chapter 9.

Exercise 2-11. Compare the performance of `lookup` and `nrlookup`. How expensive is recursion compared to iteration? □

Exercise 2-12. Use in-order traversal to create a sort routine. What time complexity does it have? Under what conditions might it behave poorly? How does its performance compare to our quicksort and a library version? □

Exercise 2-13. Devise and implement a set of tests for verifying that the tree routines are correct. □

2.9 Hash Tables

Hash tables are one of the great inventions of computer science. They combine arrays, lists, and some mathematics to create an efficient structure for storing and retrieving dynamic data. The typical application is a *symbol table*, which associates some value (the *data*) with each member of a dynamic set of strings (the *keys*). Your favorite compiler almost certainly uses a hash table to manage information about each variable in your program. Your web browser may well use a hash table to keep track of recently-used pages, and your connection to the Internet probably uses one to cache recently-used domain names and their IP addresses.

The idea is to pass the key through a *hash function* to generate a *hash value* that will be evenly distributed through a modest-sized integer range. The hash value is used to index a table where the information is stored. Java provides a standard interface to hash tables. In C and C++ the usual style is to associate with each hash value (or "bucket") a list of the items that share that hash, as this figure illustrates:

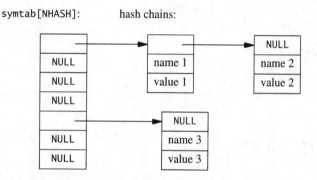

In practice, the hash function is pre-defined and an appropriate size of array is allocated, often at compile time. Each element of the array is a list that *chains* together the items that share a hash value. In other words, a hash table of *n* items is an array of lists whose average length is *n*/(array size). Retrieving an item is an $O(1)$ operation provided we pick a good hash function and the lists don't grow too long.

Because a hash table is an array of lists, the element type is the same as for a list:

```
typedef struct Nameval Nameval;
struct Nameval {
    char    *name;
    int     value;
    Nameval *next;        /* in chain */
};

Nameval *symtab[NHASH]; /* a symbol table */
```

The list techniques we discussed in Section 2.7 can be used to maintain the individual hash chains. Once you've got a good hash function, it's smooth sailing: just pick the hash bucket and walk along the list looking for a perfect match. Here is the code for a hash table lookup/insert routine. If the item is found, it is returned. If the item is not found and the `create` flag is set, `lookup` adds the item to the table. Again, this does not create a copy of the name, assuming that the caller has made a safe copy instead.

```c
/* lookup: find name in symtab, with optional create */
Nameval* lookup(char *name, int create, int value)
{
    int h;
    Nameval *sym;

    h = hash(name);
    for (sym = symtab[h]; sym != NULL; sym = sym->next)
        if (strcmp(name, sym->name) == 0)
            return sym;
    if (create) {
        sym = (Nameval *) emalloc(sizeof(Nameval));
        sym->name = name; /* assumed allocated elsewhere */
        sym->value = value;
        sym->next = symtab[h];
        symtab[h] = sym;
    }
    return sym;
}
```

This combination of lookup and optional insertion is common. Without it, there is duplication of effort; one must write

```c
if (lookup("name") == NULL)
    additem(newitem("name", value));
```

and the hash is computed twice.

How big should the array be? The general idea is to make it big enough that each hash chain will have at most a few elements, so that lookup will be $O(1)$. For instance, a compiler might have an array size of a few thousand, since a large source file has a few thousand lines, and we don't expect more than about one new identifier per line of code.

We must now decide what the hash function, `hash`, should calculate. The function must be deterministic and should be fast and distribute the data uniformly throughout the array. One of the most common hashing algorithms for strings builds a hash value by adding each byte of the string to a multiple of the hash so far. The multiplication spreads bits from the new byte through the value so far; at the end of the loop, the result should be a thorough mixing of the input bytes. Empirically, the values 31 and 37 have proven to be good choices for the multiplier in a hash function for ASCII strings.

```c
enum { MULTIPLIER = 31 };
```

```
/* hash: compute hash value of string */
unsigned int hash(char *str)
{
    unsigned int h;
    unsigned char *p;

    h = 0;
    for (p = (unsigned char *) str; *p != '\0'; p++)
        h = MULTIPLIER * h + *p;
    return h % NHASH;
}
```

The calculation uses unsigned characters because whether char is signed is not specified by C and C++, and we want the hash value to remain positive.

The hash function returns the result modulo the size of the array. If the hash function distributes key values uniformly, the precise array size doesn't matter. It's hard to be certain that a hash function is dependable, though, and even the best function may have trouble with some input sets, so it's wise to make the array size a prime number to give a bit of extra insurance by guaranteeing that the array size, the hash multiplier, and likely data values have no common factor.

Experiments show that for a wide variety of strings it's hard to construct a hash function that does appreciably better than the one above, but it's easy to make one that does worse. An early release of Java had a hash function for strings that was more efficient if the string was long. The hash function saved time by examining only 8 or 9 characters at regular intervals throughout strings longer than 16 characters, starting at the beginning. Unfortunately, although the hash function was faster, it had bad statistical properties that canceled any performance gain. By skipping pieces of the string, it tended to miss the only distinguishing part. File names begin with long identical prefixes—the directory name—and may differ only in the last few characters (.java versus .class). URLs usually begin with http://www. and end with .html, so they tend to differ only in the middle. The hash function would often examine only the non-varying part of the name, resulting in long hash chains that slowed down searching. The problem was resolved by replacing the hash with one equivalent to the one we have shown (with a multiplier of 37), which examines every character of the string.

A hash function that's good for one input set (say, short variable names) might be poor for another (URLs), so a potential hash function should be tested on a variety of typical inputs. Does it hash short strings well? Long strings? Equal length strings with minor variations?

Strings aren't the only things we can hash. We could hash the three coordinates of a particle in a physical simulation, reducing the storage to a linear table (O(number of particles)) instead of a three-dimensional array ($O(xsize \times ysize \times zsize)$).

One remarkable use of hashing is Gerard Holzmann's Supertrace program for analyzing protocols and concurrent systems. Supertrace takes the full information for each possible state of the system under analysis and hashes the information to generate the address of a single bit in memory. If that bit is on, the state has been seen before; if not, it hasn't. Supertrace uses a hash table many megabytes long, but stores only a single bit in each bucket. There is no chaining; if two states *collide* by hashing to the same value, the program won't notice. Supertrace depends on the probability of collision being low (it doesn't need to be zero because Supertrace is probabilistic, not exact). The hash function is therefore particularly careful; it uses a *cyclic redundancy check,* a function that produces a thorough mix of the data.

Hash tables are excellent for symbol tables, since they provide expected $O(1)$ access to any element. They do have a few limitations. If the hash function is poor or the table size is too small, the lists can grow long. Since the lists are unsorted, this leads to $O(n)$ behavior. The elements are not directly accessible in sorted order, but it is easy to count them, allocate an array, fill it with pointers to the elements, and sort that. Still, when used properly, the constant-time lookup, insertion, and deletion properties of a hash table are unmatched by other techniques.

Exercise 2-14. Our hash function is an excellent general-purpose hash for strings. Nonetheless, peculiar data might cause poor behavior. Construct a data set that causes our hash function to perform badly. Is it easier to find a bad set for different values of NHASH? □

Exercise 2-15. Write a function to access the successive elements of the hash table in unsorted order. □

Exercise 2-16. Change lookup so that if the average list length becomes more than x, the array is grown automatically by a factor of y and the hash table is rebuilt. □

Exercise 2-17. Design a hash function for storing the coordinates of points in 2 dimensions. How easily does your function adapt to changes in the type of the coordinates, for example from integer to floating point or from Cartesian to polar coordinates, or to changes from 2 to higher dimensions? □

2.10 Summary

There are several steps to choosing an algorithm. First, assess potential algorithms and data structures. Consider how much data the program is likely to process. If the problem involves modest amounts of data, choose simple techniques; if the data could grow, eliminate designs that will not scale up to large inputs. Then, use a library or language feature if you can. Failing that, write or borrow a short, simple, easy to understand implementation. Try it. If measurements prove it to be too slow, only then should you upgrade to a more advanced technique.

Although there are many data structures, some vital to good performance in special circumstances, most programs are based largely on arrays, lists, trees, and hash tables. Each of these supports a set of primitive operations, usually including: create a new element, find an element, add an element somewhere, perhaps delete an element, and apply some operation to all elements.

Each operation has an expected computation time that often determines how suitable this data type (or implementation) is for a particular application. Arrays support constant-time access to any element but do not grow or shrink gracefully. Lists adjust well to insertions and deletions, but take $O(n)$ time to access random elements. Trees and hash tables provide a good compromise: rapid access to specific items combined with easy growth, so long as some balance criterion is maintained.

There are other more sophisticated data structures for specialized problems, but this basic set is sufficient to build the great majority of software.

Supplementary Reading

Bob Sedgewick's family of *Algorithms* books (Addison-Wesley) is an excellent place to find accessible treatments of a variety of useful algorithms. The third edition of *Algorithms in C++* (1998) has a good discussion of hash functions and table sizes. Don Knuth's *The Art of Computer Programming* (Addison-Wesley) is the definitive source for rigorous analyses of many algorithms; Volume 3 (2nd Edition, 1998) covers sorting and searching.

Supertrace is described in *Design and Validation of Computer Protocols* by Gerard Holzmann (Prentice Hall, 1991).

Jon Bentley and Doug McIlroy describe the creation of a fast and robust quicksort in "Engineering a sort function," *Software—Practice and Experience*, **23**, 1, pp. 1249-1265, 1993.

3

Design and Implementation

Show me your flowcharts and conceal your tables, and I shall continue to be mystified. Show me your tables, and I won't usually need your flowcharts; they'll be obvious.

Frederick P. Brooks, Jr., *The Mythical Man Month*

As the quotation from Brooks's classic book suggests, the design of the data structures is the central decision in the creation of a program. Once the data structures are laid out, the algorithms tend to fall into place, and the coding is comparatively easy.

This point of view is oversimplified but not misleading. In the previous chapter we examined the basic data structures that are the building blocks of most programs. In this chapter we will combine such structures as we work through the design and implementation of a modest-sized program. We will show how the problem influences the data structures, and how the code that follows is straightforward once we have the data structures mapped out.

One aspect of this point of view is that the choice of programming language is relatively unimportant to the overall design. We will design the program in the abstract and then write it in C, Java, C++, Awk, and Perl. Comparing the implementations demonstrates how languages can help or hinder, and ways in which they are unimportant. Program design can certainly be colored by a language but is not usually dominated by it.

The problem we have chosen is unusual, but in basic form it is typical of many programs: some data comes in, some data goes out, and the processing depends on a little ingenuity.

Specifically, we're going to generate random English text that reads well. If we emit random letters or random words, the result will be nonsense. For example, a program that randomly selects letters (and blanks, to separate words) might produce this:

```
xptmxgn xusaja  afqnzgxl  lhidlwcd rjdjuvpydrlwnjy
```

which is not very convincing. If we weight the letters by their frequency of appearance in English text, we might get this:

```
idtefoae tcs trder jcii ofdslnqetacp t ola
```

which isn't a great deal better. Words chosen from the dictionary at random don't make much more sense:

```
polydactyl equatorial splashily jowl verandah circumscribe
```

For better results, we need a statistical model with more structure, such as the frequency of appearance of whole phrases. But where can we find such statistics?

We could grab a large body of English and study it in detail, but there is an easier and more entertaining approach. The key observation is that we can use any existing text to construct a statistical model of the language *as used in that text*, and from that generate random text that has similar statistics to the original.

3.1 The Markov Chain Algorithm

An elegant way to do this sort of processing is a technique called a *Markov chain algorithm*. If we imagine the input as a sequence of overlapping phrases, the algorithm divides each phrase into two parts, a multi-word *prefix* and a single *suffix* word that follows the prefix. A Markov chain algorithm emits output phrases by randomly choosing the suffix that follows the prefix, according to the statistics of (in our case) the original text. Three-word phrases work well—a two-word prefix is used to select the suffix word:

> set w_1 and w_2 to the first two words in the text
> print w_1 and w_2
> loop:
>> randomly choose w_3, one of the successors of prefix w_1 w_2 in the text
>> print w_3
>> replace w_1 and w_2 by w_2 and w_3
>> repeat loop

To illustrate, suppose we want to generate random text based on a few sentences paraphrased from the epigraph above, using two-word prefixes:

```
Show your flowcharts and conceal your tables and I will be
mystified. Show your tables and your flowcharts will be
obvious. (end)
```

These are some of the pairs of input words and the words that follow them:

Input prefix:	*Suffix words that follow:*
`Show your`	`flowcharts tables`
`your flowcharts`	`and will`
`flowcharts and`	`conceal`
`flowcharts will`	`be`
`your tables`	`and and`
`will be`	`mystified. obvious.`
`be mystified.`	`Show`
`be obvious.`	*(end)*

A Markov algorithm processing this text will begin by printing `Show your` and will then randomly pick either `flowcharts` or `tables`. If it chooses the former, the current prefix becomes `your flowcharts` and the next word will be `and` or `will`. If it chooses `tables`, the next word will be `and`. This continues until enough output has been generated or until the end-marker is encountered as a suffix.

Our program will read a piece of English text and use a Markov chain algorithm to generate new text based on the frequency of appearance of phrases of a fixed length. The number of words in the prefix, which is two in our example, is a parameter. Making the prefix shorter tends to produce less coherent prose; making it longer tends to reproduce the input text verbatim. For English text, using two words to select a third is a good compromise; it seems to recreate the flavor of the input while adding its own whimsical touch.

What is a word? The obvious answer is a sequence of alphabetic characters, but it is desirable to leave punctuation attached to the words so ''words'' and ''words.'' are different. This helps to improve the quality of the generated prose by letting punctuation, and therefore (indirectly) grammar, influence the word choice, although it also permits unbalanced quotes and parentheses to sneak in. We will therefore define a ''word'' as anything between white space, a decision that places no restriction on input language and leaves punctuation attached to the words. Since most programming languages have facilities to split text into white-space-separated words, this is also easy to implement.

Because of the method, all words, all two-word phrases, and all three-word phrases in the output must have appeared in the input, but there should be many four-word and longer phrases that are synthesized. Here are a few sentences produced by the program we will develop in this chapter, when given the text of Chapter VII of *The Sun Also Rises* by Ernest Hemingway:

> As I started up the undershirt onto his chest black, and big stomach muscles bulging under the light. "You see them?" Below the line where his ribs stopped were two raised white welts. "See on the forehead." "Oh, Brett, I love you." "Let's not talk. Talking's all bilge. I'm going away tomorrow." "Tomorrow?" "Yes. Didn't I say so? I am." "Let's have a drink, then."

We were lucky here that punctuation came out correctly; that need not happen.

3.2 Data Structure Alternatives

How much input do we intend to deal with? How fast must the program run? It seems reasonable to ask our program to read in a whole book, so we should be prepared for input sizes of $n = 100,000$ words or more. The output will be hundreds or perhaps thousands of words, and the program should run in a few seconds instead of minutes. With 100,000 words of input text, n is fairly large so the algorithms can't be too simplistic if we want the program to be fast.

The Markov algorithm must see all the input before it can begin to generate output, so it must store the entire input in some form. One possibility is to read the whole input and store it in a long string, but we clearly want the input broken down into words. If we store it as an array of pointers to words, output generation is simple: to produce each word, scan the input text to see what possible suffix words follow the prefix that was just emitted, and then choose one at random. However, that means scanning all 100,000 input words for each word we generate; 1,000 words of output means hundreds of millions of string comparisons, which will not be fast.

Another possibility is to store only unique input words, together with a list of where they appear in the input so that we can locate successor words more quickly. We could use a hash table like the one in Chapter 2, but that version doesn't directly address the needs of the Markov algorithm, which must quickly locate all the suffixes of a given prefix.

We need a data structure that better represents a prefix and its associated suffixes. The program will have two passes, an input pass that builds the data structure representing the phrases, and an output pass that uses the data structure to generate the random output. In both passes, we need to look up a prefix (quickly): in the input pass to update its suffixes, and in the output pass to select at random from the possible suffixes. This suggests a hash table whose keys are prefixes and whose values are the sets of suffixes for the corresponding prefixes.

For purposes of description, we'll assume a two-word prefix, so each output word is based on the pair of words that precede it. The number of words in the prefix doesn't affect the design and the programs should handle any prefix length, but selecting a number makes the discussion concrete. The prefix and the set of all its possible suffixes we'll call a *state*, which is standard terminology for Markov algorithms.

Given a prefix, we need to store all the suffixes that follow it so we can access them later. The suffixes are unordered and added one at a time. We don't know how many there will be, so we need a data structure that grows easily and efficiently, such as a list or a dynamic array. When we are generating output, we need to be able to choose one suffix at random from the set of suffixes associated with a particular prefix. Items are never deleted.

What happens if a phrase appears more than once? For example, 'might appear twice' might appear twice but 'might appear once' only once. This could be represented by putting 'twice' twice in the suffix list for 'might appear' or by putting it in once, with an associated counter set to 2. We've tried it with and without counters;

without is easier, since adding a suffix doesn't require checking whether it's there already, and experiments showed that the difference in run-time was negligible.

In summary, each state comprises a prefix and a list of suffixes. This information is stored in a hash table, with prefix as key. Each prefix is a fixed-size set of words. If a suffix occurs more than once for a given prefix, each occurrence will be included separately in the list.

The next decision is how to represent the words themselves. The easy way is to store them as individual strings. Since most text has many words appearing multiple times, it would probably save storage if we kept a second hash table of single words, so the text of each word was stored only once. This would also speed up hashing of prefixes, since we could compare pointers rather than individual characters: unique strings have unique addresses. We'll leave that design as an exercise; for now, strings will be stored individually.

3.3 Building the Data Structure in C

Let's begin with a C implementation. The first step is to define some constants.

```
enum {
    NPREF   = 2,     /* number of prefix words */
    NHASH   = 4093,  /* size of state hash table array */
    MAXGEN  = 10000  /* maximum words generated */
};
```

This declaration defines the number of words (NPREF) for the prefix, the size of the hash table array (NHASH), and an upper limit on the number of words to generate (MAXGEN). If NPREF is a compile-time constant rather than a run-time variable, storage management is simpler. The array size is set fairly large because we expect to give the program large input documents, perhaps a whole book. We chose NHASH = 4093 so that if the input has 10,000 distinct prefixes (word pairs), the average chain will be very short, two or three prefixes. The larger the size, the shorter the expected length of the chains and thus the faster the lookup. This program is really a toy, so the performance isn't critical, but if we make the array too small the program will not handle our expected input in reasonable time; on the other hand, if we make it too big it might not fit in the available memory.

The prefix can be stored as an array of words. The elements of the hash table will be represented as a State data type, associating the Suffix list with the prefix:

```
typedef struct State State;
typedef struct Suffix Suffix;
struct State {  /* prefix + suffix list */
    char    *pref[NPREF];   /* prefix words */
    Suffix  *suf;           /* list of suffixes */
    State   *next;          /* next in hash table */
};
```

```
struct Suffix { /* list of suffixes */
    char    *word;              /* suffix */
    Suffix  *next;              /* next in list of suffixes */
};

State   *statetab[NHASH];    /* hash table of states */
```

Pictorially, the data structures look like this:

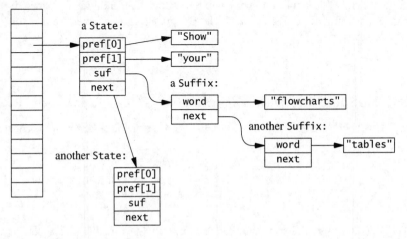

We need a hash function for prefixes, which are arrays of strings. It is simple to modify the string hash function from Chapter 2 to loop over the strings in the array, thus in effect hashing the concatenation of the strings:

```
/* hash: compute hash value for array of NPREF strings */
unsigned int hash(char *s[NPREF])
{
    unsigned int h;
    unsigned char *p;
    int i;

    h = 0;
    for (i = 0; i < NPREF; i++)
        for (p = (unsigned char *) s[i]; *p != '\0'; p++)
            h = MULTIPLIER * h + *p;
    return h % NHASH;
}
```

A similar modification to the lookup routine completes the implementation of the hash table:

```
/* lookup: search for prefix; create if requested. */
/*   returns pointer if present or created; NULL if not. */
/*   creation doesn't strdup so strings mustn't change later. */
State* lookup(char *prefix[NPREF], int create)
{
    int i, h;
    State *sp;

    h = hash(prefix);
    for (sp = statetab[h]; sp != NULL; sp = sp->next) {
        for (i = 0; i < NPREF; i++)
            if (strcmp(prefix[i], sp->pref[i]) != 0)
                break;
        if (i == NPREF)        /* found it */
            return sp;
    }
    if (create) {
        sp = (State *) emalloc(sizeof(State));
        for (i = 0; i < NPREF; i++)
            sp->pref[i] = prefix[i];
        sp->suf = NULL;
        sp->next = statetab[h];
        statetab[h] = sp;
    }
    return sp;
}
```

Notice that lookup doesn't make a copy of the incoming strings when it creates a new state; it just stores pointers in sp->pref[]. Callers of lookup must guarantee that the data won't be overwritten later. For example, if the strings are in an I/O buffer, a copy must be made before lookup is called; otherwise, subsequent input could over-write the data that the hash table points to. Decisions about who owns a resource shared across an interface arise often. We will explore this topic at length in the next chapter.

Next we need to build the hash table as the file is read:

```
/* build: read input, build prefix table */
void build(char *prefix[NPREF], FILE *f)
{
    char buf[100], fmt[10];

    /* create a format string; %s could overflow buf */
    sprintf(fmt, "%%%ds", sizeof(buf)-1);
    while (fscanf(f, fmt, buf) != EOF)
        add(prefix, estrdup(buf));
}
```

The peculiar call to sprintf gets around an irritating problem with fscanf, which is otherwise perfect for the job. A call to fscanf with format %s will read the next white-space-delimited word from the file into the buffer, but there is no limit on size: a long word might overflow the input buffer, wreaking havoc. If the buffer is 100 bytes long (which is far beyond what we expect ever to appear in normal text), we can use the format %99s (leaving one byte for the terminal '\0'), which tells fscanf to stop after 99 bytes. A long word will be broken into pieces, which is unfortunate but safe. We could declare

```
?    enum { BUFSIZE = 100 };
?    char    fmt[] = "%99s"; /* BUFSIZE-1 */
```

but that requires two constants for one arbitrary decision—the size of the buffer—and introduces the need to maintain their relationship. The problem can be solved once and for all by creating the format string dynamically with sprintf, so that's the approach we take.

The two arguments to build are the prefix array holding the previous NPREF words of input and a FILE pointer. It passes the prefix and a copy of the input word to add, which adds the new entry to the hash table and advances the prefix:

```
/* add: add word to suffix list, update prefix */
void add(char *prefix[NPREF], char *suffix)
{
    State *sp;

    sp = lookup(prefix, 1);  /* create if not found */
    addsuffix(sp, suffix);
    /* move the words down the prefix */
    memmove(prefix, prefix+1, (NPREF-1)*sizeof(prefix[0]));
    prefix[NPREF-1] = suffix;
}
```

The call to memmove is the idiom for deleting from an array. It shifts elements 1 through NPREF-1 in the prefix down to positions 0 through NPREF-2, deleting the first prefix word and opening a space for a new one at the end.

The addsuffix routine adds the new suffix:

```
/* addsuffix: add to state. suffix must not change later */
void addsuffix(State *sp, char *suffix)
{
    Suffix *suf;

    suf = (Suffix *) emalloc(sizeof(Suffix));
    suf->word = suffix;
    suf->next = sp->suf;
    sp->suf = suf;
}
```

We split the action of updating the state into two functions: add performs the general service of adding a suffix to a prefix, while addsuffix performs the implementation-specific action of adding a word to a suffix list. The add routine is used by build, but addsuffix is used internally only by add; it is an implementation detail that might change and it seems better to have it in a separate function, even though it is called in only one place.

3.4 Generating Output

With the data structure built, the next step is to generate the output. The basic idea is as before: given a prefix, select one of its suffixes at random, print it, then advance the prefix. This is the steady state of processing; we must still figure out how to start and stop the algorithm. Starting is easy if we remember the words of the first prefix and begin with them. Stopping is easy, too. We need a marker word to terminate the algorithm. After all the regular input, we can add a terminator, a ''word'' that is guaranteed not to appear in any input:

```
build(prefix, stdin);
add(prefix, NONWORD);
```

NONWORD should be some value that will never be encountered in regular input. Since the input words are delimited by white space, a ''word'' of white space will serve, such as a newline character:

```
char NONWORD[] = "\n";  /* cannot appear as real word */
```

One more worry: what happens if there is insufficient input to start the algorithm? There are two approaches to this sort of problem, either exit prematurely if there is insufficient input, or arrange that there is always enough and don't bother to check. In this program, the latter approach works well.

We can initialize building and generating with a fabricated prefix, which guarantees there is always enough input for the program. To prime the loops, initialize the prefix array to be all NONWORD words. This has the nice benefit that the first word of the input file will be the first *suffix* of the fake prefix, so the generation loop needs to print only the suffixes it produces.

In case the output is unmanageably long, we can terminate the algorithm after some number of words are produced or when we hit NONWORD as a suffix, whichever comes first.

Adding a few NONWORDs to the ends of the data simplifies the main processing loops of the program significantly; it is an example of the technique of adding *sentinel* values to mark boundaries.

As a rule, try to handle irregularities and exceptions and special cases in data. Code is harder to get right so the control flow should be as simple and regular as possible.

The generate function uses the algorithm we sketched originally. It produces one word per line of output, which can be grouped into longer lines with a word processor; Chapter 9 shows a simple formatter called fmt for this task.

With the use of the initial and final NONWORD strings, generate starts and stops properly:

```
/* generate: produce output, one word per line */
void generate(int nwords)
{
    State *sp;
    Suffix *suf;
    char *prefix[NPREF], *w;
    int i, nmatch;

    for (i = 0; i < NPREF; i++) /* reset initial prefix */
        prefix[i] = NONWORD;

    for (i = 0; i < nwords; i++) {
        sp = lookup(prefix, 0);
        nmatch = 0;
        for (suf = sp->suf; suf != NULL; suf = suf->next)
            if (rand() % ++nmatch == 0) /* prob = 1/nmatch */
                w = suf->word;
        if (strcmp(w, NONWORD) == 0)
            break;
        printf("%s\n", w);
        memmove(prefix, prefix+1, (NPREF-1)*sizeof(prefix[0]));
        prefix[NPREF-1] = w;
    }
}
```

Notice the algorithm for selecting one item at random when we don't know how many
items there are. The variable nmatch counts the number of matches as the list is
scanned. The expression

```
rand() % ++nmatch == 0
```

increments nmatch and is then true with probability 1/nmatch. Thus the first matching item is selected with probability 1, the second will replace it with probability 1/2,
the third will replace the survivor with probability 1/3, and so on. At any time, each
one of the k matching items seen so far has been selected with probability $1/k$.

At the beginning, we set the prefix to the starting value, which is guaranteed to
be installed in the hash table. The first Suffix values we find will be the first words
of the document, since they are the unique follow-on to the starting prefix. After that,
random suffixes will be chosen. The loop calls lookup to find the hash table entry for
the current prefix, then chooses a random suffix, prints it, and advances the prefix.

If the suffix we choose is NONWORD, we're done, because we have chosen the state
that corresponds to the end of the input. If the suffix is not NONWORD, we print it, then
drop the first word of the prefix with a call to memmove, promote the suffix to be the
last word of the prefix, and loop.

Now we can put all this together into a main routine that reads the standard input
and generates at most a specified number of words:

```
/* markov main: markov-chain random text generation */
int main(void)
{
    int i, nwords = MAXGEN;
    char *prefix[NPREF];              /* current input prefix */

    for (i = 0; i < NPREF; i++) /* set up initial prefix */
        prefix[i] = NONWORD;
    build(prefix, stdin);
    add(prefix, NONWORD);
    generate(nwords);
    return 0;
}
```

This completes our C implementation. We will return at the end of the chapter to a comparison of programs in different languages. The great strengths of C are that it gives the programmer complete control over implementation, and programs written in it tend to be fast. The cost, however, is that the C programmer must do more of the work, allocating and reclaiming memory, creating hash tables and linked lists, and the like. C is a razor-sharp tool, with which one can create an elegant and efficient program or a bloody mess.

Exercise 3-1. The algorithm for selecting a random item from a list of unknown length depends on having a good random number generator. Design and carry out experiments to determine how well the method works in practice. ☐

Exercise 3-2. If each input word is stored in a second hash table, the text is only stored once, which should save space. Measure some documents to estimate how much. This organization would allow us to compare pointers rather than strings in the hash chains for prefixes, which should run faster. Implement this version and measure the change in speed and memory consumption. ☐

Exercise 3-3. Remove the statements that place sentinel NONWORDs at the beginning and end of the data, and modify generate so it starts and stops properly without them. Make sure it produces correct output for input with 0, 1, 2, 3, and 4 words. Compare this implementation to the version using sentinels. ☐

3.5 Java

Our second implementation of the Markov chain algorithm is in Java. Object-oriented languages like Java encourage one to pay particular attention to the interfaces between the components of the program, which are then encapsulated as independent data items called objects or classes, with associated functions called methods.

Java has a richer library than C, including a set of *container classes* to group existing objects in various ways. One example is a Vector that provides a dynamically-growable array that can store any Object type. Another example is the Hashtable class, with which one can store and retrieve values of one type using objects of another type as keys.

In our application, `Vectors` of strings are the natural choice to hold prefixes and suffixes. We can use a `Hashtable` whose keys are prefix vectors and whose values are suffix vectors. The terminology for this type of construction is a *map* from prefixes to suffixes; in Java, we need no explicit `State` type because `Hashtable` implicitly connects (maps) prefixes to suffixes. This design is different from the C version, in which we installed `State` structures that held both prefix and suffix list, and hashed on the prefix to recover the full `State`.

A `Hashtable` provides a put method to store a key-value pair, and a get method to retrieve the value for a key:

```
Hashtable h = new Hashtable();
h.put(key, value);
Sometype v = (Sometype) h.get(key);
```

Our implementation has three classes. The first class, `Prefix`, holds the words of the prefix:

```
class Prefix {
    public Vector pref; // NPREF adjacent words from input
    ...
```

The second class, `Chain`, reads the input, builds the hash table, and generates the output; here are its class variables:

```
class Chain {
    static final int NPREF = 2; // size of prefix
    static final String NONWORD = "\n";
                    // "word" that can't appear
    Hashtable statetab = new Hashtable();
                    // key = Prefix, value = suffix Vector
    Prefix prefix = new Prefix(NPREF, NONWORD);
                    // initial prefix
    Random rand = new Random();
    ...
```

The third class is the public interface; it holds `main` and instantiates a `Chain`:

```
class Markov {
    static final int MAXGEN = 10000; // maximum words generated
    public static void main(String[] args) throws IOException
    {
        Chain chain = new Chain();
        int nwords = MAXGEN;

        chain.build(System.in);
        chain.generate(nwords);
    }
}
```

When an instance of class `Chain` is created, it in turn creates a hash table and sets up the initial prefix of NPREF NONWORDs. The `build` function uses the library function `StreamTokenizer` to parse the input into words separated by white space characters. The three calls before the loop set the tokenizer into the proper state for our definition of "word."

```
// Chain build: build State table from input stream
void build(InputStream in) throws IOException
{
    StreamTokenizer st = new StreamTokenizer(in);

    st.resetSyntax();                       // remove default rules
    st.wordChars(0, Character.MAX_VALUE);   // turn on all chars
    st.whitespaceChars(0, ' ');             // except up to blank
    while (st.nextToken() != st.TT_EOF)
        add(st.sval);
    add(NONWORD);
}
```

The `add` function retrieves the vector of suffixes for the current prefix from the hash table; if there are none (the vector is null), add creates a new vector and a new prefix to store in the hash table. In either case, it adds the new word to the suffix vector and advances the prefix by dropping the first word and adding the new word at the end.

```
// Chain add: add word to suffix list, update prefix
void add(String word)
{
    Vector suf = (Vector) statetab.get(prefix);
    if (suf == null) {
        suf = new Vector();
        statetab.put(new Prefix(prefix), suf);
    }
    suf.addElement(word);
    prefix.pref.removeElementAt(0);
    prefix.pref.addElement(word);
}
```

Notice that if `suf` is null, add installs a new `Prefix` in the hash table, rather than `prefix` itself. This is because the `Hashtable` class stores items by reference, and if we don't make a copy, we could overwrite data in the table. This is the same issue that we had to deal with in the C program.

The generation function is similar to the C version, but slightly more compact because it can index a random vector element directly instead of looping through a list.

```
// Chain generate: generate output words
void generate(int nwords)
{
    prefix = new Prefix(NPREF, NONWORD);
    for (int i = 0; i < nwords; i++) {
        Vector s = (Vector) statetab.get(prefix);
        int r = Math.abs(rand.nextInt()) % s.size();
        String suf = (String) s.elementAt(r);
        if (suf.equals(NONWORD))
            break;
        System.out.println(suf);
        prefix.pref.removeElementAt(0);
        prefix.pref.addElement(suf);
    }
}
```

The two constructors of Prefix create new instances from supplied data. The first copies an existing Prefix, and the second creates a prefix from n copies of a string; we use it to make NPREF copies of NONWORD when initializing:

```
// Prefix constructor: duplicate existing prefix
Prefix(Prefix p)
{
    pref = (Vector) p.pref.clone();
}

// Prefix constructor: n copies of str
Prefix(int n, String str)
{
    pref = new Vector();
    for (int i = 0; i < n; i++)
        pref.addElement(str);
}
```

Prefix also has two methods, hashCode and equals, that are called implicitly by the implementation of Hashtable to index and search the table. It is the need to have an explicit class for these two methods for Hashtable that forced us to make Prefix a full-fledged class, rather than just a Vector like the suffix.

The hashCode method builds a single hash value by combining the set of hashCodes for the elements of the vector:

```
static final int MULTIPLIER = 31;    // for hashCode()

// Prefix hashCode: generate hash from all prefix words
public int hashCode()
{
    int h = 0;

    for (int i = 0; i < pref.size(); i++)
        h = MULTIPLIER * h + pref.elementAt(i).hashCode();
    return h;
}
```

and `equals` does an elementwise comparison of the words in two prefixes:

```
// Prefix equals: compare two prefixes for equal words
public boolean equals(Object o)
{
    Prefix p = (Prefix) o;

    for (int i = 0; i < pref.size(); i++)
        if (!pref.elementAt(i).equals(p.pref.elementAt(i)))
            return false;
    return true;
}
```

The Java program is significantly smaller than the C program and takes care of more details; `Vectors` and the `Hashtable` are the obvious examples. In general, storage management is easy since vectors grow as needed and garbage collection takes care of reclaiming memory that is no longer referenced. But to use the `Hashtable` class, we still need to write functions `hashCode` and `equals`, so Java isn't taking care of all the details.

Comparing the way the C and Java programs represent and operate on the same basic data structure, we see that the Java version has better separation of functionality. For example, to switch from `Vectors` to arrays would be easy. In the C version, everything knows what everything else is doing: the hash table operates on arrays that are maintained in various places, `lookup` knows the layout of the `State` and `Suffix` structures, and everyone knows the size of the prefix array.

```
% java Markov <jr_chemistry.txt | fmt
Wash the blackboard.  Watch it dry.  The water goes
into the air.  When water goes into the air it
evaporates.  Tie a damp cloth to one end of a solid or
liquid.  Look around.  What are the solid things?
Chemical changes take place when something burns.  If
the burning material has liquids, they are stable and
the sponge rise.  It looked like dough, but it is
burning.  Break up the lump of sugar into small pieces
and put them together again in the bottom of a liquid.
```

Exercise 3-4. Revise the Java version of `markov` to use an array instead of a `Vector` for the prefix in the `State` class. □

3.6 C++

Our third implementation is in C++. Since C++ is almost a superset of C, it can be used as if it were C with a few notational conveniences, and our original C version of markov is also a legal C++ program. A more appropriate use of C++, however, would be to define classes for the objects in the program, more or less as we did in Java; this would let us hide implementation details. We decided to go even further by using the Standard Template Library or STL, since the STL has built-in mechanisms that will do much of what we need. The ISO standard for C++ includes the STL as part of the language definition.

The STL provides containers such as vectors, lists, and sets, and a family of fundamental algorithms for searching, sorting, inserting, and deleting. Using the template features of C++, every STL algorithm works on a variety of containers, including both user-defined types and built-in types like integers. Containers are expressed as C++ templates that are instantiated for specific data types; for example, there is a vector container that can be used to make particular types like vector<int> or vector<string>. All vector operations, including standard algorithms for sorting, can be used on such data types.

In addition to a vector container that is similar to Java's Vector, the STL provides a deque container. A deque (pronounced ''deck'') is a double-ended queue that matches what we do with prefixes: it holds NPREF elements, and lets us pop the first element and add a new one to the end, in $O(1)$ time for both. The STL deque is more general than we need, since it permits push and pop at either end, but the performance guarantees make it an obvious choice.

The STL also provides an explicit map container, based on balanced trees, that stores key-value pairs and provides $O(\log n)$ retrieval of the value associated with any key. Maps might not be as efficient as $O(1)$ hash tables, but it's nice not to have to write any code whatsoever to use them. (Some non-standard C++ libraries include a hash or hash_map container whose performance may be better.)

We also use the built-in comparison functions, which in this case will do string comparisons using the individual strings in the prefix.

With these components in hand, the code goes together smoothly. Here are the declarations:

```
typedef deque<string> Prefix;
map<Prefix, vector<string> > statetab; // prefix -> suffixes
```

The STL provides a template for deques; the notation deque<string> specializes it to a deque whose elements are strings. Since this type appears several times in the program, we used a typedef to give it the name Prefix. The map type that stores prefixes and suffixes occurs only once, however, so we did not give it a separate name; the map declaration declares a variable statetab that is a map from prefixes to vectors of strings. This is more convenient than either C or Java, because we don't need to provide a hash function or equals method.

The main routine initializes the prefix, reads the input (from standard input, called cin in the C++ iostream library), adds a tail, and generates the output, exactly as in the earlier versions:

```
// markov main: markov-chain random text generation
int main(void)
{
    int nwords = MAXGEN;
    Prefix prefix;                          // current input prefix

    for (int i = 0; i < NPREF; i++) // set up initial prefix
        add(prefix, NONWORD);
    build(prefix, cin);
    add(prefix, NONWORD);
    generate(nwords);
    return 0;
}
```

The function build uses the iostream library to read the input one word at a time:

```
// build: read input words, build state table
void build(Prefix& prefix, istream& in)
{
    string buf;

    while (in >> buf)
        add(prefix, buf);
}
```

The string buf will grow as necessary to handle input words of arbitrary length.

The add function shows more of the advantages of using the STL:

```
// add: add word to suffix list, update prefix
void add(Prefix& prefix, const string& s)
{
    if (prefix.size() == NPREF) {
        statetab[prefix].push_back(s);
        prefix.pop_front();
    }
    prefix.push_back(s);
}
```

Quite a bit is going on under these apparently simple statements. The map container overloads subscripting (the [] operator) to behave as a lookup operation. The expression statetab[prefix] does a lookup in statetab with prefix as key and returns a reference to the desired entry; the vector is created if it does not exist already. The push_back member functions of vector and deque push a new string onto the back end of the vector or deque; pop_front pops the first element off the deque.

Generation is similar to the previous versions:

```
// generate: produce output, one word per line
void generate(int nwords)
{
    Prefix prefix;
    int i;

    for (i = 0; i < NPREF; i++) // reset initial prefix
        add(prefix, NONWORD);

    for (i = 0; i < nwords; i++) {
        vector<string>& suf = statetab[prefix];
        const string& w = suf[rand() % suf.size()];
        if (w == NONWORD)
            break;
        cout << w << "\n";
        prefix.pop_front();        // advance
        prefix.push_back(w);
    }
}
```

Overall, this version seems especially clear and elegant—the code is compact, the data structure is visible and the algorithm is completely transparent. Sadly, there is a price to pay: this version runs much slower than the original C version, though it is not the slowest. We'll come back to performance measurements shortly.

Exercise 3-5. The great strength of the STL is the ease with which one can experiment with different data structures. Modify the C++ version of Markov to use various structures to represent the prefix, suffix list, and state table. How does performance change for the different structures? □

Exercise 3-6. Write a C++ version that uses only classes and the `string` data type but no other advanced library facilities. Compare it in style and speed to the STL versions. □

3.7 Awk and Perl

To round out the exercise, we also wrote the program in two popular scripting languages, Awk and Perl. These provide the necessary features for this application, associative arrays and string handling.

An *associative array* is a convenient packaging of a hash table; it looks like an array but its subscripts are arbitrary strings or numbers, or comma-separated lists of them. It is a form of map from one data type to another. In Awk, all arrays are associative; Perl has both conventional indexed arrays with integer subscripts and associative arrays, which are called ''hashes,'' a name that suggests how they are implemented.

The Awk and Perl implementations are specialized to prefixes of length 2.

```
# markov.awk: markov chain algorithm for 2-word prefixes
BEGIN { MAXGEN = 10000; NONWORD = "\n"; w1 = w2 = NONWORD }
{   for (i = 1; i <= NF; i++) {      # read all words
        statetab[w1,w2,++nsuffix[w1,w2]] = $i
        w1 = w2
        w2 = $i
    }
}
END {
    statetab[w1,w2,++nsuffix[w1,w2]] = NONWORD  # add tail
    w1 = w2 = NONWORD
    for (i = 0; i < MAXGEN; i++) {  # generate
        r = int(rand()*nsuffix[w1,w2]) + 1  # nsuffix >= 1
        p = statetab[w1,w2,r]
        if (p == NONWORD)
            exit
        print p
        w1 = w2             # advance chain
        w2 = p
    }
}
```

Awk is a pattern-action language: the input is read a line at a time, each line is matched against the patterns, and for each match the corresponding action is executed. There are two special patterns, BEGIN and END, that match before the first line of input and after the last.

An action is a block of statements enclosed in braces. In the Awk version of Markov, the BEGIN block initializes the prefix and a couple of other variables.

The next block has no pattern, so by default it is executed once for each input line. Awk automatically splits each input line into fields (white-space delimited words) called $1 through $NF; the variable NF is the number of fields. The statement

```
statetab[w1,w2,++nsuffix[w1,w2]] = $i
```

builds the map from prefix to suffixes. The array nsuffix counts suffixes and the element nsuffix[w1,w2] counts the number of suffixes associated with that prefix. The suffixes themselves are stored in array elements statetab[w1,w2,1], statetab[w1,w2,2], and so on.

When the END block is executed, all the input has been read. At that point, for each prefix there is an element of nsuffix containing the suffix count, and there are that many elements of statetab containing the suffixes.

The Perl version is similar, but uses an anonymous array instead of a third subscript to keep track of suffixes; it also uses multiple assignment to update the prefix. Perl uses special characters to indicate the types of variables: $ marks a scalar and @ an indexed array, while brackets [] are used to index arrays and braces {} to index hashes.

```
# markov.pl: markov chain algorithm for 2-word prefixes

$MAXGEN = 10000;
$NONWORD = "\n";
$w1 = $w2 = $NONWORD;            # initial state
while (<>) {                     # read each line of input
    foreach (split) {
        push(@{$statetab{$w1}{$w2}}, $_);
        ($w1, $w2) = ($w2, $_); # multiple assignment
    }
}
push(@{$statetab{$w1}{$w2}}, $NONWORD);     # add tail

$w1 = $w2 = $NONWORD;
for ($i = 0; $i < $MAXGEN; $i++) {
    $suf = $statetab{$w1}{$w2}; # array reference
    $r = int(rand @$suf);       # @$suf is number of elems
    exit if (($t = $suf->[$r]) eq $NONWORD);
    print "$t\n";
    ($w1, $w2) = ($w2, $t);     # advance chain
}
```

As in the previous programs, the map is stored using the variable statetab. The heart of the program is the line

```
        push(@{$statetab{$w1}{$w2}}, $_);
```

which pushes a new suffix onto the end of the (anonymous) array stored at statetab{$w1}{$w2}. In the generation phase, $statetab{$w1}{$w2} is a reference to an array of suffixes, and $suf->[$r] points to the r-th suffix.

Both the Perl and Awk programs are short compared to the three earlier versions, but they are harder to adapt to handle prefixes that are not exactly two words. The core of the C++ STL implementation (the add and generate functions) is of comparable length and seems clearer. Nevertheless, scripting languages are often a good choice for experimental programming, for making prototypes, and even for production use if run-time is not a major issue.

Exercise 3-7. Modify the Awk and Perl versions to handle prefixes of any length. Experiment to determine what effect this change has on performance. □

3.8 Performance

We have several implementations to compare. We timed the programs on the Book of Psalms from the King James Bible, which has 42,685 words (5,238 distinct words, 22,482 prefixes). This text has enough repeated phrases (''Blessed is the ...'')

that one suffix list has more than 400 elements, and there are a few hundred chains with dozens of suffixes, so it is a good test data set.

> Blessed is the man of the net. Turn thee unto me, and raise me up, that I may tell all my fears. They looked unto him, he heard. My praise shall be blessed. Wealth and riches shall be saved. Thou hast dealt well with thy hid treasure: they are cast into a standing water, the flint into a standing water, and dry ground into watersprings.

The times in the following table are the number of seconds for generating 10,000 words of output; one machine is a 250MHz MIPS R10000 running Irix 6.4 and the other is a 400MHz Pentium II with 128 megabytes of memory running Windows NT. Run-time is almost entirely determined by the input size; generation is very fast by comparison. The table also includes the approximate program size in lines of source code.

	250MHz R10000	400MHz Pentium II	Lines of source code
C	0.36 sec	0.30 sec	150
Java	4.9	9.2	105
C++/STL/deque	2.6	11.2	70
C++/STL/list	1.7	1.5	70
Awk	2.2	2.1	20
Perl	1.8	1.0	18

The C and C++ versions were compiled with optimizing compilers, while the Java runs had just-in-time compilers enabled. The Irix C and C++ times are the fastest obtained from three different compilers; similar results were observed on Sun SPARC and DEC Alpha machines. The C version of the program is fastest by a large factor; Perl comes second. The times in the table are a snapshot of our experience with a particular set of compilers and libraries, however, so you may see very different results in your environment.

Something is clearly wrong with the STL deque version on Windows. Experiments showed that the deque that represents the prefix accounts for most of the run-time, although it never holds more than two elements; we would expect the central data structure, the map, to dominate. Switching from a deque to a list (which is a doubly-linked list in the STL) improves the time dramatically. On the other hand, switching from a map to a (non-standard) hash container made no difference on Irix; hashes were not available on our Windows machine. It is a testament to the fundamental soundness of the STL design that these changes required only substituting the word list for the word deque or hash for map in two places and recompiling. We conclude that the STL, which is a new component of C++, still suffers from immature implementations. The performance is unpredictable between implementations of the STL and between individual data structures. The same is true of Java, where implementations are also changing rapidly.

There are some interesting challenges in testing a program that is meant to produce voluminous random output. How do we know it works at all? How do we know it works all the time? Chapter 6, which discusses testing, contains some suggestions and describes how we tested the Markov programs.

3.9 Lessons

The Markov program has a long history. The first version was written by Don P. Mitchell, adapted by Bruce Ellis, and applied to humorous deconstructionist activities throughout the 1980s. It lay dormant until we thought to use it in a university course as an illustration of program design. Rather than dusting off the original, we rewrote it from scratch in C to refresh our memories of the various issues that arise, and then wrote it again in several other languages, using each language's unique idioms to express the same basic idea. After the course, we reworked the programs many times to improve clarity and presentation.

Over all that time, however, the basic design has remained the same. The earliest version used the same approach as the ones we have presented here, although it did employ a second hash table to represent individual words. If we were to rewrite it again, we would probably not change much. The design of a program is rooted in the layout of its data. The data structures don't define every detail, but they do shape the overall solution.

Some data structure choices make little difference, such as lists versus growable arrays. Some implementations generalize better than others—the Perl and Awk code could be readily modified to one- or three-word prefixes but parameterizing the choice would be awkward. As befits object-oriented languages, tiny changes to the C++ and Java implementations would make the data structures suitable for objects other than English text, for instance programs (where white space would be significant), or notes of music, or even mouse clicks and menu selections for generating test sequences.

Of course, while the data structures are much the same, there is a wide variation in the general appearance of the programs, in the size of the source code, and in performance. Very roughly, higher-level languages give slower programs than lower level ones, although it's unwise to generalize other than qualitatively. Big building-blocks like the C++ STL or the associative arrays and string handling of scripting languages can lead to more compact code and shorter development time. These are not without price, although the performance penalty may not matter much for programs, like Markov, that run for only a few seconds.

Less clear, however, is how to assess the loss of control and insight when the pile of system-supplied code gets so big that one no longer knows what's going on underneath. This is the case with the STL version; its performance is unpredictable and there is no easy way to address that. One immature implementation we used needed to be repaired before it would run our program. Few of us have the resources or the energy to track down such problems and fix them.

This is a pervasive and growing concern in software: as libraries, interfaces, and tools become more complicated, they become less understood and less controllable. When everything works, rich programming environments can be very productive, but when they fail, there is little recourse. Indeed, we may not even realize that something is wrong if the problems involve performance or subtle logic errors.

The design and implementation of this program illustrate a number of lessons for larger programs. First is the importance of choosing simple algorithms and data structures, the simplest that will do the job in reasonable time for the expected problem size. If someone else has already written them and put them in a library for you, that's even better; our C++ implementation profited from that.

Following Brooks's advice, we find it best to start detailed design with data structures, guided by knowledge of what algorithms might be used; with the data structures settled, the code goes together easily.

It's hard to design a program completely and then build it; constructing real programs involves iteration and experimentation. The act of building forces one to clarify decisions that had previously been glossed over. That was certainly the case with our programs here, which have gone through many changes of detail. As much as possible, start with something simple and evolve it as experience dictates. If our goal had been just to write a personal version of the Markov chain algorithm for fun, we would almost surely have written it in Awk or Perl—though not with as much polishing as the ones we showed here—and let it go at that.

Production code takes much more effort than prototypes do, however. If we think of the programs presented here as *production code* (since they have been polished and thoroughly tested), production quality requires one or two orders of magnitude more effort than a program intended for personal use.

Exercise 3-8. We have seen versions of the Markov program in a wide variety of languages, including Scheme, Tcl, Prolog, Python, Generic Java, ML, and Haskell; each presents its own challenges and advantages. Implement the program in your favorite language and compare its general flavor and performance. □

Supplementary Reading

The Standard Template Library is described in a variety of books, including *Generic Programming and the STL*, by Matthew Austern (Addison-Wesley, 1998). The definitive reference on C++ itself is *The C++ Programming Language*, by Bjarne Stroustrup (3rd edition, Addison-Wesley, 1997). For Java, we refer to *The Java Programming Language, 2nd Edition* by Ken Arnold and James Gosling (Addison-Wesley, 1998). The best description of Perl is *Programming Perl, 2nd Edition*, by Larry Wall, Tom Christiansen, and Randal Schwartz (O'Reilly, 1996).

The idea behind *design patterns* is that there are only a few distinct design constructs in most programs in the same way that there are only a few basic data structures; very loosely, it is the design analog of the code idioms that we discussed in Chapter 1. The standard reference is *Design Patterns: Elements of Reusable Object-Oriented Software*, by Erich Gamma, Richard Helm, Ralph Johnson, and John Vlissides (Addison-Wesley, 1995).

The picaresque adventures of the markov program, originally called shaney, were described in the ''Computing Recreations'' column of the June, 1989 *Scientific American*. The article was republished in *The Magic Machine*, by A. K. Dewdney (W. H. Freeman, 1990).

4

Interfaces

Before I built a wall I'd ask to know
What I was walling in or walling out,
And to whom I was like to give offence.
Something there is that doesn't love a wall,
That wants it down.

Robert Frost, *Mending Wall*

The essence of design is to balance competing goals and constraints. Although there may be many tradeoffs when one is writing a small self-contained system, the ramifications of particular choices remain within the system and affect only the individual programmer. But when code is to be used by others, decisions have wider repercussions.

Among the issues to be worked out in a design are

- Interfaces: what services and access are provided? The interface is in effect a contract between supplier and customer. The desire is to provide services that are uniform and convenient, with enough functionality to be easy to use but not so much as to become unwieldy.

- Information hiding: what information is visible and what is private? An interface must provide straightforward access to the components while hiding details of the implementation so they can be changed without affecting users.

- Resource management: who is responsible for managing memory and other limited resources? Here, the main problems are allocating and freeing storage, and managing shared copies of information.

- Error handling: who detects errors, who reports them, and how? When an error is detected, what recovery is attempted?

In Chapter 2 we looked at the individual pieces—the data structures—from which a system is built. In Chapter 3, we looked at how to combine those into a small program. The topic now turns to the interfaces between components that might come from different sources. In this chapter we illustrate interface design by building a

85

library of functions and data structures for a common task. Along the way, we will present some principles of design. Typically there are an enormous number of decisions to be made, but most are made almost unconsciously. Without these principles, the result is often the sort of haphazard interfaces that frustrate and impede programmers every day.

4.1 Comma-Separated Values

Comma-separated values, or CSV, is the term for a natural and widely used representation for tabular data. Each row of a table is a line of text; the fields on each line are separated by commas. The table at the end of the previous chapter might begin this way in CSV format:

```
,"250MHz","400MHz","Lines of"
,"R10000","Pentium II","source code"
C,0.36 sec,0.30 sec,150
Java,4.9,9.2,105
```

This format is read and written by programs such as spreadsheets; not coincidentally, it also appears on web pages for services such as stock price quotations. A popular web page for stock quotes presents a display like this:

Symbol	Last Trade		Change		Volume
LU	2:19PM	86-1/4	+4-1/16	+4.94%	5,804,800
T	2:19PM	60-11/16	−1-3/16	−1.92%	2,468,000
MSFT	2:24PM	106-9/16	+1-3/8	+1.31%	11,474,900

Download Spreadsheet Format

Retrieving numbers by interacting with a web browser is effective but time-consuming. It's a nuisance to invoke a browser, wait, watch a barrage of advertisements, type a list of stocks, wait, wait, wait, then watch another barrage, all to get a few numbers. To process the numbers further requires even more interaction; selecting the ''Download Spreadsheet Format'' link retrieves a file that contains much the same information in lines of CSV data like these (edited to fit):

```
"LU",86.25,"11/4/1998","2:19PM",+4.0625,
       83.9375,86.875,83.625,5804800
"T",60.6875,"11/4/1998","2:19PM",-1.1875,
       62.375,62.625,60.4375,2468000
"MSFT",106.5625,"11/4/1998","2:24PM",+1.375,
       105.8125,107.3125,105.5625,11474900
```

Conspicuous by its absence in this process is the principle of letting the machine do the work. Browsers let your computer access data on a remote server, but it would be more convenient to retrieve the data without forced interaction. Underneath all the button-pushing is a purely textual procedure—the browser reads some HTML, you type some text, the browser sends that to a server and reads some HTML back. With the right tools and language, it's easy to retrieve the information automatically. Here's a program in the language Tcl to access the stock quote web site and retrieve CSV data in the format above, preceded by a few header lines:

```
# getquotes.tcl: stock prices for Lucent, AT&T, Microsoft
set so [socket quote.yahoo.com 80]    ;# connect to server
set q "/d/quotes.csv?s=LU+T+MSFT&f=sl1d1t1c1ohgv"
puts $so "GET $q HTTP/1.0\r\n\r\n"     ;# send request
flush $so
puts [read $so]                        ;# read & print reply
```

The cryptic sequence f=... that follows the ticker symbols is an undocumented control string, analogous to the first argument of printf, that determines what values to retrieve. By experiment, we determined that s identifies the stock symbol, l1 the last price, c1 the change since yesterday, and so on. What's important isn't the details, which are subject to change anyway, but the possibility of automation: retrieving the desired information and converting it into the form we need without any human intervention. We can let the machine do the work.

It typically takes a fraction of a second to run getquotes, far less than interacting with a browser. Once we have the data, we will want to process it further. Data formats like CSV work best if there are convenient libraries for converting to and from the format, perhaps allied with some auxiliary processing such as numerical conversions. But we do not know of an existing public library to handle CSV, so we will write one ourselves.

In the next few sections, we will build three versions of a library to read CSV data and convert it into an internal representation. Along the way, we'll talk about issues that arise when designing software that must work with other software. For example, there does not appear to be a standard definition of CSV, so the implementation cannot be based on a precise specification, a common situation in the design of interfaces.

4.2 A Prototype Library

We are unlikely to get the design of a library or interface right on the first attempt. As Fred Brooks once wrote, "plan to throw one away; you will, anyhow." Brooks was writing about large systems but the idea is relevant for any substantial piece of software. It's not usually until you've built and used a version of the program that you understand the issues well enough to get the design right.

In this spirit, we will approach the construction of a library for CSV by building one to throw away, a *prototype*. Our first version will ignore many of the difficulties of a thoroughly engineered library, but will be complete enough to be useful and to let us gain some familiarity with the problem.

Our starting point is a function `csvgetline` that reads one line of CSV data from a file into a buffer, splits it into fields in an array, removes quotes, and returns the number of fields. Over the years, we have written similar code in almost every language we know, so it's a familiar task. Here is a prototype version in C; we've marked it as questionable because it is just a prototype:

```
char buf[200];      /* input line buffer */
char *field[20];    /* fields */

/* csvgetline: read and parse line, return field count */
/* sample input: "LU",86.25,"11/4/1998","2:19PM",+4.0625 */
int csvgetline(FILE *fin)
{
    int nfield;
    char *p, *q;

    if (fgets(buf, sizeof(buf), fin) == NULL)
        return -1;
    nfield = 0;
    for (q = buf; (p=strtok(q, ",\n\r")) != NULL; q = NULL)
        field[nfield++] = unquote(p);
    return nfield;
}
```

The comment at the top of the function includes an example of the input format that the program accepts; such comments are helpful for programs that parse messy input.

The CSV format is too complicated to be parsed easily by `scanf` so we use the C standard library function `strtok`. Each call of `strtok(p,s)` returns a pointer to the first token within p consisting of characters not in s; `strtok` terminates the token by overwriting the following character of the original string with a null byte. On the first call, `strtok`'s first argument is the string to scan; subsequent calls use `NULL` to indicate that scanning should resume where it left off in the previous call. This is a poor interface. Because `strtok` stores a variable in a secret place between calls, only one sequence of calls may be active at one time; unrelated interleaved calls will interfere with each other.

Our function `unquote` removes the leading and trailing quotes that appear in the sample input above. It does not handle nested quotes, however, so although sufficient for a prototype, it's not general.

```
/* unquote: remove leading and trailing quote */
char *unquote(char *p)
{
    if (p[0] == '"') {
        if (p[strlen(p)-1] == '"')
            p[strlen(p)-1] = '\0';
        p++;
    }
    return p;
}
```

A simple test program helps verify that `csvgetline` works:

```
?    /* csvtest main: test csvgetline function */
?    int main(void)
?    {
?        int i, nf;
?
?        while ((nf = csvgetline(stdin)) != -1)
?            for (i = 0; i < nf; i++)
?                printf("field[%d] = '%s'\n", i, field[i]);
?        return 0;
?    }
```

The `printf` encloses the fields in matching single quotes, which demarcate them and help to reveal bugs that handle white space incorrectly.

We can now run this on the output produced by `getquotes.tcl`:

```
% getquotes.tcl | csvtest
...
field[0] = 'LU'
field[1] = '86.375'
field[2] = '11/5/1998'
field[3] = '1:01PM'
field[4] = '-0.125'
field[5] = '86'
field[6] = '86.375'
field[7] = '85.0625'
field[8] = '2888600'
field[0] = 'T'
field[1] = '61.0625'
...
```

(We have edited out the HTTP header lines.)

Now we have a prototype that seems to work on data of the sort we showed above. But it might be prudent to try it on something else as well, especially if we plan to let others use it. We found another web site that downloads stock quotes and obtained a file of similar information but in a different form: carriage returns (\r) rather than newlines to separate records, and no terminating carriage return at the end of the file. We've edited and formatted it to fit on the page:

```
"Ticker","Price","Change","Open","Prev Close","Day High",
    "Day Low","52 Week High","52 Week Low","Dividend",
    "Yield","Volume","Average Volume","P/E"
"LU",86.313,-0.188,86.000,86.500,86.438,85.063,108.50,
    36.18,0.16,0.1,2946700,9675000,N/A
"T",61.125,0.938,60.375,60.188,61.125,60.000,68.50,
    46.50,1.32,2.1,3061000,4777000,17.0
"MSFT",107.000,1.500,105.313,105.500,107.188,105.250,
    119.62,59.00,N/A,N/A,7977300,16965000,51.0
```

With this input, our prototype failed miserably.

We designed our prototype after examining one data source, and we tested it originally only on data from that same source. Thus we shouldn't be surprised when the first encounter with a different source reveals gross failings. Long input lines, many fields, and unexpected or missing separators all cause trouble. This fragile prototype might serve for personal use or to demonstrate the feasibility of an approach, but no more than that. It's time to rethink the design before we try another implementation.

We made a large number of decisions, both implicit and explicit, in the prototype. Here are some of the choices that were made, not always in the best way for a general-purpose library. Each raises an issue that needs more careful attention.

- The prototype doesn't handle long input lines or lots of fields. It can give wrong answers or crash because it doesn't even check for overflows, let alone return sensible values in case of errors.
- The input is assumed to consist of lines terminated by newlines.
- Fields are separated by commas and surrounding quotes are removed. There is no provision for embedded quotes or commas.
- The input line is not preserved; it is overwritten by the process of creating fields.
- No data is saved from one input line to the next; if something is to be remembered, a copy must be made.
- Access to the fields is through a global variable, the `field` array, which is shared by `csvgetline` and functions that call it; there is no control over access to the field contents or the pointers. There is also no attempt to prevent access beyond the last field.
- The global variables make the design unsuitable for a multi-threaded environment or even for two sequences of interleaved calls.
- The caller must open and close files explicitly; `csvgetline` reads only from open files.
- Input and splitting are inextricably linked: each call reads a line and splits it into fields, regardless of whether the application needs that service.
- The return value is the number of fields on the line; each line must be split to compute this value. There is also no way to distinguish errors from end of file.
- There is no way to change any of these properties without changing the code.

This long yet incomplete list illustrates some of the possible design tradeoffs. Each decision is woven through the code. That's fine for a quick job, like parsing one fixed format from a known source. But what if the format changes, or a comma appears within a quoted string, or the server produces a long line or a lot of fields?

It may seem easy to cope, since the ''library'' is small and only a prototype anyway. Imagine, however, that after sitting on the shelf for a few months or years the code becomes part of a larger program whose specification changes over time. How will `csvgetline` adapt? If that program is used by others, the quick choices made in the original design may spell trouble that surfaces years later. This scenario is representative of the history of many bad interfaces. It is a sad fact that a lot of quick and dirty code ends up in widely-used software, where it remains dirty and often not as quick as it should have been anyway.

4.3 A Library for Others

Using what we learned from the prototype, we now want to build a library worthy of general use. The most obvious requirement is that we must make csvgetline more robust so it will handle long lines or many fields; it must also be more careful in the parsing of fields.

To create an interface that others can use, we must consider the issues listed at the beginning of this chapter: interfaces, information hiding, resource management, and error handling. The interplay among these strongly affects the design. Our separation of these issues is a bit arbitrary, since they are interrelated.

Interface. We decided on three basic operations:

    char *csvgetline(FILE *): read a new CSV line

    char *csvfield(int n): return the n-th field of the current line

    int csvnfield(void): return the number of fields on the current line

What function value should csvgetline return? It is desirable to return as much useful information as convenient, which suggests returning the number of fields, as in the prototype. But then the number of fields must be computed even if the fields aren't being used. Another possible value is the input line length, which is affected by whether the trailing newline is preserved. After several experiments, we decided that csvgetline will return a pointer to the original line of input, or NULL if end of file has been reached.

We will remove the newline at the end of the line returned by csvgetline, since it can easily be restored if necessary.

The definition of a field is complicated; we have tried to match what we observe empirically in spreadsheets and other programs. A field is a sequence of zero or more characters. Fields are separated by commas. Leading and trailing blanks are preserved. A field may be enclosed in double-quote characters, in which case it may contain commas. A quoted field may contain double-quote characters, which are represented by a doubled double-quote; the CSV field "x""y" defines the string x"y. Fields may be empty; a field specified as "" is empty, and identical to one specified by adjacent commas.

Fields are numbered from zero. What if the user asks for a non-existent field by calling csvfield(-1) or csvfield(100000)? We could return "" (the empty string) because this can be printed and compared; programs that process variable numbers of fields would not have to take special precautions to deal with non-existent ones. But that choice provides no way to distinguish empty from non-existent. A second choice would be to print an error message or even abort; we will discuss shortly why this is not desirable. We decided to return NULL, the conventional value for a non-existent string in C.

Information hiding. The library will impose no limits on input line length or number of fields. To achieve this, either the caller must provide the memory or the callee (the library) must allocate it. The caller of the library function fgets passes in an array and a maximum size. If the line is longer than the buffer, it is broken into pieces. This behavior is unsatisfactory for the CSV interface, so our library will allocate memory as it discovers that more is needed.

Thus only csvgetline knows about memory management; nothing about the way that it organizes memory is accessible from outside. The best way to provide that isolation is through a function interface: csvgetline reads the next line, no matter how big, csvfield(n) returns a pointer to the bytes of the n-th field of the current line, and csvnfield returns the number of fields on the current line.

We will have to grow memory as longer lines or more fields arrive. Details of how that is done are hidden in the csv functions; no other part of the program knows how this works, for instance whether the library uses small arrays that grow, or very large arrays, or something completely different. Nor does the interface reveal when memory is freed.

If the user calls only csvgetline, there's no need to split into fields; lines can be split on demand. Whether field-splitting is eager (done right away when the line is read) or lazy (done only when a field or count is needed) or very lazy (only the requested field is split) is another implementation detail hidden from the user.

Resource management. We must decide who is responsible for shared information. Does csvgetline return the original data or make a copy? We decided that the return value of csvgetline is a pointer to the original input, which will be overwritten when the next line is read. Fields will be built in a copy of the input line, and csvfield will return a pointer to the field within the copy. With this arrangement, the user must make another copy if a particular line or field is to be saved or changed, and it is the user's responsibility to release that storage when it is no longer needed.

Who opens and closes the input file? Whoever opens an input file should do the corresponding close: matching tasks should be done at the same level or place. We will assume that csvgetline is called with a FILE pointer to an already-open file that the caller will close when processing is complete.

Managing the resources shared or passed across the boundary between a library and its callers is a difficult task, and there are often sound but conflicting reasons to prefer various design choices. Errors and misunderstandings about the shared responsibilities are a frequent source of bugs.

Error handling. Because csvgetline returns NULL, there is no good way to distinguish end of file from an error like running out of memory; similarly, access to a non-existent field causes no error. By analogy with ferror, we could add another function csvgeterror to the interface to report the most recent error, but for simplicity we will leave it out of this version.

As a principle, library routines should not just die when an error occurs; error status should be returned to the caller for appropriate action. Nor should they print messages or pop up dialog boxes, since they may be running in an environment where a message would interfere with something else. Error handling is a topic worth a separate discussion of its own, later in this chapter.

Specification. The choices made above should be collected in one place as a specification of the services that csvgetline provides and how it is to be used. In a large project, the specification precedes the implementation, because specifiers and implementers are usually different people and may be in different organizations. In practice, however, work often proceeds in parallel, with specification and code evolving together, although sometimes the ''specification'' is written only after the fact to describe approximately what the code does.

The best approach is to write the specification early and revise it as we learn from the ongoing implementation. The more accurate and careful a specification is, the more likely that the resulting program will work well. Even for personal programs, it is valuable to prepare a reasonably thorough specification because it encourages consideration of alternatives and records the choices made.

For our purposes, the specification would include function prototypes and a detailed prescription of behavior, responsibilities and assumptions:

> Fields are separated by commas.
> A field may be enclosed in double-quote characters "...".
> A quoted field may contain commas but not newlines.
> A quoted field may contain double-quote characters ", represented by "".
> Fields may be empty; "" and an empty string both represent an empty field.
> Leading and trailing white space is preserved.

> ```
> char *csvgetline(FILE *f);
> ```
>   reads one line from open input file f;
>   assumes that input lines are terminated by \r, \n, \r\n, or EOF.
>   returns pointer to line, with terminator removed, or NULL if EOF occurred.
>   line may be of arbitrary length; returns NULL if memory limit exceeded.
>   line must be treated as read-only storage;
>   caller must make a copy to preserve or change contents.

> ```
> char *csvfield(int n);
> ```
>   fields are numbered from 0.
>   returns n-th field from last line read by csvgetline;
>   returns NULL if n < 0 or beyond last field.
>   fields are separated by commas.
>   fields may be surrounded by "..."; such quotes are removed;
>   within "...", "" is replaced by " and comma is not a separator.
>   in unquoted fields, quotes are regular characters.
>   there can be an arbitrary number of fields of any length;
>   returns NULL if memory limit exceeded.
>   field must be treated as read-only storage;
>   caller must make a copy to preserve or change contents.
>   behavior undefined if called before csvgetline is called.

```
int csvnfield(void);
```
        returns number of fields on last line read by `csvgetline`.
        behavior undefined if called before `csvgetline` is called.

This specification still leaves open questions. For example, what values should be returned by `csvfield` and `csvnfield` if they are called after `csvgetline` has encountered EOF? How should ill-formed fields be handled? Nailing down all such puzzles is difficult even for a tiny system, and very challenging for a large one, though it is important to try. One often doesn't discover oversights and omissions until implementation is underway.

The rest of this section contains a new implementation of `csvgetline` that matches the specification. The library is broken into two files, a header `csv.h` that contains the function declarations that represent the public part of the interface, and an implementation file `csv.c` that contains the code. Users include `csv.h` in their source code and link their compiled code with the compiled version of `csv.c`; the source need never be visible.

Here is the header file:

```
/* csv.h: interface for csv library */

extern char *csvgetline(FILE *f); /* read next input line */
extern char *csvfield(int n);     /* return field n */
extern int csvnfield(void);       /* return number of fields */
```

The internal variables that store text and the internal functions like `split` are declared `static` so they are visible only within the file that contains them. This is the simplest way to hide information in a C program.

```
enum { NOMEM = -2 };           /* out of memory signal */

static char *line     = NULL;  /* input chars */
static char *sline    = NULL;  /* line copy used by split */
static int  maxline   = 0;     /* size of line[] and sline[] */
static char **field   = NULL;  /* field pointers */
static int  maxfield  = 0;     /* size of field[] */
static int  nfield    = 0;     /* number of fields in field[] */

static char fieldsep[] = ","; /* field separator chars */
```

The variables are initialized statically as well. These initial values are used to test whether to create or grow arrays.

These declarations describe a simple data structure. The `line` array holds the input line; the `sline` array is created by copying characters from `line` and terminating each field. The `field` array points to entries in `sline`. This diagram shows the state of these three arrays after the input line ab,"cd","e""f",,"g,h" has been processed. Shaded elements in `sline` are not part of any field.

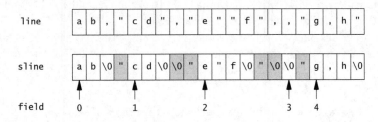

Here is the function csvgetline itself:

```
/* csvgetline: get one line, grow as needed */
/* sample input: "LU",86.25,"11/4/1998","2:19PM",+4.0625 */
char *csvgetline(FILE *fin)
{
    int i, c;
    char *newl, *news;

    if (line == NULL) {          /* allocate on first call */
        maxline = maxfield = 1;
        line = (char *) malloc(maxline);
        sline = (char *) malloc(maxline);
        field = (char **) malloc(maxfield*sizeof(field[0]));
        if (line == NULL || sline == NULL || field == NULL) {
            reset();
            return NULL;          /* out of memory */
        }
    }
    for (i=0; (c=getc(fin))!=EOF && !endofline(fin,c); i++) {
        if (i >= maxline-1) {   /* grow line */
            maxline *= 2;        /* double current size */
            newl = (char *) realloc(line, maxline);
            news = (char *) realloc(sline, maxline);
            if (newl == NULL || news == NULL) {
                reset();
                return NULL;     /* out of memory */
            }
            line = newl;
            sline = news;
        }
        line[i] = c;
    }
    line[i] = '\0';
    if (split() == NOMEM) {
        reset();
        return NULL;                /* out of memory */
    }
    return (c == EOF && i == 0) ? NULL : line;
}
```

An incoming line is accumulated in line, which is grown as necessary by a call to realloc; the size is doubled on each growth, as in Section 2.6. The sline array is kept the same size as line; csvgetline calls split to create the field pointers in a separate array field, which is also grown as needed.

As is our custom, we start the arrays very small and grow them on demand, to guarantee that the array-growing code is exercised. If allocation fails, we call reset to restore the globals to their starting state, so a subsequent call to csvgetline has a chance of succeeding:

```
/* reset: set variables back to starting values */
static void reset(void)
{
    free(line); /* free(NULL) permitted by ANSI C */
    free(sline);
    free(field);
    line = NULL;
    sline = NULL;
    field = NULL;
    maxline = maxfield = nfield = 0;
}
```

The endofline function handles the problem that an input line may be terminated by a carriage return, a newline, both, or even EOF:

```
/* endofline: check for and consume \r, \n, \r\n, or EOF */
static int endofline(FILE *fin, int c)
{
    int eol;

    eol = (c=='\r' || c=='\n');
    if (c == '\r') {
        c = getc(fin);
        if (c != '\n' && c != EOF)
            ungetc(c, fin); /* read too far; put c back */
    }
    return eol;
}
```

A separate function is necessary, since the standard input functions do not handle the rich variety of perverse formats encountered in real inputs.

Our prototype used strtok to find the next token by searching for a separator character, normally a comma, but this made it impossible to handle quoted commas. A major change in the implementation of split is necessary, though its interface need not change. Consider these input lines:

```
"","",""
,"",
,"",
,,
```

Each line has three empty fields. Making sure that split parses them and other odd inputs correctly complicates it significantly, an example of how special cases and boundary conditions can come to dominate a program.

```
/* split: split line into fields */
static int split(void)
{
    char *p, **newf;
    char *sepp; /* pointer to temporary separator character */
    int sepc;   /* temporary separator character */

    nfield = 0;
    if (line[0] == '\0')
        return 0;
    strcpy(sline, line);
    p = sline;

    do {
        if (nfield >= maxfield) {
            maxfield *= 2;              /* double current size */
            newf = (char **) realloc(field,
                        maxfield * sizeof(field[0]));
            if (newf == NULL)
                return NOMEM;
            field = newf;
        }
        if (*p == '"')
            sepp = advquoted(++p);  /* skip initial quote */
        else
            sepp = p + strcspn(p, fieldsep);
        sepc = sepp[0];
        sepp[0] = '\0';                 /* terminate field */
        field[nfield++] = p;
        p = sepp + 1;
    } while (sepc == ',');

    return nfield;
}
```

The loop grows the array of field pointers if necessary, then calls one of two other functions to locate and process the next field. If the field begins with a quote, advquoted finds the field and returns a pointer to the separator that ends the field. Otherwise, to find the next comma we use the library function strcspn(p,s), which searches a string p for the next occurrence of any character in string s; it returns the number of characters skipped over.

Quotes within a field are represented by two adjacent quotes, so advquoted squeezes those into a single one; it also removes the quotes that surround the field. Some complexity is added by an attempt to cope with plausible inputs that don't match the specification, such as "abc"def. In such cases, we append whatever follows the second quote until the next separator as part of this field. Microsoft Excel appears to use a similar algorithm.

```
/* advquoted: quoted field; return pointer to next separator */
static char *advquoted(char *p)
{
    int i, j;

    for (i = j = 0; p[j] != '\0'; i++, j++) {
        if (p[j] == '"' && p[++j] != '"') {
            /* copy up to next separator or \0 */
            int k = strcspn(p+j, fieldsep);
            memmove(p+i, p+j, k);
            i += k;
            j += k;
            break;
        }
        p[i] = p[j];
    }
    p[i] = '\0';
    return p + j;
}
```

Since the input line is already split, csvfield and csvnfield are trivial:

```
/* csvfield:  return pointer to n-th field */
char *csvfield(int n)
{
    if (n < 0 || n >= nfield)
        return NULL;
    return field[n];
}

/* csvnfield:  return number of fields */
int csvnfield(void)
{
    return nfield;
}
```

Finally, we can modify the test driver to exercise this version of the library; since it keeps a copy of the input line, which the prototype does not, it can print the original line before printing the fields:

```
/* csvtest main: test CSV library */
int main(void)
{
    int i;
    char *line;

    while ((line = csvgetline(stdin)) != NULL) {
        printf("line = '%s'\n", line);
        for (i = 0; i < csvnfield(); i++)
            printf("field[%d] = '%s'\n", i, csvfield(i));
    }
    return 0;
}
```

This completes our C version. It handles arbitrarily large inputs and does something sensible even with perverse data. The price is that it is more than four times as long as the first prototype and some of the code is intricate. Such expansion of size and complexity is a typical result of moving from prototype to production.

Exercise 4-1. There are several degrees of laziness for field-splitting; among the possibilities are to split all at once but only when some field is requested, to split only the field requested, or to split up to the field requested. Enumerate possibilities, assess their potential difficulty and benefits, then write them and measure their speeds. □

Exercise 4-2. Add a facility so separators can be changed (a) to an arbitrary class of characters; (b) to different separators for different fields; (c) to a regular expression (see Chapter 9). What should the interface look like? □

Exercise 4-3. We chose to use the static initialization provided by C as the basis of a one-time switch: if a pointer is NULL on entry, initialization is performed. Another possibility is to require the user to call an explicit initialization function, which could include suggested initial sizes for arrays. Implement a version that combines the best of both. What is the role of reset in your implementation? □

Exercise 4-4. Design and implement a library for creating CSV-formatted data. The simplest version might take an array of strings and print them with quotes and commas. A more sophisticated version might use a format string analogous to printf. Look at Chapter 9 for some suggestions on notation. □

4.4 A C++ Implementation

In this section we will write a C++ version of the CSV library to address some of the remaining limitations of the C version. This will entail some changes to the specification, of which the most important is that the functions will handle C++ strings instead of C character arrays. The use of C++ strings will automatically resolve some of the storage management issues, since the library functions will manage the memory for us. In particular, the field routines will return strings that can be modified by the caller, a more flexible design than the previous version.

A class Csv defines the public face, while neatly hiding the variables and functions of the implementation. Since a class object contains all the state for an instance, we can instantiate multiple Csv variables; each is independent of the others so multiple CSV input streams can operate at the same time.

```
class Csv { // read and parse comma-separated values
    // sample input: "LU",86.25,"11/4/1998","2:19PM",+4.0625

  public:
    Csv(istream& fin = cin, string sep = ",") :
        fin(fin), fieldsep(sep) {}

    int getline(string&);
    string getfield(int n);
    int getnfield() const { return nfield; }

  private:
    istream& fin;              // input file pointer
    string line;               // input line
    vector<string> field;      // field strings
    int nfield;                // number of fields
    string fieldsep;           // separator characters

    int split();
    int endofline(char);
    int advplain(const string& line, string& fld, int);
    int advquoted(const string& line, string& fld, int);
};
```

Default parameters for the constructor are defined so a default Csv object will read
from the standard input stream and use the normal field separator; either can be
replaced with explicit values.

To manage strings, the class uses the standard C++ string and vector classes
rather than C-style strings. There is no non-existent state for a string: ''empty''
means only that the length is zero, and there is no equivalent of NULL, so we can't use
that as an end of file signal. Thus Csv::getline returns the input line through an
argument by reference, reserving the function value itself for end of file and error
reports.

```
// getline: get one line, grow as needed
int Csv::getline(string& str)
{
    char c;

    for (line = ""; fin.get(c) && !endofline(c); )
        line += c;
    split();
    str = line;
    return !fin.eof();
}
```

The += operator is overloaded to append a character to a string.

Minor changes are needed in endofline. Again, we have to read the input a character at a time, since none of the standard input routines can handle the variety of
inputs.

```
// endofline: check for and consume \r, \n, \r\n, or EOF
int Csv::endofline(char c)
{
    int eol;

    eol = (c=='\r' || c=='\n');
    if (c == '\r') {
        fin.get(c);
        if (!fin.eof() && c != '\n')
            fin.putback(c); // read too far
    }
    return eol;
}
```

Here is the new version of `split`:

```
// split: split line into fields
int Csv::split()
{
    string fld;
    int i, j;

    nfield = 0;
    if (line.length() == 0)
        return 0;
    i = 0;

    do {
        if (i < line.length() && line[i] == '"')
            j = advquoted(line, fld, ++i);  // skip quote
        else
            j = advplain(line, fld, i);
        if (nfield >= field.size())
            field.push_back(fld);
        else
            field[nfield] = fld;
        nfield++;
        i = j + 1;
    } while (j < line.length());

    return nfield;
}
```

Since `strcspn` doesn't work on C++ strings, we must change both `split` and `advquoted`. The new version of `advquoted` uses the C++ standard function `find_first_of` to locate the next occurrence of a separator character. The call `s.find_first_of(fieldsep,j)` searches the string `s` for the first instance of any character in `fieldsep` that occurs at or after position `j`. If it fails to find an instance, it returns an index beyond the end of the string, so we must bring it back within range. The inner `for` loop that follows appends characters up to the separator to the field being accumulated in `fld`.

```
// advquoted: quoted field; return index of next separator
int Csv::advquoted(const string& s, string& fld, int i)
{
    int j;

    fld = "";
    for (j = i; j < s.length(); j++) {
        if (s[j] == '"' && s[++j] != '"') {
            int k = s.find_first_of(fieldsep, j);
            if (k > s.length()) // no separator found
                k = s.length();
            for (k -= j; k-- > 0; )
                fld += s[j++];
            break;
        }
        fld += s[j];
    }
    return j;
}
```

The function find_first_of is also used in a new function advplain, which advances over a plain unquoted field. Again, this change is required because C string functions like strcspn cannot be applied to C++ strings, which are an entirely different data type.

```
// advplain: unquoted field; return index of next separator
int Csv::advplain(const string& s, string& fld, int i)
{
    int j;

    j = s.find_first_of(fieldsep, i); // look for separator
    if (j > s.length())               // none found
        j = s.length();
    fld = string(s, i, j-i);
    return j;
}
```

As before, Csv::getfield is trivial, while Csv::getnfield is so short that it is implemented in the class definition.

```
// getfield: return n-th field
string Csv::getfield(int n)
{
    if (n < 0 || n >= nfield)
        return "";
    else
        return field[n];
}
```

Our test program is a simple variant of the earlier one:

```
// Csvtest main: test Csv class
int main(void)
{
    string line;
    Csv csv;
    while (csv.getline(line) != 0) {
        cout << "line = '" << line <<"'\n";
        for (int i = 0; i < csv.getnfield(); i++)
            cout << "field[" << i << "] = '"
                 << csv.getfield(i) << "'\n";
    }
    return 0;
}
```

The usage is different than with the C version, though only in a minor way. Depending on the compiler, the C++ version is anywhere from 40 percent to four times slower than the C version on a large input file of 30,000 lines with about 25 fields per line. As we saw when comparing versions of markov, this variability is a reflection on library maturity. The C++ source program is about 20 percent shorter.

Exercise 4-5. Enhance the C++ implementation to overload subscripting with operator[] so that fields can be accessed as csv[i]. □

Exercise 4-6. Write a Java version of the CSV library, then compare the three implementations for clarity, robustness, and speed. □

Exercise 4-7. Repackage the C++ version of the CSV code as an STL iterator. □

Exercise 4-8. The C++ version permits multiple independent Csv instances to operate concurrently without interfering, a benefit of encapsulating all the state in an object that can be instantiated multiple times. Modify the C version to achieve the same effect by replacing the global data structures with structures that are allocated and initialized by an explicit csvnew function. □

4.5 Interface Principles

In the previous sections we were working out the details of an interface, which is the detailed boundary between code that provides a service and code that uses it. An interface defines what some body of code does for its users, how the functions and perhaps data members can be used by the rest of the program. Our CSV interface provides three functions—read a line, get a field, and return the number of fields—which are the only operations that can be performed.

To prosper, an interface must be well suited for its task—simple, general, regular, predictable, robust—and it must adapt gracefully as its users and its implementation change. Good interfaces follow a set of principles. These are not independent or even consistent, but they help us describe what happens across the boundary between two pieces of software.

Hide implementation details. The implementation behind the interface should be hidden from the rest of the program so it can be changed without affecting or breaking anything. There are several terms for this kind of organizing principle; information hiding, encapsulation, abstraction, modularization, and the like all refer to related ideas. An interface should hide details of the implementation that are irrelevant to the client (user) of the interface. Details that are invisible can be changed without affecting the client, perhaps to extend the interface, make it more efficient, or even replace its implementation altogether.

The basic libraries of most programming languages provide familiar examples, though not always especially well-designed ones. The C standard I/O library is among the best known: a couple of dozen functions that open, close, read, write, and otherwise manipulate files. The implementation of file I/O is hidden behind a data type FILE*, whose properties one might be able to see (because they are often spelled out in <stdio.h>) but should not exploit.

If the header file does not include the actual structure declaration, just the name of the structure, this is sometimes called an *opaque type*, since its properties are not visible and all operations take place through a pointer to whatever real object lurks behind.

Avoid global variables; wherever possible it is better to pass references to all data through function arguments.

We strongly recommend against publicly visible data in all forms; it is too hard to maintain consistency of values if users can change variables at will. Function interfaces make it easier to enforce access rules, but this principle is often violated. The predefined I/O streams like stdin and stdout are almost always defined as elements of a global array of FILE structures:

```
extern FILE    __iob[_NFILE];
#define stdin  (&__iob[0])
#define stdout (&__iob[1])
#define stderr (&__iob[2])
```

This makes the implementation completely visible; it also means that one can't assign to stdin, stdout or stderr, even though they look like variables. The peculiar name __iob uses the ANSI C convention of two leading underscores for private names that must be visible, which makes the names less likely to conflict with names in a program.

Classes in C++ and Java are better mechanisms for hiding information; they are central to the proper use of those languages. The container classes of the C++ Standard Template Library that we used in Chapter 3 carry this even further: aside from some performance guarantees there is no information about implementation, and library creators can use any mechanism they like.

Choose a small orthogonal set of primitives. An interface should provide as much functionality as necessary but no more, and the functions should not overlap excessively in their capabilities. Having lots of functions may make the library easier to use—whatever one needs is there for the taking. But a large interface is harder to write and maintain, and sheer size may make it hard to learn and use as well. ''Application program interfaces'' or APIs are sometimes so huge that no mortal can be expected to master them.

In the interest of convenience, some interfaces provide multiple ways of doing the same thing, a tendency that should be resisted. The C standard I/O library provides at least four different functions that will write a single character to an output stream:

```
char c;
putc(c, fp);
fputc(c, fp);
fprintf(fp, "%c", c);
fwrite(&c, sizeof(char), 1, fp);
```

If the stream is `stdout`, there are several more possibilities. These are convenient, but not all are necessary.

Narrow interfaces are to be preferred to wide ones, at least until one has strong evidence that more functions are needed. Do one thing, and do it well. Don't add to an interface just because it's possible to do so, and don't fix the interface when it's the implementation that's broken. For instance, rather than having `memcpy` for speed and `memmove` for safety, it would be better to have one function that was always safe, and fast when it could be.

Don't reach behind the user's back. A library function should not write secret files and variables or change global data, and it should be circumspect about modifying data in its caller. The `strtok` function fails several of these criteria. It is a bit of a surprise that `strtok` writes null bytes into the middle of its input string. Its use of the null pointer as a signal to pick up where it left off last time implies secret data held between calls, a likely source of bugs, and it precludes concurrent uses of the function. A better design would provide a single function that tokenizes an input string. For similar reasons, our second C version can't be used for two input streams; see Exercise 4-8.

The use of one interface should not demand another one just for the convenience of the interface designer or implementer. Instead, make the interface self-contained, or failing that, be explicit about what external services are required. Otherwise, you place a maintenance burden on the client. An obvious example is the pain of managing huge lists of header files in C and C++ source; header files can be thousands of lines long and include dozens of other headers.

Do the same thing the same way everywhere. Consistency and regularity are important. Related things should be achieved by related means. The basic `str...` functions in the C library are easy to use without documentation because they all behave about the same: data flows from right to left, the same direction as in an assignment statement, and they all return the resulting string. On the other hand, in the C Standard I/O library it is hard to predict the order of arguments to functions. Some have the FILE* argument first, some last; others have various orders for size and number of elements. The algorithms for STL containers present a very uniform interface, so it is easy to predict how to use an unfamiliar function.

External consistency, behaving like something else, is also a goal. For example, the mem... functions were designed after the str... functions in C, but borrowed their style. The standard I/O functions fread and fwrite would be easier to remember if they looked like the read and write functions they were based on. Unix command-line options are introduced by a minus sign, but a given option letter may mean completely different things, even between related programs.

If wildcards like the * in *.exe are all expanded by a command interpreter, behavior is uniform. If they are expanded by individual programs, non-uniform behavior is likely. Web browsers take a single mouse click to follow a link, but other applications take two clicks to start a program or follow a link; the result is that many people automatically click twice regardless.

These principles are easier to follow in some environments than others, but they still stand. For instance, it's hard to hide implementation details in C, but a good programmer will not exploit them, because to do so makes the details part of the interface and violates the principle of information hiding. Comments in header files, names with special forms (such as __iob), and so on are ways of encouraging good behavior when it can't be enforced.

No matter what, there is a limit to how well we can do in designing an interface. Even the best interfaces of today may eventually become the problems of tomorrow, but good design can push tomorrow off a while longer.

4.6 Resource Management

One of the most difficult problems in designing the interface for a library (or a class or a package) is to manage resources that are owned by the library or that are shared by the library and those who call it. The most obvious such resource is memory—who is responsible for allocating and freeing storage?—but other shared resources include open files and the state of variables whose values are of common interest. Roughly, the issues fall into the categories of initialization, maintaining state, sharing and copying, and cleaning up.

The prototype of our CSV package used static initialization to set the initial values for pointers, counts, and the like. But this choice is limiting since it prevents restarting the routines in their initial state once one of the functions has been called. An alternative is to provide an initialization function that sets all internal values to the correct initial values. This permits restarting, but relies on the user to call it explicitly. The reset function in the second version could be made public for this purpose.

In C++ and Java, constructors are used to initialize data members of classes. Properly defined constructors ensure that all data members are initialized and that there is no way to create an uninitialized class object. A group of constructors can support various kinds of initializers; we might provide Csv with one constructor that takes a file name and another that takes an input stream.

What about copies of information managed by a library, such as the input lines and fields? Our C csvgetline program provides direct access to the input strings (line and fields) by returning pointers to them. This unrestricted access has several drawbacks. It's possible for the user to overwrite memory so as to render other information invalid; for example, an expression like

```
strcpy(csvfield(1), csvfield(2));
```

could fail in a variety of ways, most likely by overwriting the beginning of field 2 if field 2 is longer than field 1. The user of the library must make a copy of any information to be preserved beyond the next call to csvgetline; in the following sequence, the pointer might well be invalid at the end if the second csvgetline causes a reallocation of its line buffer.

```
char *p;

csvgetline(fin);
p = csvfield(1);
csvgetline(fin);
/* p could be invalid here */
```

The C++ version is safer because the strings are copies that can be changed at will.

Java uses references to refer to objects, that is, any entity other than one of the basic types like int. This is more efficient than making a copy, but one can be fooled into thinking that a reference is a copy; we had a bug like that in an early version of our Java markov program and this issue is a perennial source of bugs involving strings in C. Clone methods provide a way to make a copy when necessary.

The other side of initialization or construction is finalization or destruction— cleaning up and recovering resources when some entity is no longer needed. This is particularly important for memory, since a program that fails to recover unused memory will eventually run out. Much modern software is embarrassingly prone to this fault. Related problems occur when open files are to be closed: if data is being buffered, the buffer may have to be flushed (and its memory reclaimed). For standard C library functions, flushing happens automatically when the program terminates normally, but it must otherwise be programmed. The C and C++ standard function atexit provides a way to get control just before a program terminates normally; interface implementers can use this facility to schedule cleanup.

Free a resource in the same layer that allocated it. One way to control resource allocation and reclamation is to have the same library, package, or interface that allocates

a resource be responsible for freeing it. Another way of saying this is that the allocation state of a resource should not change across the interface. Our CSV libraries read
data from files that have already been opened, so they leave them open when they are
done. The caller of the library needs to close the files.

C++ constructors and destructors help enforce this rule. When a class instance
goes out of scope or is explicitly destroyed, the destructor is called; it can flush
buffers, recover memory, reset values, and do whatever else is necessary. Java does
not provide an equivalent mechanism. Although it is possible to define a finalization
method for a class, there is no assurance that it will run at all, let alone at a particular
time, so cleanup actions cannot be guaranteed to occur, although it is often reasonable
to assume they will.

Java does provide considerable help with memory management because it has
built-in *garbage collection*. As a program runs, it allocates new objects. There is no
way to deallocate them explicitly, but the run-time system keeps track of which
objects are still in use and which are not, and periodically returns unused ones to the
available memory pool.

There are a variety of techniques for garbage collection. Some schemes keep track
of the number of uses of each object, its *reference count*, and free an object when its
reference count goes to zero. This technique can be used explicitly in C and C++ to
manage shared objects. Other algorithms periodically follow a trail from the allocation pool to all referenced objects. Objects that are found this way are still in use;
objects that are not referred to by any other object are not in use and can be reclaimed.

The existence of automatic garbage collection does *not* mean that there are no
memory-management issues in a design. We still have to determine whether interfaces return references to shared objects or copies of them, and this affects the entire
program. Nor is garbage collection free—there is overhead to maintain information
and to reclaim unused memory, and collection may happen at unpredictable times.

All of these problems become more complicated if a library is to be used in an
environment where more than one thread of control can be executing its routines at
the same time, as in a multi-threaded Java program.

To avoid problems, it is necessary to write code that is *reentrant*, which means
that it works regardless of the number of simultaneous executions. Reentrant code
will avoid global variables, static local variables, and any other variable that could be
modified while another thread is using it. The key to good multi-thread design is to
separate the components so they share nothing except through well-defined interfaces.
Libraries that inadvertently expose variables to sharing destroy the model. (In a
multi-thread program, strtok is a disaster, as are other functions in the C library that
store values in internal static memory.) If variables might be shared, they must be
protected by some kind of locking mechanism to ensure that only one thread at a time
accesses them. Classes are a big help here because they provide a focus for discussing sharing and locking models. Synchronized methods in Java provide a way for
one thread to lock an entire class or instance of a class against simultaneous modifica-

tion by some other thread; synchronized blocks permit only one thread at a time to execute a section of code.

Multi-threading adds significant complexity to programming issues, and is too big a topic for us to discuss in detail here.

4.7 Abort, Retry, Fail?

In the previous chapters we used functions like eprintf and estrdup to handle errors by displaying a message before terminating execution. For example, eprintf behaves like fprintf(stderr,...), but exits the program with an error status after reporting the error. It uses the <stdarg.h> header and the vfprintf library routine to print the arguments represented by the ... in the prototype. The stdarg library must be initialized by a call to va_start and terminated by va_end. We will use more of this interface in Chapter 9.

```c
#include <stdarg.h>
#include <string.h>
#include <errno.h>

/* eprintf: print error message and exit */
void eprintf(char *fmt, ...)
{
    va_list args;

    fflush(stdout);
    if (progname() != NULL)
        fprintf(stderr, "%s: ", progname());

    va_start(args, fmt);
    vfprintf(stderr, fmt, args);
    va_end(args);

    if (fmt[0] != '\0' && fmt[strlen(fmt)-1] == ':')
        fprintf(stderr, " %s", strerror(errno));
    fprintf(stderr, "\n");
    exit(2); /* conventional value for failed execution */
}
```

If the format argument ends with a colon, eprintf calls the standard C function strerror, which returns a string containing any additional system error information that might be available. We also wrote weprintf, similar to eprintf, that displays a warning but does not exit. The printf-like interface is convenient for building up strings that might be printed or displayed in a dialog box.

Similarly, estrdup tries to make a copy of a string, and exits with a message (via eprintf) if it runs out of memory:

```
/* estrdup: duplicate a string, report if error */
char *estrdup(char *s)
{
    char *t;

    t = (char *) malloc(strlen(s)+1);
    if (t == NULL)
        eprintf("estrdup(\"%.20s\") failed:", s);
    strcpy(t, s);
    return t;
}
```

and `emalloc` provides a similar service for calls to `malloc`:

```
/* emalloc: malloc and report if error */
void *emalloc(size_t n)
{
    void *p;

    p = malloc(n);
    if (p == NULL)
        eprintf("malloc of %u bytes failed:", n);
    return p;
}
```

A matching header file called `eprintf.h` declares these functions:

```
/* eprintf.h: error wrapper functions */
extern  void    eprintf(char *, ...);
extern  void    weprintf(char *, ...);
extern  char    *estrdup(char *);
extern  void    *emalloc(size_t);
extern  void    *erealloc(void *, size_t);
extern  char    *progname(void);
extern  void    setprogname(char *);
```

This header is included in any file that calls one of the error functions. Each error message also includes the name of the program if it has been set by the caller; this is set and retrieved by the trivial functions `setprogname` and `progname`, declared in the header file and defined in the source file with `eprintf`:

```
static char *name = NULL;  /* program name for messages */

/* setprogname: set stored name of program */
void setprogname(char *str)
{
    name = estrdup(str);
}

/* progname: return stored name of program */
char *progname(void)
{
    return name;
}
```

Typical usage looks like this:

```
int main(int argc, char *argv[])
{
    setprogname("markov");
    ...
    f = fopen(argv[i], "r");
    if (f == NULL)
        eprintf("can't open %s:", argv[i]);
    ...
}
```

which prints output like this:

```
markov: can't open psalm.txt: No such file or directory
```

We find these wrapper functions convenient for our own programming, since they unify error handling and their very existence encourages us to catch errors instead of ignoring them. There is nothing special about our design, however, and you might prefer some variant for your own programs.

Suppose that rather than writing functions for our own use, we are creating a library for others to use in their programs. What should a function in that library do if an unrecoverable error occurs? The functions we wrote earlier in this chapter display a message and die. This is acceptable behavior for many programs, especially small stand-alone tools and applications. For other programs, however, quitting is wrong since it prevents the rest of the program from attempting any recovery; for instance, a word processor must recover from errors so it does not lose the document that you are typing. In some situations a library routine should not even display a message, since the program may be running in an environment where a message will interfere with displayed data or disappear without a trace. A useful alternative is to record diagnostic output in an explicit "log file," where it can be monitored independently.

Detect errors at a low level, handle them at a high level. As a general principle, errors should be detected at as low a level as possible, but handled at a high level. In most cases, the caller should determine how to handle an error, not the callee. Library routines can help in this by failing gracefully; that reasoning led us to return NULL for a non-existent field rather than aborting. Similarly, csvgetline returns NULL no matter how many times it is called after the first end of file.

Appropriate return values are not always obvious, as we saw in the earlier discussion about what csvgetline should return. We want to return as much useful information as possible, but in a form that is easy for the rest of the program to use. In C, C++ and Java, that means returning something as the function value, and perhaps other values through reference (pointer) arguments. Many library functions rely on the ability to distinguish normal values from error values. Input functions like getchar return a char for valid data, and some non-char value like EOF for end of file or error.

This mechanism doesn't work if the function's legal return values take up all possible values. For example a mathematical function like log can return any floating-point number. In IEEE floating point, a special value called NaN (''not a number'') indicates an error and can be returned as an error signal.

Some languages, such as Perl and Tcl, provide a low-cost way to group two or more values into a *tuple*. In such languages, a function value and any error state can be easily returned together. The C++ STL provides a pair data type that can also be used in this way.

It is desirable to distinguish various exceptional values like end of file and error states if possible, rather than lumping them together into a single value. If the values can't readily be separated, another option is to return a single ''exception'' value and provide another function that returns more detail about the last error.

This is the approach used in Unix and in the C standard library, where many system calls and library functions return -1 but also set a global variable called errno that encodes the specific error; strerror returns a string associated with the error number. On our system, this program:

```
#include <stdio.h>
#include <string.h>
#include <errno.h>
#include <math.h>

/* errno main: test errno */
int main(void)
{
    double f;

    errno = 0;   /* clear error state */
    f = log(-1.23);
    printf("%f %d %s\n", f, errno, strerror(errno));
    return 0;
}
```

prints

```
nan0x10000000 33 Domain error
```

As shown, errno must be cleared first; then if an error occurs, errno will be set to a non-zero value.

Use exceptions only for exceptional situations. Some languages provide *exceptions* to catch unusual situations and recover from them; they provide an alternate flow of control when something bad happens. Exceptions should not be used for handling expected return values. Reading from a file will eventually produce an end of file; this should be handled with a return value, not by an exception.

In Java, one writes

```
String fname = "someFileName";
try {
    FileInputStream in = new FileInputStream(fname);
    int c;
    while ((c = in.read()) != -1)
        System.out.print((char) c);
    in.close();
} catch (FileNotFoundException e) {
    System.err.println(fname + " not found");
} catch (IOException e) {
    System.err.println("IOException: " + e);
    e.printStackTrace();
}
```

The loop reads characters until end of file, an expected event that is signaled by a return value of -1 from read. If the file can't be opened, that raises an exception, however, rather than setting the input stream to null as would be done in C or C++. Finally, if some other I/O error happens in the try block, it is also exceptional, and it is caught by the IOException clause.

Exceptions are often overused. Because they distort the flow of control, they can lead to convoluted constructions that are prone to bugs. It is hardly exceptional to fail to open a file; generating an exception in this case strikes us as over-engineering. Exceptions are best reserved for truly unexpected events, such as file systems filling up or floating-point errors.

For C programs, the pair of functions setjmp and longjmp provide a much lower-level service upon which an exception mechanism can be built, but they are sufficiently arcane that we won't go into them here.

What about recovery of resources when an error occurs? Should a library attempt a recovery when something goes wrong? Not usually, but it might do a service by making sure that it leaves information in as clean and harmless a state as possible. Certainly unused storage should be reclaimed. If variables might be still accessible, they should be set to sensible values. A common source of bugs is trying to use a pointer that points to freed storage. If error-handling code sets pointers to zero after freeing what they point to, this won't go undetected. The reset function in the second version of the CSV library was an attempt to address these issues. In general, aim to keep the library usable after an error has occurred.

4.8 User Interfaces

Thus far we have talked mainly about interfaces among the components of a program or between programs. But there is another important kind of interface, between a program and its human users.

Most of the example programs in this book are text-based, so their user interfaces tend to be straightforward. As we discussed in the previous section, errors should be detected and reported, and recovery attempted where it makes sense. Error output should include all available information and should be as meaningful as possible out of context; a diagnostic should not say

```
estrdup failed
```

when it could say

```
markov: estrdup("Derrida") failed: Memory limit reached
```

It costs nothing to add the extra information as we did in `estrdup`, and it may help a user to identify a problem or provide valid input.

Programs should display information about proper usage when an error is made, as shown in functions like

```
/* usage: print usage message and exit */
void usage(void)
{
    fprintf(stderr, "usage: %s [-d] [-n nwords]"
        " [-s seed] [files ...]\n", progname());
    exit(2);
}
```

The program name identifies the source of the message, which is especially important if this is part of a larger process. If a program presents a message that just says `syntax error` or `estrdup failed`, the user might have no idea who said it.

The text of error messages, prompts, and dialog boxes should state the form of valid input. Don't say that a parameter is too large; report the valid range of values. When possible, the text should be valid input itself, such as the full command line with the parameter set properly. In addition to steering users toward proper use, such output can be captured in a file or by a mouse sweep and then used to run some further process. This points out a weakness of dialog boxes: their contents are hard to grab for later use.

One effective way to create a good user interface for input is by designing a specialized language for setting parameters, controlling actions, and so on; a good notation can make a program easy to use while it helps organize an implementation. Language-based interfaces are the subject of Chapter 9.

Defensive programming, that is, making sure that a program is invulnerable to bad input, is important both for protecting users against themselves and also as a security mechanism. This is discussed more in Chapter 6, which talks about program testing.

For most people, graphical interfaces are *the* user interface for their computers. Graphical user interfaces are a huge topic, so we will say only a few things that are germane to this book. First, graphical interfaces are hard to create and make "right" since their suitability and success depend strongly on human behavior and expectations. Second, as a practical matter, if a system has a user interface, there is usually more code to handle user interaction than there is in whatever algorithms do the work.

Nevertheless, familiar principles apply to both the external design and the internal implementation of user interface software. From the user's standpoint, style issues like simplicity, clarity, regularity, uniformity, familiarity, and restraint all contribute to an interface that is easy to use; the absence of such properties usually goes along with unpleasant or awkward interfaces.

Uniformity and regularity are desirable, including consistent use of terms, units, formats, layouts, fonts, colors, sizes, and all the other options that a graphical system makes available. How many different English words are used to exit from a program or close a window? The choices range from Abandon to control-Z, with at least a dozen between. This inconsistency is confusing to a native speaker and baffling for others.

Within graphics code, interfaces are particularly important, since these systems are large, complicated, and driven by a very different input model than scanning sequential text. Object-oriented programming excels at graphical user interfaces, since it provides a way to encapsulate all the state and behaviors of windows, using inheritance to combine similarities in base classes while separating differences in derived classes.

Supplementary Reading

Although a few of its technical details are now dated, *The Mythical Man Month*, by Frederick P. Brooks, Jr. (Addison-Wesley, 1975; Anniversary Edition 1995), is delightful reading and contains insights about software development that are as valuable today as when it was originally published.

Almost every book on programming has something useful to say about interface design. One practical book based on hard-won experience is *Large-Scale C++ Software Design* by John Lakos (Addison-Wesley, 1996), which discusses how to build and manage truly large C++ programs. David Hanson's *C Interfaces and Implementations* (Addison-Wesley, 1997) is a good treatment for C programs.

Steve McConnell's *Rapid Development* (Microsoft Press, 1996) is an excellent description of how to build software in teams, with an emphasis on the role of prototyping.

There are several interesting books on the design of graphical user interfaces, with a variety of different perspectives. We suggest *Designing Visual Interfaces: Communication Oriented Techniques* by Kevin Mullet and Darrell Sano (Prentice Hall, 1995), *Designing the User Interface: Strategies for Effective Human-Computer Interaction* by Ben Shneiderman (3rd edition, Addison-Wesley, 1997), *About Face: The Essentials of User Interface Design* by Alan Cooper (IDG, 1995), and *User Interface Design* by Harold Thimbleby (Addison-Wesley, 1990).

5

Debugging

bug.

    b. A defect or fault in a machine, plan, or the like. orig. *U.S.*
1889 Pall Mall Gaz. 11 Mar. 1/1 Mr. Edison, I was informed, had been up the
two previous nights discovering 'a bug' in his phonograph—an expression for
solving a difficulty, and implying that some imaginary insect has secreted itself
inside and is causing all the trouble.

                                  Oxford English Dictionary, 2nd Edition

We have presented a lot of code in the past four chapters, and we've pretended
that it all pretty much worked the first time. Naturally this wasn't true; there were
plenty of bugs. The word "bug" didn't originate with programmers, but it is certainly one of the most common terms in computing. Why should software be so
hard?

One reason is that the complexity of a program is related to the number of ways
that its components can interact, and software is full of components and interactions.
Many techniques attempt to reduce the connections between components so there are
fewer pieces to interact; examples include information hiding, abstraction and interfaces, and the language features that support them. There are also techniques for
ensuring the integrity of a software design—program proofs, modeling, requirements
analysis, formal verification—but none of these has yet changed the way software is
built; they have been successful only on small problems. The reality is that there will
always be errors that we find by testing and eliminate by debugging.

Good programmers know that they spend as much time debugging as writing so
they try to learn from their mistakes. Every bug you find can teach you how to prevent a similar bug from happening again or to recognize it if it does.

Debugging is hard and can take long and unpredictable amounts of time, so the
goal is to avoid having to do much of it. Techniques that help reduce debugging time
include good design, good style, boundary condition tests, assertions and sanity
checks in the code, defensive programming, well-designed interfaces, limited global
data, and checking tools. An ounce of prevention really is worth a pound of cure.

What is the role of language? A major force in the evolution of programming languages has been the attempt to prevent bugs through language features. Some features make classes of errors less likely: range checking on subscripts, restricted pointers or no pointers at all, garbage collection, string data types, typed I/O, and strong type-checking. On the opposite side of the coin, some features are prone to error, like goto statements, global variables, unrestricted pointers, and automatic type conversions. Programmers should know the potentially risky bits of their languages and take extra care when using them. They should also enable all compiler checks and heed the warnings.

Each language feature that prevents some problem has a cost of its own. If a higher-level language makes the simple bugs disappear automatically, the price is that it makes it easier to create higher-level bugs. No language prevents you from making mistakes.

Even though we wish it were otherwise, a majority of programming time is spent testing and debugging. In this chapter, we'll discuss how to make your debugging time as short and productive as possible; we'll come back to testing in Chapter 6.

5.1 Debuggers

Compilers for major languages usually come with sophisticated debuggers, often packaged as part of a development environment that integrates creation and editing of source code, compilation, execution, and debugging, all in a single system. Debuggers include graphical interfaces for stepping through a program one statement or function at a time, stopping at particular lines or when a specific condition occurs. They also provide facilities for formatting and displaying the values of variables.

A debugger can be invoked directly when a problem is known to exist. Some debuggers take over automatically when something unexpectedly goes wrong during program execution. It's usually easy to find out where the program was executing when it died, examine the sequence of functions that were active (the *stack trace*), and display the values of local and global variables. That much information may be sufficient to identify a bug. If not, breakpoints and stepping make it possible to re-run a failing program one step at a time to find the first place where something goes wrong.

In the right environment and in the hands of an experienced user, a good debugger can make debugging effective and efficient, if not exactly painless. With such powerful tools at one's disposal, why would anyone ever debug without them? Why do we need a whole chapter on debugging?

There are several good reasons, some objective and some based on personal experience. Some languages outside the mainstream have no debugger or provide only rudimentary debugging capabilities. Debuggers are system-dependent, so you may not have access to the familiar debugger from one system when you work on another. Some programs are not handled well by debuggers: multi-process or multi-thread programs, operating systems, and distributed systems must often be debugged by lower-level approaches. In such situations, you're on your own, without much help besides print statements and your own experience and ability to reason about code.

As a personal choice, we tend not to use debuggers beyond getting a stack trace or the value of a variable or two. One reason is that it is easy to get lost in details of complicated data structures and control flow; we find stepping through a program less productive than thinking harder and adding output statements and self-checking code at critical places. Clicking over statements takes longer than scanning the output of judiciously-placed displays. It takes less time to decide where to put print statements than to single-step to the critical section of code, even assuming we know where that is. More important, debugging statements stay with the program; debugger sessions are transient.

Blind probing with a debugger is not likely to be productive. It is more helpful to use the debugger to discover the state of the program when it fails, then think about how the failure could have happened. Debuggers can be arcane and difficult programs, and especially for beginners may provide more confusion than help. If you ask the wrong question, they will probably give you an answer, but you may not know it's misleading.

A debugger can be of enormous value, however, and you should certainly include one in your debugging toolkit; it is likely to be the first thing you turn to. But if you don't have a debugger, or if you're stuck on an especially hard problem, the techniques in this chapter will help you to debug effectively and efficiently anyway. They should make your use of your debugger more productive as well, since they are largely concerned with how to reason about errors and probable causes.

5.2 Good Clues, Easy Bugs

Oops! Something is badly wrong. My program crashed, or printed nonsense, or seems to be running forever. Now what?

Beginners have a tendency to blame the compiler, the library, or anything other than their own code. Experienced programmers would love to do the same, but they know that, realistically, most problems are their own fault.

Fortunately, most bugs are simple and can be found with simple techniques. Examine the evidence in the erroneous output and try to infer how it could have been produced. Look at any debugging output before the crash; if possible get a stack trace from a debugger. Now you know something of what happened, and where. Pause to reflect. How could that happen? Reason back from the state of the crashed program to determine what could have caused this.

Debugging involves backwards reasoning, like solving murder mysteries. Something impossible occurred, and the only solid information is that it really did occur. So we must think backwards from the result to discover the reasons. Once we have a full explanation, we'll know what to fix and, along the way, likely discover a few other things we hadn't expected.

Look for familiar patterns. Ask yourself whether this is a familiar pattern. "I've seen that before" is often the beginning of understanding, or even the whole answer. Common bugs have distinctive signatures. For instance, novice C programmers often write

```
?    int n;
?    scanf("%d", n);
```

instead of

```
     int n;
     scanf("%d", &n);
```

and this typically causes an attempt to access out-of-bounds memory when a line of input is read. People who teach C recognize the symptom instantly.

Mismatched types and conversions in `printf` and `scanf` are an endless source of easy bugs:

```
?    int n = 1;
?    double d = PI;
?    printf("%d %f\n", d, n);
```

The signature of this error is sometimes the appearance of preposterous values: huge integers or improbably large or small floating-point values. On a Sun SPARC, the output from this program is a huge number and an astronomical one (folded to fit):

```
1074340347 268156158598852001534108794260233396350\
    1936585971793218047714963795307788611480564140\
    0796821289594743537151163524101175474084764156\
    4227714083238396234301440144.000000
```

Another common error is using `%f` instead of `%lf` to read a `double` with `scanf`. Some compilers catch such mistakes by verifying that the types of `scanf` and `printf` arguments match their format strings; if all warnings are enabled, for the `printf` above, the GNU compiler `gcc` reports that

```
x.c:9: warning: int format, double arg (arg 2)
x.c:9: warning: double format, different type arg (arg 3)
```

Failing to initialize a local variable gives rise to another distinctive error. The result is often an extremely large value, the garbage left over from whatever previous value was stored in the same memory location. Some compilers will warn you, though you may have to enable the compile-time check, and they can never catch all cases. Memory returned by allocators like `malloc`, `realloc`, and `new` is likely to be garbage too; be sure to initialize it.

Examine the most recent change. What was the last change? If you're changing only one thing at a time as a program evolves, the bug most likely is either in the new code or has been exposed by it. Looking carefully at recent changes helps to localize the problem. If the bug appears in the new version and not in the old, the new code is part of the problem. This means that you should preserve at least the previous version of the program, which you believe to be correct, so that you can compare behaviors. It also means that you should keep records of changes made and bugs fixed, so you don't have to rediscover this vital information while you're trying to fix a bug. Source code control systems and other history mechanisms are helpful here.

Don't make the same mistake twice. After you fix a bug, ask whether you might have made the same mistake somewhere else. This happened to one of us just days before beginning to write this chapter. The program was a quick prototype for a colleague, and included some boilerplate for optional arguments:

```
?       for (i = 1; i < argc; i++) {
?           if (argv[i][0] != '-')  /* options finished */
?               break;
?           switch (argv[i][1]) {
?           case 'o':                 /* output filename */
?               outname = argv[i];
?               break;
?           case 'f':
?               from = atoi(argv[i]);
?               break;
?           case 't':
?               to = atoi(argv[i]);
?               break;
?           ...
```

Shortly after our colleague tried it, he reported that the output file name always had the prefix -o attached to it. This was embarrassing but easy to repair; the code should have read

```
        outname = &argv[i][2];
```

So that was fixed up and shipped off, and back came another report that the program failed to handle an argument like -f123 properly: the converted numeric value was always zero. This is the same error; the next case in the switch should have read

```
        from = atoi(&argv[i][2]);
```

Because the author was still in a hurry, he failed to notice that the same blunder occurred twice more and it took another round before all of the fundamentally identical errors were fixed.

Easy code can have bugs if its familiarity causes us to let down our guard. Even when code is so simple you could write it in your sleep, don't fall asleep while writing it.

Debug it now, not later. Being in too much of a hurry can hurt in other situations as well. Don't ignore a crash when it happens; track it down right away, since it may not happen again until it's too late. A famous example occurred on the Mars Pathfinder mission. After the flawless landing in July 1997 the spacecraft's computers tended to reset once a day or so, and the engineers were baffled. Once they tracked down the problem, they realized that they had seen that problem before. During pre-launch tests the resets had occurred, but had been ignored because the engineers were working on unrelated problems. So they were forced to deal with the problem later when the machine was tens of millions of miles away and much harder to fix.

Get a stack trace. Although debuggers can probe running programs, one of their most common uses is to examine the state of a program after death. The source line number of the failure, often part of a stack trace, is the most useful single piece of debugging information; improbable values of arguments are also a big clue (zero pointers, integers that are huge when they should be small, or negative when they should be positive, character strings that aren't alphabetic).

Here's a typical example, based on the discussion of sorting in Chapter 2. To sort an array of integers, we should call qsort with the integer comparison function icmp:

```
int arr[N];
qsort(arr, N, sizeof(arr[0]), icmp);
```

but suppose it is inadvertently passed the name of the string comparison function scmp instead:

```
?       int arr[N];
?       qsort(arr, N, sizeof(arr[0]), scmp);
```

A compiler can't detect the mismatch of types here, so disaster awaits. When we run the program, it crashes by attempting to access an illegal memory location. Running the dbx debugger produces a stack trace like this, edited to fit:

```
0 strcmp(0x1a2, 0x1c2) ["strcmp.s":31]
1 scmp(p1 = 0x10001048, p2 = 0x1000105c) ["badqs.c":13]
2 qst(0x10001048, 0x10001074, 0x400b20, 0x4) ["qsort.c":147]
3 qsort(0x10001048, 0x1c2, 0x4, 0x400b20) ["qsort.c":63]
4 main() ["badqs.c":45]
5 __istart() ["crt1tinit.s":13]
```

This says that the program died in strcmp; by inspection, the two pointers passed to strcmp are much too small, a clear sign of trouble. The stack trace gives a trail of line numbers where each function was called. Line 13 in our test file badqs.c is the call

```
return strcmp(v1, v2);
```

which identifies the failing call and points towards the error.

A debugger can also be used to display values of local or global variables that will give additional information about what went wrong.

Read before typing. One effective but under-appreciated debugging technique is to read the code very carefully and think about it for a while without making changes. There's a powerful urge to get to the keyboard and start modifying the program to see if the bug goes away. But chances are that you don't know what's really broken and will change the wrong thing, perhaps breaking something else. A listing of the critical part of program on paper can give a different perspective than what you see on the screen, and encourages you to take more time for reflection. Don't make listings as a matter of routine, though. Printing a complete program wastes trees since it's hard to see the structure when it's spread across many pages and the listing will be obsolete the moment you start editing again.

Take a break for a while; sometimes what you see in the source code is what you meant rather than what you wrote, and an interval away from it can soften your misconceptions and help the code speak for itself when you return.

Resist the urge to start typing; thinking is a worthwhile alternative.

Explain your code to someone else. Another effective technique is to explain your code to someone else. This will often cause you to explain the bug to yourself. Sometimes it takes no more than a few sentences, followed by an embarrassed "Never mind, I see what's wrong. Sorry to bother you." This works remarkably well; you can even use non-programmers as listeners. One university computer center kept a teddy bear near the help desk. Students with mysterious bugs were required to explain them to the bear before they could speak to a human counselor.

5.3 No Clues, Hard Bugs

"I haven't got a clue. What on earth is going on?" If you really haven't any idea what could be wrong, life gets tougher.

Make the bug reproducible. The first step is to make sure you can make the bug appear on demand. It's frustrating to chase down a bug that doesn't happen every time. Spend some time constructing input and parameter settings that reliably cause the problem, then wrap up the recipe so it can be run with a button push or a few keystrokes. If it's a hard bug, you'll be making it happen over and over as you track down the problem, so you'll save yourself time by making it easy to reproduce.

If the bug can't be made to happen every time, try to understand why not. Does some set of conditions make it happen more often than others? Even if you can't make it happen every time, if you can decrease the time spent waiting for it, you'll find it faster.

If a program provides debugging output, enable it. Simulation programs like the Markov chain program in Chapter 3 should include an option that produces debugging information such as the seed of the random number generator so that output can be reproduced; another option should allow for setting the seed. Many programs include such options and it is a good idea to include similar facilities in your own programs.

Divide and conquer. Can the input that causes the program to fail be made smaller or more focused? Narrow down the possibilities by creating the smallest input where the bug still shows up. What changes make the error go away? Try to find crucial test cases that focus on the error. Each test case should aim at a definitive outcome that confirms or denies a specific hypothesis about what is wrong.

Proceed by binary search. Throw away half the input and see if the output is still wrong; if not, go back to the previous state and discard the other half of the input. The same binary search process can be used on the program text itself: eliminate some part of the program that should have no relationship to the bug and see if the bug is still there. An editor with undo is helpful in reducing big test cases and big programs without losing the bug.

Study the numerology of failures. Sometimes a pattern in the numerology of failing examples gives a clue that focuses the search. We found some spelling mistakes in a newly written section of this book, where occasional letters had simply disappeared. This was mystifying. The text had been created by cutting and pasting from another file, so it seemed possible that something was wrong with the cut or paste commands in the text editor. But where to start looking for the problem? For clues we looked at the data, and noticed that the missing characters seemed uniformly distributed through the text. We measured the intervals and found that the distance between dropped characters was always 1023 bytes, a suspiciously non-random value. A search through the editor source code for numbers near 1024 found a couple of candidates. One of those was in new code, so we examined that first, and the bug was easy to spot, a classic off-by-one error where a null byte overwrote the last character in a 1024-byte buffer.

Studying the patterns of numbers related to the failure pointed us right at the bug. Elapsed time? A couple of minutes of mystification, five minutes of looking at the data to discover the pattern of missing characters, a minute to search for likely places to fix, and another minute to identify and eliminate the bug. This one would have been hopeless to find with a debugger, since it involved two multiprocess programs, driven by mouse clicks, communicating through a file system.

Display output to localize your search. If you don't understand what the program is doing, adding statements to display more information can be the easiest, most cost-effective way to find out. Put them in to verify your understanding or refine your ideas of what's wrong. For example, display "can't get here" if you think it's not possible to reach a certain point in the code; then if you see that message, move the output statements back towards the start to figure out where things first begin to go wrong. Or show "got here" messages going forward, to find the last place where things seem to be working. Each message should be distinct so you can tell which one you're looking at.

Display messages in a compact fixed format so they are easy to scan by eye or with programs like the pattern-matching tool `grep`. (A `grep`-like program is invaluable for searching text. Chapter 9 includes a simple implementation.) If you're displaying the value of a variable, format it the same way each time. In C and C++, show pointers as hexadecimal numbers with %x or %p; this will help you to see whether two pointers have the same value or are related. Learn to read pointer values and recognize likely and unlikely ones, like zero, negative numbers, odd numbers, and small numbers. Familiarity with the form of addresses will pay off when you're using a debugger, too.

If output is potentially voluminous, it might be sufficient to print single-letter outputs like A, B, ..., as a compact display of where the program went.

Write self-checking code. If more information is needed, you can write your own check function to test a condition, dump relevant variables, and abort the program:

```
/* check: test condition, print and die */
void check(char *s)
{
    if (var1 > var2) {
        printf("%s: var1 %d var2 %d\n", s, var1, var2);
        fflush(stdout); /* make sure all output is out */
        abort();        /* signal abnormal termination */
    }
}
```

We wrote check to call abort, a standard C library function that causes program execution to be terminated abnormally for analysis with a debugger. In a different application, you might want check to carry on after printing.

Next, add calls to check wherever they might be useful in your code:

```
check("before suspect");
/* ... suspect code ... */
check("after suspect");
```

After a bug is fixed, don't throw check away. Leave it in the source, commented out or controlled by a debugging option, so that it can be turned on again when the next difficult problem appears.

For harder problems, check might evolve to do verification and display of data structures. This approach can be generalized to routines that perform ongoing consistency checks of data structures and other information. In a program with intricate data structures, it's a good idea to write these checks *before* problems happen, as components of the program proper, so they can be turned on when trouble starts. Don't use them only when debugging; leave them installed during all stages of program development. If they're not expensive, it might be wise to leave them always enabled. Large programs like telephone switching systems often devote a significant amount of code to "audit" subsystems that monitor information and equipment, and report or even fix problems if they occur.

Write a log file. Another tactic is to write a *log file* containing a fixed-format stream of debugging output. When a crash occurs, the log records what happened just before the crash. Web servers and other network programs maintain extensive logs of traffic so they can monitor themselves and their clients; this fragment (edited to fit) comes from a local system:

```
[Sun Dec 27 16:19:24 1998]
HTTPd: access to /usr/local/httpd/cgi-bin/test.html
    failed for m1.cs.bell-labs.com,
    reason: client denied by server (CGI non-executable)
    from http://m2.cs.bell-labs.com/cgi-bin/test.pl
```

Be sure to flush I/O buffers so the final log records appear in the log file. Output functions like printf normally buffer their output to print it efficiently; abnormal termination may discard this buffered output. In C, a call to fflush guarantees that all output is written before the program dies; there are analogous flush functions for output streams in C++ and Java. Or, if you can afford the overhead, you can avoid the flushing problem altogether by using unbuffered I/O for log files. The standard functions setbuf and setvbuf control buffering; setbuf(fp, NULL) turns off buffering on the stream fp. The standard error streams (stderr, cerr, System.err) are normally unbuffered by default.

Draw a picture. Sometimes pictures are more effective than text for testing and debugging. Pictures are especially helpful for understanding data structures, as we saw in Chapter 2, and of course when writing graphics software, but they can be used for all kinds of programs. Scatter plots display misplaced values more effectively than columns of numbers. A histogram of data reveals anomalies in exam grades, random numbers, bucket sizes in allocators and hash tables, and the like.

If you don't understand what's happening inside your program, try annotating the data structures with statistics and plotting the result. The following graphs plot, for the C markov program in Chapter 3, hash chain lengths on the x axis and the number of elements in chains of that length on the y axis. The input data is our standard test, the Book of Psalms (42,685 words, 22,482 prefixes). The first two graphs are for the good hash multipliers of 31 and 37 and the third is for the awful multiplier of 128. In the first two cases, no chain is longer than 15 or 16 elements and most elements are in chains of length 5 or 6. In the third, the distribution is broader, the longest chain has 187 elements, and there are thousands of elements in chains longer than 20.

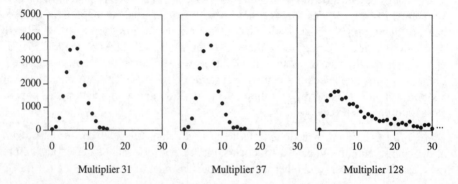

Multiplier 31   Multiplier 37   Multiplier 128

Use tools. Make good use of the facilities of the environment where you are debugging. For example, a file comparison program like diff compares the outputs from successful and failed debugging runs so you can focus on what has changed. If your debugging output is long, use grep to search it or an editor to examine it. Resist the temptation to send debugging output to a printer: computers scan voluminous output better than people do. Use shell scripts and other tools to automate the processing of the output from debugging runs.

Write trivial programs to test hypotheses or confirm your understanding of how something works. For instance, is it valid to free a NULL pointer?

```
int main(void)
{
    free(NULL);
    return 0;
}
```

Source code control programs like RCS keep track of versions of code so you can see what has changed and revert to previous versions to restore a known state. Besides indicating what has changed recently, they can also identify sections of code that have a long history of frequent modification; these are often a good place for bugs to lurk.

Keep records. If the search for a bug goes on for any length of time, you will begin to lose track of what you tried and what you learned. If you record your tests and results, you are less likely to overlook something or to think that you have checked some possibility when you haven't. The act of writing will help you remember the problem the next time something similar comes up, and will also serve when you're explaining it to someone else.

5.4 Last Resorts

What do you do if none of this advice helps? This may be the time to use a good debugger to step through the program. If your mental model of how something works is just plain wrong, so you're looking in the wrong place entirely, or looking in the right place but not seeing the problem, a debugger forces you to think differently. These ''mental model'' bugs are among the hardest to find; the mechanical aid is invaluable.

Sometimes the misconception is simple: incorrect operator precedence, or the wrong operator, or indentation that doesn't match the actual structure, or a scope error where a local name hides a global name or a global name intrudes into a local scope. For example, programmers often forget that & and | have lower precedence than == and !=. They write

```
?    if (x & 1 == 0)
?        ...
```

and can't figure out why this is always false. Occasionally a slip of the finger converts a single = into two or vice versa:

```
?     while ((c == getchar()) != EOF)
?         if (c = '\n')
?             break;
```

Or extra code is left behind during editing:

```
?     for (i = 0; i < n; i++);
?         a[i++] = 0;
```

Or hasty typing creates a problem:

```
?     switch (c) {
?         case '<':
?             mode = LESS;
?             break;
?         case '>':
?             mode = GREATER;
?             break;
?         defualt:
?             mode = EQUAL;
?             break;
?     }
```

Sometimes the error involves arguments in the wrong order in a situation where type-checking can't help, like writing

```
?     memset(p, n, 0);     /* store n 0's in p */
```

instead of

```
      memset(p, 0, n);     /* store n 0's in p */
```

Sometimes something changes behind your back—global or shared variables are modified and you don't realize that some other routine can touch them.

Sometimes your algorithm or data structure has a fatal flaw and you just can't see it. While preparing material on linked lists, we wrote a package of list functions to create new elements, link them to the front or back of lists, and so on; these functions appear in Chapter 2. Of course we wrote a test program to make sure everything was correct. The first few tests worked but then one failed spectacularly. In essence, this was the testing program:

```
?     while (scanf("%s %d", name, &value) != EOF) {
?         p = newitem(name, value);
?         list1 = addfront(list1, p);
?         list2 = addend(list2, p);
?     }
?     for (p = list1; p != NULL; p = p->next)
?         printf("%s %d\n", p->name, p->value);
```

It was surprisingly difficult to see that the first loop was putting the same node p on both lists so the pointers were hopelessly scrambled by the time we got to printing.

It's tough to find this kind of bug, because your brain takes you right around the mistake. Thus a debugger is a help, since it forces you to go in a different direction, to follow what the program *is* doing, not what you think it is doing. Often the underlying problem is something wrong with the structure of the whole program, and to see the error you need to return to your starting assumptions.

Notice, by the way, that in the list example the error was in the test code, which made the bug that much harder to find. It is frustratingly easy to waste time chasing bugs that aren't there, because the test program is wrong, or by testing the wrong version of the program, or by failing to update or recompile before testing.

If you can't find a bug after considerable work, take a break. Clear your mind, do something else. Talk to a friend and ask for help. The answer might appear out of the blue, but if not, you won't be stuck in the same rut in the next debugging session.

Once in a long while, the problem really is the compiler or a library or the operating system or even the hardware, especially if something changed in the environment just before a bug appeared. You should never start by blaming one of these, but when everything else has been eliminated, that might be all that's left. We once had to move a large text-formatting program from its original Unix home to a PC. The program compiled without incident, but behaved in an extremely odd way: it dropped roughly every second character of its input. Our first thought was that this must be some property of using 16-bit integers instead of 32-bit, or perhaps some strange byte-order problem. But by printing out the characters seen by the main loop, we finally tracked it down to an error in the standard header file `ctype.h` provided by the compiler vendor. It implemented `isprint` as a function macro:

```
?     #define isprint(c) ((c) >= 040 && (c) < 0177)
```

and the main input loop was basically

```
?     while (isprint(c = getchar()))
?         ...
```

Each time an input character was blank (octal 40, a poor way to write ' ') or greater, which was most of the time, `getchar` was called a second time because the macro evaluated its argument twice, and the first input character disappeared forever. The original code was not as clean as it should have been—there's too much in the loop condition—but the vendor's header file was inexcusably wrong.

One can still find instances of this problem today; this macro comes from a different vendor's current header files:

```
?     #define __iscsym(c) (isalnum(c) || ((c) == '_'))
```

Memory "leaks"—the failure to reclaim memory that is no longer in use—are a significant source of erratic behavior. Another problem is forgetting to close files, until the table of open files is full and the program cannot open any more. Programs with leaks tend to fail mysteriously because they run out of some resource but the specific failure can't be reproduced.

Occasionally hardware itself goes bad. The floating-point flaw in the 1994 Pentium processor that caused certain computations to produce wrong answers was a highly publicized and costly bug in the design of the hardware, but once it had been identified, it was of course reproducible. One of the strangest bugs we ever saw involved a calculator program, long ago on a two-processor system. Sometimes the expression 1/2 would print 0.5 and sometimes it would print some consistent but utterly wrong value like 0.7432; there was no pattern as to whether one got the right answer or the wrong one. The problem was eventually traced to a failure of the floating-point unit in one of the processors. As the calculator program was randomly executed on one processor or the other, answers were either correct or nonsense.

Many years ago we used a machine whose internal temperature could be estimated from the number of low-order bits it got wrong in floating-point calculations. One of the circuit cards was loose; as the machine got warmer, the card tilted further out of its socket, and more data bits were disconnected from the backplane.

5.5 Non-reproducible Bugs

Bugs that won't stand still are the most difficult to deal with, and usually the problem isn't as obvious as failing hardware. The very fact that the behavior is non-deterministic is itself information, however; it means that the error is not likely to be a flaw in your algorithm but that in some way your code is using information that changes each time the program runs.

Check whether all variables have been initialized; you may be picking up a random value from whatever was previously stored in the same memory location. Local variables of functions and memory obtained from allocators are the most likely culprits in C and C++. Set all variables to known values; if there's a random number seed that is normally set from the time of day, force it to a constant, like zero.

If the bug changes behavior or even disappears when debugging code is added, it may be a memory allocation error—somewhere you have written outside of allocated memory, and the addition of debugging code changes the layout of storage enough to change the effect of the bug. Most output functions, from printf to dialog windows, allocate memory themselves, further muddying the waters.

If the crash site seems far away from anything that could be wrong, the most likely problem is overwriting memory by storing into a memory location that isn't used until much later. Sometimes this is a dangling pointer problem, where a pointer to a local variable is inadvertently returned from a function, then used. Returning the address of a local variable is a recipe for delayed disaster:

```
?      char *msg(int n, char *s)
?      {
?          char buf[100];
?
?          sprintf(buf, "error %d: %s\n", n, s);
?          return buf;
?      }
```

By the time the pointer returned by msg is used, it no longer points to meaningful storage. You must allocate storage with malloc, use a static array, or require the caller to provide the space.

Using a dynamically allocated value after it has been freed has similar symptoms. We mentioned this in Chapter 2 when we wrote freeall. This code is wrong:

```
?      for (p = listp; p != NULL; p = p->next)
?          free(p);
```

Once memory has been freed, it must not be used since its contents may have changed and there is no guarantee that p->next still points to the right place.

In some implementations of malloc and free, freeing an item twice corrupts the internal data structures but doesn't cause trouble until much later, when a subsequent call slips on the mess made earlier. Some allocators come with debugging options that can be set to check the consistency of the arena at each call; turn them on if you have a non-deterministic bug. Failing that, you can write your own allocator that does some of its own consistency checking or logs all calls for separate analysis. An allocator that doesn't have to run fast is easy to write, so this strategy is feasible when the situation is dire. There are also excellent commercial products that check memory management and catch errors and leaks; writing your own malloc and free can give you some of their benefits if you don't have access to them.

When a program works for one person but fails for another, something must depend on the external environment of the program. This might include files read by the program, file permissions, environment variables, search path for commands, defaults, or startup files. It's hard to be a consultant for these situations, since you have to become the other person to duplicate the environment of the broken program.

Exercise 5-1. Write a version of malloc and free that can be used for debugging storage-management problems. One approach is to check the entire workspace on each call of malloc and free; another is to write logging information that can be processed by another program. Either way, add markers to the beginning and end of each allocated block to detect overruns at either end. □

5.6 Debugging Tools

Debuggers aren't the only tools that help find bugs. A variety of programs can help us wade through voluminous output to select important bits, find anomalies, or rearrange data to make it easier to see what's going on. Many of these programs are part of the standard toolkit; some are written to help find a particular bug or to analyze a specific program.

In this section we will describe a simple program called `strings` that is especially useful for looking at files that are mostly non-printing characters, such as executables or the mysterious binary formats favored by some word processors. There is often valuable information hidden within, like the text of a document, or error messages and undocumented options, or the names of files and directories, or the names of functions a program might call.

We also find `strings` helpful for locating text in other binary files. Image files often contain ASCII strings that identify the program that created them, and compressed files and archives (such as zip files) may contain file names; `strings` will find these too.

Unix systems provide an implementation of `strings` already, although it's a little different from this one. It recognizes when its input is a program and examines only the text and data segments, ignoring the symbol table. Its -a option forces it to read the whole file.

In effect, `strings` extracts the ASCII text from a binary file so the text can be read or processed by other programs. If an error message carries no identification, it may not be evident what program produced it, let alone why. In that case, searching through likely directories with a command like

```
% strings *.exe *.dll | grep 'mystery message'
```

might locate the producer.

The `strings` function reads a file and prints all runs of at least MINLEN = 6 printable characters.

```
/* strings: extract printable strings from stream */
void strings(char *name, FILE *fin)
{
    int c, i;
    char buf[BUFSIZ];

    do {    /* once for each string */
        for (i = 0; (c = getc(fin)) != EOF; ) {
            if (!isprint(c))
                break;
            buf[i++] = c;
            if (i >= BUFSIZ)
                break;
        }
        if (i >= MINLEN) /* print if long enough */
            printf("%s:%.*s\n", name, i, buf);
    } while (c != EOF);
}
```

The `printf` format string `%.*s` takes the string length from the next argument (`i`), since the string (`buf`) is not null-terminated.

The do-while loop finds and then prints each string, terminating at EOF. Checking for end of file at the bottom allows the `getc` and string loops to share a termination condition and lets a single `printf` handle end of string, end of file, and string too long.

A standard-issue outer loop with a test at the top, or a single `getc` loop with a more complex body, would require duplicating the `printf`. This function started life that way, but it had a bug in the `printf` statement. We fixed that in one place but forgot to fix two others. ("Did I make the same mistake somewhere else?") At that point, it became clear that the program needed to be rewritten so there was less duplicated code; that led to the do-while.

The main routine of `strings` calls the `strings` function for each of its argument files:

```
/* strings main: find printable strings in files */
int main(int argc, char *argv[])
{
    int i;
    FILE *fin;

    setprogname("strings");
    if (argc == 1)
        eprintf("usage: strings filenames");
    else {
        for (i = 1; i < argc; i++) {
            if ((fin = fopen(argv[i], "rb")) == NULL)
                weprintf("can't open %s:", argv[i]);
            else {
                strings(argv[i], fin);
                fclose(fin);
            }
        }
    }
    return 0;
}
```

You might be surprised that `strings` doesn't read its standard input if no files are named. Originally it did. To explain why it doesn't now, we need to tell a debugging story.

The obvious test case for `strings` is to run the program on itself. This worked fine on Unix, but under Windows 95 the command

```
C:\> strings <strings.exe
```

produced exactly five lines of output:

```
!This program cannot be run in DOS mode.
'.rdata
@.data
.idata
.reloc
```

The first line looks like an error message and we wasted some time before realizing it's actually a string in the program, and the output is correct, at least as far as it goes. It's not unknown to have a debugging session derailed by misunderstanding the source of a message.

But there should be more output. Where is it? Late one night, the light finally dawned. ("I've seen that before!") This is a portability problem that is described in more detail in Chapter 8. We had originally written the program to read only from its standard input using getchar. On Windows, however, getchar returns EOF when it encounters a particular byte (0x1A or control-Z) in text mode input and this was causing the early termination.

This is absolutely legal behavior, but not what we were expecting given our Unix background. The solution is to open the file in binary mode using the mode "rb". But stdin is already open and there is no standard way to change its mode. (Functions like fdopen or setmode could be used but they are not part of the C standard.) Ultimately we face a set of unpalatable alternatives: force the user to provide a file name so it works properly on Windows but is unconventional on Unix; silently produce wrong answers if a Windows user attempts to read from standard input; or use conditional compilation to make the behavior adapt to different systems, at the price of reduced portability. We chose the first option so the same program works the same way everywhere.

Exercise 5-2. The strings program prints strings with MINLEN or more characters, which sometimes produces more output than is useful. Provide strings with an optional argument to define the minimum string length. □

Exercise 5-3. Write vis, which copies input to output, except that it displays non-printable bytes like backspaces, control characters, and non-ASCII characters as \Xhh where hh is the hexadecimal representation of the non-printable byte. By contrast with strings, vis is most useful for examining inputs that contain only a few non-printing characters. □

Exercise 5-4. What does vis produce if the *input* is \X0A? How could you make the output of vis unambiguous? □

Exercise 5-5. Extend vis to process a sequence of files, fold long lines at any desired column, and remove non-printable characters entirely. What other features might be consistent with the role of the program? □

5.7 Other People's Bugs

Realistically, most programmers do not have the fun of developing a brand new system from the ground up. Instead, they spend much of their time using, maintaining, modifying and thus, inevitably, debugging code written by other people.

When debugging others' code, everything that we have said about how to debug your own code applies. Before starting, though, you must first acquire some understanding of how the program is organized and how the original programmers thought and wrote. The term used in one very large software project is "discovery," which is not a bad metaphor. The task is discovering what on earth is going on in something that you didn't write.

This is a place where tools can help significantly. Text-search programs like `grep` can find all the occurrences of names. Cross-referencers give some idea of the program's structure. A display of the graph of function calls is valuable if it isn't too big. Stepping through a program a function call at a time with a debugger can reveal the sequence of events. A revision history of the program may give some clues by showing what has been done to the program over time. Frequent changes are often a sign of code that is poorly understood or subject to changing requirements, and thus potentially buggy.

Sometimes you need to track down errors in software you are not responsible for and do not have the source code for. In that case, the task is to identify and characterize the bug sufficiently well that you can report it accurately, and at the same time perhaps find a "work-around" that avoids the problem.

If you think that you have found a bug in someone else's program, the first step is to make absolutely sure it is a genuine bug, so you don't waste the author's time and lose your own credibility.

When you find a compiler bug, make sure that the error is really in the compiler and not in your own code. For example, whether a right shift operation fills with zero bits (logical shift) or propagates the sign bit (arithmetic shift) is unspecified in C and C++, so novices sometimes think it's an error if a construct like

```
?     i = -1;
?     printf("%d\n", i >> 1);
```

yields an unexpected answer. But this is a portability issue, because this statement can legitimately behave differently on different systems. Try your test on multiple systems and be sure you understand what happens; check the language definition to be sure.

Make sure the bug is new. Do you have the latest version of the program? Is there a list of bug fixes? Most software goes through multiple releases; if you find a bug in version 4.0b1, it might well be fixed or replaced by a new one in version 4.04b2. In any case, few programmers have much enthusiasm for fixing bugs in anything but the current version of a program.

Finally, put yourself in the shoes of the person who receives your report. You want to provide the owner with as good a test case as you can manage. It's not very helpful if the bug can be demonstrated only with large inputs, or an elaborate environment, or multiple supporting files. Strip the test down to a minimal and self-contained case. Include other information that could possibly be relevant, like the version of the program itself, and of the compiler, operating system, and hardware. For the buggy version of isprint mentioned in Section 5.4, we could provide this as a test program:

```
/* test program for isprint bug */
int main(void)
{
    int c;

    while (isprint(c = getchar()) || c != EOF)
        printf("%c", c);
    return 0;
}
```

Any line of printable text will serve as a test case, since the output will contain only half the input:

```
% echo 1234567890 | isprint_test
24680
%
```

The best bug reports are the ones that need only a line or two of input on a plain vanilla system to demonstrate the fault, and that include a fix. Send the kind of bug report you'd like to receive yourself.

5.8 Summary

With the right attitude debugging can be fun, like solving a puzzle, but whether we enjoy it or not, debugging is an art that we will practice regularly. Still, it would be nice if bugs didn't happen, so we try to avoid them by writing code well in the first place. Well-written code has fewer bugs to begin with and those that remain are easier to find.

Once a bug has been seen, the first thing to do is to think hard about the clues it presents. How could it have come about? Is it something familiar? Was something just changed in the program? Is there something special about the input data that provoked it? A few well-chosen test cases and a few print statements in the code may be enough.

If there aren't good clues, hard thinking is still the best first step, to be followed by systematic attempts to narrow down the location of the problem. One step is cutting down the input data to make a small input that fails; another is cutting out code to eliminate regions that can't be related. It's possible to insert checking code that gets turned on only after the program has executed some number of steps, again to try to localize the problem. All of these are instances of a general strategy, divide and conquer, which is as effective in debugging as it is in politics and war.

Use other aids as well. Explaining your code to someone else (even a teddy bear) is wonderfully effective. Use a debugger to get a stack trace. Use some of the commercial tools that check for memory leaks, array bounds violations, suspect code, and the like. Step through your program when it has become clear that you have the wrong mental picture of how the code works.

Know yourself, and the kinds of errors you make. Once you have found and fixed a bug, make sure that you eliminate other bugs that might be similar. Think about what happened so you can avoid making that kind of mistake again.

Supplementary Reading

Steve Maguire's *Writing Solid Code* (Microsoft Press, 1993) and Steve McConnell's *Code Complete* (Microsoft Press, 1993) both have much good advice on debugging.

6

Testing

In ordinary computational practice by hand or by desk machines, it is the custom to check every step of the computation and, when an error is found, to localize it by a backward process starting from the first point where the error is noted.

Norbert Wiener, *Cybernetics*

Testing and debugging are often spoken as a single phrase but they are not the same thing. To over-simplify, debugging is what you do when you know that a program is broken. Testing is a determined, systematic attempt to break a program that you think is working.

Edsger Dijkstra made the famous observation that testing can demonstrate the presence of bugs, but not their absence. His hope is that programs can be made correct by construction, so that there are no errors and thus no need for testing. Though this is a fine goal, it is not yet realistic for substantial programs. So in this chapter we'll focus on how to test to find errors rapidly, efficiently, and effectively.

Thinking about potential problems as you code is a good start. Systematic testing, from easy tests to elaborate ones, helps ensure that programs begin life working correctly and remain correct as they grow. Automation helps to eliminate manual processes and encourages extensive testing. And there are plenty of tricks of the trade that programmers have learned from experience.

One way to write bug-free code is to generate it by a program. If some programming task is understood so well that writing the code seems mechanical, then it should be mechanized. A common case occurs when a program can be generated from a specification in some specialized language. For example, we compile high-level languages into assembly code; we use regular expressions to specify patterns of text; we use notations like SUM(A1:A50) to represent operations over a range of cells in a spreadsheet. In such cases, if the generator or translator is correct and if the specification is correct, the resulting program will be correct too. We will cover this rich topic

139

in more detail in Chapter 9; in this chapter we will talk briefly about ways to create tests from compact specifications.

6.1 Test as You Write the Code

The earlier a problem is found, the better. If you think systematically about what you are writing as you write it, you can verify simple properties of the program as it is being constructed, with the result that your code will have gone through one round of testing before it is even compiled. Certain kinds of bugs never come to life.

Test code at its boundaries. One technique is *boundary condition testing*: as each small piece of code is written—a loop or a conditional statement, for example—check right then that the condition branches the right way or that the loop goes through the proper number of times. This process is called boundary condition testing because you are probing at the natural boundaries within the program and data, such as non-existent or empty input, a single input item, an exactly full array, and so on. The idea is that most bugs occur at boundaries. If a piece of code is going to fail, it will likely fail at a boundary. Conversely, if it works at its boundaries, it's likely to work elsewhere too.

This fragment, modeled on fgets, reads characters until it finds a newline or fills a buffer:

```
?       int i;
?       char s[MAX];
?
?       for (i = 0; (s[i] = getchar()) != '\n' && i < MAX-1; ++i)
?           ;
?       s[--i] = '\0';
```

Imagine that you have just written this loop. Now simulate it mentally as it reads a line. The first boundary to test is the simplest: an empty line. If you start with a line that contains only a single newline, it's easy to see that the loop stops on the first iteration with i set to zero, so the last line decrements i to -1 and thus writes a null byte into s[-1], which is before the beginning of the array. Boundary condition testing finds the error.

If we rewrite the loop to use the conventional idiom for filling an array with input characters, it looks like this:

```
?       for (i = 0; i < MAX-1; i++)
?           if ((s[i] = getchar()) == '\n')
?               break;
?       s[i] = '\0';
```

Repeating the original boundary test, it's easy to verify that a line with just a newline is handled correctly: i is zero, the first input character breaks out of the loop, and

'\0' is stored in s[0]. Similar checking for inputs of one and two characters followed by a newline give us confidence that the loop works near that boundary.

There are other boundary conditions to check, though. If the input contains a long line or no newlines, that is protected by the check that i stays less than MAX-1. But what if the input is empty, so the first call to getchar returns EOF? We must check for that:

```
?    for (i = 0; i < MAX-1; i++)
?        if ((s[i] = getchar()) == '\n' || s[i] == EOF)
?            break;
?    s[i] = '\0';
```

Boundary condition testing can catch lots of bugs, but not all of them. We will return to this example in Chapter 8, where we will show that it still has a portability bug.

The next step is to check input at the other boundary, where the array is nearly full, exactly full, and over-full, particularly if the newline arrives at the same time. We won't write out the details here, but it's a good exercise. Thinking about the boundaries raises the question of what to do when the buffer fills before a '\n' occurs; this gap in the specification should be resolved early, and testing boundaries helps to identify it.

Boundary condition checking is effective for finding off-by-one errors. With practice, it becomes second nature, and many trivial bugs are eliminated before they ever happen.

Test pre- and post-conditions. Another way to head off problems is to verify that expected or necessary properties hold before (pre-condition) and after (post-condition) some piece of code executes. Making sure that input values are within range is a common example of testing a pre-condition. This function for computing the average of n elements in an array has a problem if n is less than or equal to zero:

```
?    double avg(double a[], int n)
?    {
?        int i;
?        double sum;
?
?        sum = 0.0;
?        for (i = 0; i < n; i++)
?            sum += a[i];
?        return sum / n;
?    }
```

What should avg do if n is zero? An array with no elements is a meaningful concept although its average value is not. Should avg let the system catch the division by zero? Abort? Complain? Quietly return some innocuous value? What if n is negative, which is nonsensical but not impossible? As suggested in Chapter 4, our preference would probably be to return 0 as the average if n is less than or equal to zero:

```
    return n <= 0 ? 0.0 : sum/n;
```

but there's no single right answer.

The one guaranteed wrong answer is to ignore the problem. An article in the November, 1998 *Scientific American* describes an incident aboard the USS *Yorktown*, a guided-missile cruiser. A crew member mistakenly entered a zero for a data value, which resulted in a division by zero, an error that cascaded and eventually shut down the ship's propulsion system. The *Yorktown* was dead in the water for a couple of hours because a program didn't check for valid input.

Use assertions. C and C++ provide an assertion facility in `<assert.h>` that encourages adding pre- and post-condition tests. Since a failed assertion aborts the program, these are usually reserved for situations where a failure is really unexpected and there's no way to recover. We might augment the code above with an assertion before the loop:

```
assert(n > 0);
```

If the assertion is violated, it will cause the program to abort with a standard message:

```
Assertion failed: n > 0, file avgtest.c, line 7
Abort(crash)
```

Assertions are particularly helpful for validating properties of interfaces because they draw attention to inconsistencies between caller and callee and may even indicate who's at fault. If the assertion that n is greater than zero fails when the function is called, it points the finger at the caller rather than at avg itself as the source of trouble. If an interface changes but we forget to fix some routine that depends on it, an assertion may catch the mistake before it causes real trouble.

Program defensively. A useful technique is to add code to handle "can't happen" cases, situations where it is not logically possible for something to happen but (because of some failure elsewhere) it might anyway. Adding a test for zero or negative array lengths to avg was one example. As another example, a program processing grades might expect that there would be no negative or huge values but should check anyway:

```
if (grade < 0 || grade > 100)   /* can't happen */
    letter = '?';
else if (grade >= 90)
    letter = 'A';
else
    ...
```

This is an example of *defensive programming*: making sure that a program protects itself against incorrect use or illegal data. Null pointers, out of range subscripts, division by zero, and other errors can be detected early and warned about or deflected. Defensive programming (no pun intended) might well have caught the zero-divide problem on the *Yorktown*.

Check error returns. One often-overlooked defense is to check the error returns from library functions and system calls. Return values from input routines such as `fread` and `fscanf` should always be checked for errors, as should any file open call such as `fopen`. If a read or open fails, computation cannot proceed correctly.

Checking the return code from output functions like `fprintf` or `fwrite` will catch the error that results from trying to write a file when there is no space left on the disk. It may be sufficient to check the return value from `fclose`, which returns EOF if any error occurred during any operation, and zero otherwise.

```
fp = fopen(outfile, "w");
while (...)                    /* write output to outfile */
    fprintf(fp, ...);
if (fclose(fp) == EOF) {     /* any errors? */
    /* some output error occurred */
}
```

Output errors can be serious. If the file being written is the new version of a precious file, this check will save you from removing the old file if the new one was not written successfully.

The effort of testing as you go is minimal and pays off handsomely. Thinking about testing as you write a program will lead to better code, because that's when you know best what the code should do. If instead you wait until something breaks, you will probably have forgotten how the code works. Working under pressure, you will need to figure it out again, which takes time, and the fixes will be less thorough and more fragile because your refreshed understanding is likely to be incomplete.

Exercise 6-1. Check out these examples at their boundaries, then fix them as necessary according to the principles of style in Chapter 1 and the advice in this chapter.

(a) This is supposed to compute factorials:

```
?     int factorial(int n)
?     {
?         int fac;
?         fac = 1;
?         while (n--)
?             fac *= n;
?         return fac;
?     }
```

(b) This is supposed to print the characters of a string one per line:

```
?     i = 0;
?     do {
?         putchar(s[i++]);
?         putchar('\n');
?     } while (s[i] != '\0');
```

(c) This is meant to copy a string from source to destination:

```
?       void strcpy(char *dest, char *src)
?       {
?           int i;
?
?           for (i = 0; src[i] != '\0'; i++)
?               dest[i] = src[i];
?       }
```

(d) Another string copy, which attempts to copy n characters from s to t:

```
?       void strncpy(char *t, char *s, int n)
?       {
?           while (n > 0 && *s != '\0') {
?               *t = *s;
?               t++;
?               s++;
?               n--;
?           }
?       }
```

(e) A numerical comparison:

```
?       if (i > j)
?           printf("%d is greater than %d.\n", i, j);
?       else
?           printf("%d is smaller than %d.\n", i, j);
```

(f) A character class test:

```
?       if (c >= 'A' && c <= 'Z') {
?           if (c <= 'L')
?               cout << "first half of alphabet";
?           else
?               cout << "second half of alphabet";
?       }
```

□

Exercise 6-2. As we are writing this book in late 1998, the Year 2000 problem looms as perhaps the biggest boundary condition problem ever.
(a) What dates would you use to check whether a system is likely to work in the year 2000? Supposing that tests are expensive to perform, in what order would you do your tests after trying January 1, 2000 itself?
(b) How would you test the standard function ctime, which returns a string representation of the date in this form:

```
Fri Dec 31 23:58:27 EST 1999\n\0
```

Suppose your program calls ctime. How would you write your code to defend against a flawed implementation?

(c) Describe how you would test a calendar program that prints output like this:

```
    January 2000
 S  M Tu  W Th  F  S
                    1
 2  3  4  5  6  7  8
 9 10 11 12 13 14 15
16 17 18 19 20 21 22
23 24 25 26 27 28 29
30 31
```

(d) What other time boundaries can you think of in systems that you use, and how would you test to see whether they are handled correctly? □

6.2 Systematic Testing

It's important to test a program systematically so you know at each step what you are testing and what results you expect. You need to be orderly so you don't overlook anything, and you must keep records so you know how much you have done.

Test incrementally. Testing should go hand in hand with program construction. A "big bang" where one writes the whole program, then tests it all at once, is much harder and more time-consuming than an incremental approach. Write part of a program, test it, add some more code, test that, and so on. If you have two packages that have been written and tested independently, test that they work together when you finally connect them.

For instance, when we were testing the CSV programs in Chapter 4, the first step was to write just enough code to read the input; this let us validate input processing. The next step was to split input lines at commas. Once these parts were working, we moved on to fields with quotes, and then gradually worked up to testing everything.

Test simple parts first. The incremental approach also applies to how you test features. Tests should focus first on the simplest and most commonly executed features of a program; only when those are working properly should you move on. This way, at each stage, you expose more to testing and build confidence that basic mechanisms are working correctly. Easy tests find the easy bugs. Each test does the minimum to ferret out the next potential problem. Although each bug is harder to trigger than its predecessor, it is not necessarily harder to fix.

In this section, we'll talk about ways to choose effective tests and in what order to apply them; in the next two sections, we'll talk about how to mechanize the process so that it can be carried out efficiently. The first step, at least for small programs or individual functions, is an extension of the boundary condition testing that we described in the previous section: systematic testing of small cases.

Suppose we have a function that performs binary search in an array of integers. We would begin with these tests, arranged in order of increasing complexity:

- search an array with no elements
- search an array with one element and a trial value that is
    - less than the single element in the array
    - equal to the single element
    - greater than the single element
- search an array with two elements and trial values that
    - check all five possible positions
- check behavior with duplicate elements in the array and trial values
    - less than the value in the array
    - equal to the value
    - greater than the value
- search an array with three elements as with two elements
- search an array with four elements as with two and three

If the function gets past this unscathed, it's likely to be in good shape, but it could still be tested further.

This set of tests is small enough to perform by hand, but it is better to create a *test scaffold* to mechanize the process. The following driver program is about as simple as we can manage. It reads input lines that contain a key to search for and an array size; it creates an array of that size containing values 1, 3, 5, ...; and it searches the array for the key.

```c
/* bintest main: scaffold for testing binsearch */
int main(void)
{
    int i, key, nelem, arr[1000];

    while (scanf("%d %d", &key, &nelem) != EOF) {
        for (i = 0; i < nelem; i++)
            arr[i] = 2*i + 1;
        printf("%d\n", binsearch(key, arr, nelem));
    }
    return 0;
}
```

This is simpleminded but it shows that a useful test scaffold need not be big, and it is easily extended to perform more of these tests and require less manual intervention.

Know what output to expect. For all tests, it's necessary to know what the right answer is; if you don't, you're wasting your time. This might seem obvious, since for many programs it's easy to tell whether the program is working. For example, either a copy of a file is a copy or it isn't. The output from a sort is sorted or it isn't; it must also be a permutation of the original input.

Most programs are more difficult to characterize—compilers (does the output properly translate the input?), numerical algorithms (is the answer within error tolerance?), graphics (are the pixels in the right places?), and so on. For these, it's especially important to validate the output by comparing it with known values.

- To test a compiler, compile and run the test files. The test programs should in turn generate output, and their results should be compared to known ones.
- To test a numerical program, generate test cases that explore the edges of the algorithm, trivial cases as well as hard ones. Where possible, write code that verifies that output properties are sane. For example, the output of a numerical integrator can be tested for continuity, and for agreement with closed-form solutions.
- To test a graphics program, it's not enough to see if it can draw a box; instead read the box back from the screen and check that its edges are exactly where they should be.

If the program has an inverse, check that its application recovers the input. Encryption and decryption are inverses, so if you encrypt something and can't decrypt it, something is wrong. Similarly, lossless compression and expansion algorithms should be inverses. Programs that bundle files together should extract them unchanged. Sometimes there are multiple methods for inversion; check all combinations.

Verify conservation properties. Many programs preserve some property of their inputs. Tools like wc (count lines, words, and characters) and sum (compute a checksum) can verify that outputs are of the same size, have the same number of words, contain the same bytes in some order, and the like. Other programs compare files for identity (cmp) or report differences (diff). These programs or similar ones are readily available for most environments, and are well worth acquiring.

A byte-frequency program can be used to check for conservation of data and also to spot anomalies like non-text characters in supposedly text-only files; here's a version that we call freq:

```c
#include <stdio.h>
#include <ctype.h>
#include <limits.h>

unsigned long count[UCHAR_MAX+1];

/* freq main: display byte frequency counts */
int main(void)
{
    int c;
    while ((c = getchar()) != EOF)
        count[c]++;

    for (c = 0; c <= UCHAR_MAX; c++)
        if (count[c] != 0)
            printf("%.2x  %c  %lu\n",
                c, isprint(c) ? c : '-', count[c]);
    return 0;
}
```

Conservation properties can be verified within a program, too. A function that counts the elements in a data structure provides a trivial consistency check. A hash table should have the property that every element inserted into it can be retrieved. This condition is easy to check with a function that dumps the contents of the table into a file or an array. At any time, the number of insertions into a data structure minus the number of deletions must equal the number of elements contained, a condition that is easy to verify.

Compare independent implementations. Independent implementations of a library or program should produce the same answers. For example, two compilers should produce programs that behave the same way on the same machine, at least in most situations.

Sometimes an answer can be computed in two different ways, or you might be able to write a trivial version of a program to use as a slow but independent comparison. If two unrelated programs get the same answers, there is a good chance that they are correct; if they get different answers, at least one is wrong.

One of the authors once worked with another person on a compiler for a new machine. The work of debugging the code generated by the compiler was split: one person wrote the software that encoded instructions for the target machine, and the other wrote the disassembler for the debugger. This meant that any error of interpretation or implementation of the instruction set was unlikely to be duplicated between the two components. When the compiler miscoded an instruction, the disassembler was sure to notice. All the early output of the compiler was run through the disassembler and verified against the compiler's own debugging printouts. This strategy worked very well in practice, instantly catching mistakes in both pieces. The only difficult, protracted debugging occurred when both people interpreted an ambiguous phrase in the architecture description in the same incorrect way.

Measure test coverage. One goal of testing is to make sure that every statement of a program has been executed sometime during the sequence of tests; testing cannot be considered complete unless every line of the program has been exercised by at least one test. Complete coverage is often quite difficult to achieve. Even leaving aside "can't happen" statements, it is hard to use normal inputs to force a program to go through particular statements.

There are commercial tools for measuring coverage. Profilers, often included as part of compiler suites, provide a way to compute a statement frequency count for each program statement that indicates the coverage achieved by specific tests.

We tested the Markov program of Chapter 3 with a combination of these techniques. The last section of this chapter describes those tests in detail.

Exercise 6-3. Describe how you would test `freq`. □

Exercise 6-4. Design and implement a version of `freq` that measures the frequencies of other types of data values, such as 32-bit integers or floating-point numbers. Can you make one version of the program handle a variety of types elegantly? □

6.3 Test Automation

It's tedious and unreliable to do much testing by hand; proper testing involves lots of tests, lots of inputs, and lots of comparisons of outputs. Testing should therefore be done by programs, which don't get tired or careless. It's worth taking the time to write a script or trivial program that encapsulates all the tests, so a complete test suite can be run by (literally or figuratively) pushing a single button. The easier a test suite is to run, the more often you'll run it and the less likely you'll skip it when time is short. We wrote a test suite that verifies all the programs we wrote for this book, and ran it every time we made changes; parts of the suite ran automatically after each successful compilation.

Automate regression testing. The most basic form of automation is *regression testing*, which performs a sequence of tests that compare the new version of something with the previous version. When fixing problems, there's a natural tendency to check only that the fix works; it's easy to overlook the possibility that the fix broke something else. The intent of regression testing is to make sure that the behavior hasn't changed except in expected ways.

Some systems are rich in tools that help with such automation; scripting languages allow us to write short scripts to run test sequences. On Unix, file comparators like diff and cmp compare outputs; sort brings common elements together; grep filters test outputs; wc, sum, and freq summarize outputs. Together, these make it easy to create *ad hoc* test scaffolds, maybe not enough for large programs but entirely adequate for a program maintained by an individual or a small group.

Here is a script for regression testing a killer application program called ka. It runs the old version (old_ka) and the new version (new_ka) for a large number of different test data files, and complains about each one for which the outputs are not identical. It is written for a Unix shell but could easily be transcribed to Perl or other scripting language:

```
for i in ka_data.*           # loop over test data files
do
    old_ka $i >out1          # run the old version
    new_ka $i >out2          # run the new version
    if ! cmp -s out1 out2    # compare output files
    then
        echo $i: BAD         # different: print error message
    fi
done
```

A test script should usually run silently, producing output only if something unexpected occurs, as this one does. We could instead choose to print each file name as it is being tested, and to follow it with an error message if something goes wrong. Such indications of progress help to identify problems like an infinite loop or a test script that is failing to run the right tests, but the extra chatter is annoying if the tests are running properly.

The -s argument causes cmp to report status but produce no output. If the files compare equal, cmp returns a true status, ! cmp is false, and nothing is printed. If the old and new outputs differ, however, cmp returns false and the file name and a warning are printed.

There is an implicit assumption in regression testing that the previous version of the program computes the right answer. This must be carefully checked at the beginning of time, and the invariant scrupulously maintained. If an erroneous answer ever sneaks into a regression test, it's very hard to detect and everything that depends on it will be wrong thereafter. It's good practice to check the regression test itself periodically to make sure it is still valid.

Create self-contained tests. Self-contained tests that carry their own inputs and expected outputs provide a complement to regression tests. Our experience testing Awk may be instructive. Many language constructions are tested by running specified inputs through tiny programs and checking that the right output is produced. The following part of a large collection of miscellaneous tests verifies one tricky increment expression. This test runs the new version of Awk (newawk) on a short Awk program to produce output in one file, writes the correct output to another file with echo, compares the files, and reports an error if they differ.

```
# field increment test: $i++ means ($i)++, not $(i++)

echo 3 5 | newawk '{i = 1; print $i++; print $1, i}' >out1

echo '3
4 1' >out2  # correct answer

if ! cmp -s out1 out2   # outputs are different
then
     echo 'BAD: field increment test failed'
fi
```

The first comment is part of the test input; it documents what the test is testing.

Sometimes it is possible to construct a large number of tests with modest effort. For simple expressions, we created a small, specialized language for describing tests, input data, and expected outputs. Here is a short sequence that tests some of the ways that the numeric value 1 can be represented in Awk:

```
try {if ($1 == 1) print "yes"; else print "no"}
1        yes
1.0      yes
1E0      yes
0.1E1    yes
10E-1    yes
01       yes
+1       yes
10E-2    no
10       no
```

The first line is a program to be tested (everything after the word `try`). Each subsequent line is a set of inputs and the expected output, separated by tabs. The first test says that if the first input field is 1 the output should be `yes`. The first seven tests should all print `yes` and the last two tests should print `no`.

An Awk program (what else?) converts each test into a complete Awk program, then runs each input through it, and compares actual output to expected output; it reports only those cases where the answer is wrong.

Similar mechanisms are used to test the regular expression matching and substitution commands. A little language for writing tests makes it easy to create a lot of them; using a program to write a program to test a program has high leverage. (Chapter 9 has more to say about little languages and the use of programs that write programs.)

Overall, there are about a thousand tests for Awk; the whole set can be run with a single command, and if everything goes well, no output is produced. Whenever a feature is added or a bug is fixed, new tests are added to verify correct operation. Whenever the program is changed, even in a trivial way, the whole test suite is run; it takes only a few minutes. It sometimes catches completely unexpected errors, and has saved the authors of Awk from public embarrassment many times.

What should you do when you discover an error? If it was not found by an existing test, create a new test that does uncover the problem and verify the test by running it with the broken version of the code. The error may suggest further tests or a whole new class of things to check. Or perhaps it is possible to add defenses to the program that would catch the error internally.

Never throw away a test. It can help you decide whether a bug report is valid or describes something already fixed. Keep a record of bugs, changes, and fixes; it will help you identify old problems and fix new ones. In most commercial programming shops, such records are mandatory. For your personal programming, they are a small investment that will pay off repeatedly.

Exercise 6-5. Design a test suite for `printf`, using as many mechanical aids as possible. □

6.4 Test Scaffolds

Our discussion so far is based largely on testing a single stand-alone program in its completed form. This is not the only kind of test automation, however, nor is it the most likely way to test parts of a big program during construction, especially if you are part of a team. Nor is it the most effective way to test small components that are buried in something larger.

To test a component in isolation, it's usually necessary to create some kind of framework or *scaffold* that provides enough support and interface to the rest of the system that the part under test will run. We showed a tiny example for testing binary search earlier in this chapter.

It's easy to build scaffolds for testing mathematical functions, string functions, sort routines, and so on, since the scaffolding is likely to consist mostly of setting up input parameters, calling the functions to be tested, then checking the results. It's a bigger job to create scaffolding for testing a partly-completed program.

To illustrate, we'll walk through building a test for memset, one of the mem... functions in the C/C++ standard library. These functions are often written in assembly language for a specific machine, since their performance is important. The more carefully tuned they are, however, the more likely they are to be wrong and thus the more thoroughly they should be tested.

The first step is to provide the simplest possible C versions that are known to work; these provide a benchmark for performance and, more important, for correctness. To move to a new environment, one carries the simple versions and uses them until the tuned ones are working.

The function memset(s,c,n) sets n bytes of memory to the byte c, starting at address s, and returns s. This function is easy if speed is not an issue:

```
/* memset: set first n bytes of s to c */
void *memset(void *s, int c, size_t n)
{
    size_t i;
    char *p;

    p = (char *) s;
    for (i = 0; i < n; i++)
        p[i] = c;
    return s;
}
```

But when speed is an issue, tricks like writing full words of 32 or 64 bits at a time are used. These can lead to bugs, so extensive testing is mandatory.

Testing is based on a combination of exhaustive and boundary-condition checks at likely points of failure. For memset, the boundaries include obvious values of n such as zero, one and two, but also values that are powers of two or nearby values, including both small ones and large ones like 2^{16}, which corresponds to a natural boundary in many machines, a 16-bit word. Powers of two deserve attention because one way to make memset faster is to set multiple bytes at one time; this might be done by special instructions or by trying to store a word at a time instead of a byte. Similarly, we want to check array origins with a variety of alignments in case there is some error based on starting address or length. We will place the target array inside a larger array, thus creating a buffer zone or safety margin on each side and giving us an easy way to vary the alignment.

We also want to check a variety of values for c, including zero, 0x7F (the largest signed value, assuming 8-bit bytes), 0x80 and 0xFF (probing at potential errors involving signed and unsigned characters), and some values much bigger than one byte (to be sure that only one byte is used). We should also initialize memory to some known pattern that is different from any of these character values so we can check whether memset wrote outside the valid area.

We can use the simple implementation as a standard of comparison in a test that allocates two arrays, then compares behaviors on combinations of n, c and offset within the array:

```
big = maximum left margin + maximum n + maximum right margin
s0 = malloc(big)
s1 = malloc(big)
for each combination of test parameters n, c, and offset:
    set all of s0 and s1 to known pattern
    run slow memset(s0 + offset, c, n)
    run fast memset(s1 + offset, c, n)
    check return values
    compare all of s0 and s1 byte by byte
```

An error that causes memset to write outside the limits of its array is most likely to affect bytes near the beginning or the end of the array, so leaving a buffer zone makes it easier to see damaged bytes and makes it less likely that an error will overwrite some other part of the program. To check for writing out of bounds, we compare *all* the bytes of s0 and s1, not just the n bytes that should be written.

Thus a reasonable set of tests might include all combinations of:

```
offset = 10, 11, ..., 20
c = 0, 1, 0x7F, 0x80, 0xFF, 0x11223344
n = 0, 1, 2, 3, 4, 5, 7, 8, 9, 15, 16, 17,
    31, 32, 33, ..., 65535, 65536, 65537
```

The values of n would include at least $2^i - 1$, 2^i and $2^i + 1$ for i from 0 to 16.

These values should not be wired into the main part of the test scaffold, but should appear in arrays that might be created by hand or by program. Generating them automatically is better; that makes it easy to specify more powers of two or to include more offsets and more characters.

These tests will give memset a thorough workout yet cost very little time even to create, let alone run, since there are fewer than 3500 cases for the values above. The tests are completely portable, so they can be carried to a new environment as necessary.

As a warning, consider this story. We once gave a copy of a memset tester to someone developing an operating system and libraries for a new processor. Months later, we (the authors of the original test) started using the machine and had a large application fail its test suite. We traced the problem to a subtle bug involving sign extension in the assembly language implementation of memset. For reasons unknown, the library implementer had changed the memset tester so it did not check values of c above 0x7F. Of course, the bug was isolated by running the original, working tester, once we realized that memset was a suspect.

Functions like `memset` are susceptible to exhaustive tests because they are simple enough that one can prove that the test cases exercise all possible execution paths through the code, thus giving complete coverage. For example, it is possible to test `memmove` for all combinations of overlap, direction, and alignment. This is not exhaustive in the sense of testing all possible copy operations, but it is an exhaustive test of representatives of each kind of distinct input situation.

As in any testing method, test scaffolds need the correct answer to verify the operations they are testing. An important technique, which we used in testing `memset`, is to compare a simple version that is believed correct against a new version that may be incorrect. This can be done in stages, as the following example shows.

One of the authors implemented a raster graphics library involving an operator that copied blocks of pixels from one image to another. Depending on the parameters, the operation could be a simple memory copy, or it could require converting pixel values from one color space to another, or it could require ''tiling'' where the input was copied repeatedly throughout a rectangular area, or combinations of these and other features. The specification of the operator was simple, but an efficient implementation would require lots of special code for the many cases. To make sure all that code was right demanded a sound testing strategy.

First, simple code was written by hand to perform the correct operation for a single pixel. This was used to test the library version's handling of a single pixel. Once this stage was working, the library could be trusted for single-pixel operations.

Next, hand-written code used the library a pixel at a time to build a very slow version of the operator that worked on a single horizontal row of pixels, and that was compared with the library's much more efficient handling of a row. With that working, the library could be trusted for horizontal lines.

This sequence continued, using lines to build rectangles, rectangles to build tiles, and so on. Along the way, many bugs were found, including some in the tester itself, but that's part of the effectiveness of the method: we were testing two independent implementations, building confidence in both as we went. If a test failed, the tester printed out a detailed analysis to aid understanding what went wrong, and also to verify that the tester was working properly itself.

As the library was modified and ported over the years, the tester repeatedly proved invaluable for finding bugs.

Because of its layer-by-layer approach, this tester needed to be run from scratch each time, to verify its own trust of the library. Incidentally, the tester was not exhaustive, but probabilistic: it generated random test cases which, for long enough runs, would eventually explore every cranny of the code. With the huge number of possible test cases, this strategy was more effective than trying to construct a thorough test set by hand, and much more efficient than exhaustive testing.

Exercise 6-6. Create the test scaffold for `memset` along the lines that we indicated. □

Exercise 6-7. Create tests for the rest of the `mem...` family. □

Exercise 6-8. Specify a testing regime for numerical routines like `sqrt`, `sin`, and so on, as found in `math.h`. What input values make sense? What independent checks can be performed? □

Exercise 6-9. Define mechanisms for testing the functions of the C `str...` family, like `strcmp`. Some of these functions, especially tokenizers like `strtok` and `strcspn`, are significantly more complicated than the `mem...` family, so more sophisticated tests will be called for. □

6.5 Stress Tests

High volumes of machine-generated input are another effective testing technique. Machine-generated input stresses programs differently than input written by people does. Higher volume in itself tends to break things because very large inputs cause overflow of input buffers, arrays, and counters, and are effective at finding unchecked fixed-size storage within a program. People tend to avoid ''impossible'' cases like empty inputs or input that is out of order or out of range, and are unlikely to create very long names or huge data values. Computers, by contrast, produce output strictly according to their programs and have no idea of what to avoid.

To illustrate, here is a single line of output produced by the Microsoft Visual C++ Version 5.0 compiler while compiling the C++ STL implementation of `markov`; we have edited the line so it fits:

```
xtree(114) : warning C4786: 'std::_Tree<std::deque<std::
basic_string<char,std::char_traits<char>,std::allocator
<char>>,std::allocator<std::basic_string<char,std::
   ... 1420 characters omitted
allocator<char>>>>>::iterator' : identifier was
truncated to '255' characters in the debug information
```

The compiler is warning us that it has generated a variable name that is a remarkable 1594 characters long but that only 255 characters have been preserved as debugging information. Not all programs defend themselves against such unusually long strings.

Random inputs (not necessarily legal) are another way to assault a program in the hope of breaking something. This is a logical extension of ''people don't do that'' reasoning. For example, some commercial C compilers are tested with randomly-generated but syntactically valid programs. The trick is to use the specification of the problem—in this case, the C standard—to drive a program that produces valid but bizarre test data.

Such tests rely on detection by built-in checks and defenses in the program, since it may not be possible to verify that the program is producing the right output; the goal is more to provoke a crash or a ''can't happen'' than to uncover straightforward errors. It's also a good way to test that error-handling code works. With sensible input, most errors don't happen and code to handle them doesn't get exercised; by nature, bugs tend to hide in such corners. At some point, though, this kind of testing reaches diminishing returns: it finds problems that are so unlikely to happen in real life they may not be worth fixing.

Some testing is based on explicitly malicious inputs. Security attacks often use big or illegal inputs that overwrite precious data; it is wise to look for such weak spots. A few standard library functions are vulnerable to this sort of attack. For instance, the standard library function `gets` provides no way to limit the size of an input line, so it should *never* be used; always use `fgets(buf, sizeof(buf), stdin)` instead. A bare `scanf("%s",buf)` doesn't limit the length of an input line either; it should therefore usually be used with an explicit length, such as `scanf("%20s",buf)`. In Section 3.3 we showed how to address this problem for a general buffer size.

Any routine that might receive values from outside the program, directly or indirectly, should validate its input values before using them. The following program from a textbook is supposed to read an integer typed by a user, and warn if the integer is too long. Its goal is to demonstrate how to overcome the `gets` problem, but the solution doesn't always work.

```
?    #define MAXNUM 10
?
?    int main(void)
?    {
?        char num[MAXNUM];
?
?        memset(num, 0, sizeof(num));
?        printf("Type a number: ");
?        gets(num);
?        if (num[MAXNUM-1] != 0)
?            printf("Number too big.\n");
?        /* ... */
?    }
```

If the input number is ten digits long, it will overwrite the last zero in array `num` with a non-zero value, and in theory this will be detected after the return from `gets`. Unfortunately, this is not sufficient. A malicious attacker can provide an even longer input string that overwrites some critical value, perhaps the return address for the call, so the program never returns to the `if` statement but instead executes something nefarious. Thus this kind of unchecked input is a potential security problem.

Lest you think that this is an irrelevant textbook example, in July, 1998 an error of this form was uncovered in several major electronic mail programs. As the *New York Times* reported,

> The security hole is caused by what is known as a "buffer overflow error." Programmers are supposed to include code in their software to check that incoming data are of a safe type and that the units are arriving at the right length. If a unit of data is too long, it can overrun the "buffer"—the chunk of memory set aside to hold it. In that case, the E-mail program will crash, and a hostile programmer can trick the computer into running a malicious program in its place.

This was also one of the attacks in the famous ''Internet Worm'' incident of 1988.

Programs that parse HTML forms can also be vulnerable to attacks that store very long input strings in small arrays:

```
?       static char query[1024];
?
?       char *read_form(void)
?       {
?           int qsize;
?
?           qsize = atoi(getenv("CONTENT_LENGTH"));
?           fread(query, qsize, 1, stdin);
?           return query;
?       }
```

The code assumes that the input will never be more than 1024 bytes long so, like gets, it is open to an attack that overflows its buffer.

More familiar kinds of overflow can cause trouble, too. If integers overflow silently, the result can be disastrous. Consider an allocation like

```
?       char *p;
?       p = (char *) malloc(x * y * z);
```

If the product of x, y, and z overflows, the call to malloc might produce a reasonable-sized array, but p[x] might refer to memory outside the allocated region. Suppose that ints are 16 bits and x, y, and z are each 41. Then x*y*z is 68921, which is 3385 modulo 2^{16}. So the call to malloc allocates only 3385 bytes; any reference with a subscript beyond that value will be out of bounds.

Conversion between types is another source of overflow, and catching the error may not be good enough. The Ariane 5 rocket exploded on its maiden flight in June, 1996 because the navigation package was inherited from the Ariane 4 without proper testing. The new rocket flew faster, resulting in larger values of some variables in the navigation software. Shortly after launch, an attempt to convert a 64-bit floating-point number into a 16-bit signed integer generated an overflow. The error was caught, but the code that caught it elected to shut down the subsystem. The rocket veered off course and exploded. It was unfortunate that the code that failed generated inertial reference information useful only before lift-off; had it been turned off at the moment of launch, there would have been no trouble.

On a more mundane level, binary inputs sometimes break programs that expect text inputs, especially if they assume that the input is in the 7-bit ASCII character set. It is instructive and sometimes sobering to pass binary input (such as a compiled program) to an unsuspecting program that expects text input.

Good test cases can often be used on a variety of programs. For example, any program that reads files should be tested on an empty file. Any program that reads text should be tested on binary files. Any program that reads text lines should be tested on huge lines and empty lines and input with no newlines at all. It's a good idea to keep

a collection of such test files handy, so you can test any program with them without
having to recreate the tests. Or write a program to create test files upon demand.

When Steve Bourne was writing his Unix shell (which came to be known as the
Bourne shell), he made a directory of 254 files with one-character names, one for each
byte value except '\0' and slash, the two characters that cannot appear in Unix file
names. He used that directory for all manner of tests of pattern-matching and tok-
enization. (The test directory was of course created by a program.) For years afterwards, that directory was the bane of file-tree-walking programs; it tested them to
destruction.

Exercise 6-10. Try to create a file that will crash your favorite text editor, compiler,
or other program. □

6.6 Tips for Testing

Experienced testers use many tricks and techniques to make their work more productive; this section includes some of our favorites.

Programs should check array bounds (if the language doesn't do it for them), but
the checking code might not be tested if the array sizes are large compared to typical
input. To exercise the checks, temporarily make the array sizes very small, which is
easier than creating large test cases. We used a related trick in the array-growing code
in Chapter 2 and in the CSV library in Chapter 4. In fact, we left the tiny initial values
in place, since the additional startup cost is negligible.

Make the hash function return a constant, so every element gets installed in the
same hash bucket. This will exercise the chaining mechanism; it also provides an
indication of worst-case performance.

Write a version of your storage allocator that intentionally fails early, to test your
code for recovering from out-of-memory errors. This version returns NULL after 10
calls:

```
/* testmalloc: returns NULL after 10 calls */
void *testmalloc(size_t n)
{
    static int count = 0;

    if (++count > 10)
        return NULL;
    else
        return malloc(n);
}
```

Before you ship your code, disable testing limitations that will affect performance.
We once tracked down a performance problem in a production compiler to a hash
function that always returned zero because testing code had been left installed.

Initialize arrays and variables with some distinctive value, rather than the usual default of zero; then if you access out of bounds or pick up an uninitialized variable, you are more likely to notice it. The constant 0xDEADBEEF is easy to recognize in a debugger; allocators sometimes use such values to help catch uninitialized data.

Vary your test cases, especially when making small tests by hand—it's easy to get into a rut by always testing the same thing, and you may not notice that something else has broken.

Don't keep on implementing new features or even testing existing ones if there are known bugs; they could be affecting the test results.

Test output should include all input parameter settings, so the tests can be reproduced exactly. If your program uses random numbers, have a way to set and print the starting seed, independent of whether the tests themselves are random. Make sure that test inputs and corresponding outputs are properly identified, so they can be understood and reproduced.

It's also wise to provide ways to make the amount and type of output controllable when a program is run; extra output can help during testing.

Test on multiple machines, compilers, and operating systems. Each combination potentially reveals errors that won't be seen on others, such as dependencies on byte-order, sizes of integers, treatment of null pointers, handling of carriage return and newline, and specific properties of libraries and header files. Testing on multiple machines also uncovers problems in gathering the components of a program for shipment and, as we will discuss in Chapter 8, may reveal unwitting dependencies on the development environment.

We will discuss performance testing in Chapter 7.

6.7 Who Does the Testing?

Testing that is done by the implementer or someone else with access to the source code is sometimes called white box testing. (The term is a weak analogy to black box testing, where the tester does not know how the component is implemented; ''clear box'' might be more evocative.) It is important to test your own code: don't assume that some testing organization or user will find things for you. But it's easy to delude yourself about how carefully you are testing, so try to ignore the code and think of hard cases, not easy ones. To quote Don Knuth describing how he creates tests for the TEX formatter, ''I get into the meanest, nastiest frame of mind that I can manage, and I write the nastiest [testing] code I can think of; then I turn around and embed that in even nastier constructions that are almost obscene.'' The reason for testing is to find bugs, not to declare the program working. Therefore the tests should be tough, and when they find problems, that is a vindication of your methods, not a cause for alarm.

Black box testing means that the tester has no knowledge of or access to the innards of the code. It finds different kinds of errors, because the tester has different assumptions about where to look. Boundary conditions are a good place to begin black box testing; high-volume, perverse, and illegal inputs are good follow-ons. Of course you should also test the ordinary "middle of the road" or conventional uses of the program to verify basic functionality.

Real users are the next step. New users find new bugs, because they probe the program in unexpected ways. It is important to do this kind of testing before the program is released to the world though, sadly, many programs are shipped without enough testing of any kind. Beta releases of software are an attempt to have numerous real users test a program before it is finalized, but beta releases should not be used as a substitute for thorough testing. As software systems get larger and more complex, and development schedules get shorter, however, the pressure to ship without adequate testing increases.

It's hard to test interactive programs, especially if they involve mouse input. Some testing can be done by scripts (whose properties depend on language, environment, and the like). Interactive programs should be controllable from scripts that simulate user behaviors so they can be tested by programs. One technique is to capture the actions of real users and replay them; another is to create a scripting language that describes sequences and timing of events.

Finally, give some thought to how to test the tests themselves. We mentioned in Chapter 5 the confusion caused by a faulty test program for a list package. A regression suite infected by an error will cause trouble for the rest of time. The results of a set of tests will not mean much if the tests themselves are flawed.

6.8 Testing the Markov Program

The Markov program of Chapter 3 is sufficiently intricate that it needs careful testing. It produces nonsense, which is hard to analyze for validity, and we wrote multiple versions in several languages. As a final complication, its output is random and different each time. How can we apply some of the lessons of this chapter to testing this program?

The first set of tests consists of a handful of tiny files that check boundary conditions, to make sure the program produces the right output for inputs that contain only a few words. For prefixes of length two, we use five files that contain respectively (with one word per line)

```
(empty file)
a
a b
a b c
a b c d
```

For each file, the output should be identical to the input. These checks uncovered several off-by-one errors in initializing the table and starting and stopping the generator.

A second test verified conservation properties. For two-word prefixes, every word, every pair, and every triple that appears in the output of a run must occur in the input as well. We wrote an Awk program that reads the original input into a giant array, builds arrays of all pairs and triples, then reads the Markov output into another array and compares the two:

```
# markov test:  check that all words, pairs, triples in
#    output ARGV[2] are in original input ARGV[1]
BEGIN {
    while (getline <ARGV[1] > 0)
        for (i = 1; i <= NF; i++) {
            wd[++nw] = $i    # input words
            single[$i]++
        }
    for (i = 1; i < nw; i++)
        pair[wd[i],wd[i+1]]++
    for (i = 1; i < nw-1; i++)
        triple[wd[i],wd[i+1],wd[i+2]]++

    while (getline <ARGV[2] > 0) {
        outwd[++ow] = $0     # output words
        if (!($0 in single))
            print "unexpected word", $0
    }
    for (i = 1; i < ow; i++)
        if (!((outwd[i],outwd[i+1]) in pair))
            print "unexpected pair", outwd[i], outwd[i+1]
    for (i = 1; i < ow-1; i++)
        if (!((outwd[i],outwd[i+1],outwd[i+2]) in triple))
            print "unexpected triple",
                outwd[i], outwd[i+1], outwd[i+2]
}
```

We made no attempt to build an efficient test, just to make the test program as simple as possible. It takes six or seven seconds to check a 10,000 word output file against a 42,685 word input file, not much longer than some versions of Markov take to generate it. Checking conservation caught a major error in our Java implementation: the program sometimes overwrote hash table entries because it used references instead of making copies of prefixes.

This test illustrates the principle that it can be much easier to verify a property of the output than to create the output itself. For instance it is easier to check that a file is sorted than to sort it in the first place.

A third test is statistical in nature. The input consists of the sequence

    a b c a b c ... a b d ...

with ten occurrences of abc for each abd. The output should have about 10 times as many c's as d's if the random selection is working properly. We confirm this with freq, of course.

The statistical test showed that an early version of the Java program, which associated counters with each suffix, produced 20 c's for every d, twice as many as it should have. After some head scratching, we realized that Java's random number generator returns negative as well as positive integers; the factor of two occurred because the range of values was twice as large as expected, so twice as many values would be zero modulo the counter; this favored the first element in the list, which happened to be c. The fix was to take the absolute value before the modulus. Without this test, we would never have discovered the error; to the eye, the output looked fine.

Finally, we gave the Markov program plain English text to see that it produced beautiful nonsense. Of course, we also ran this test early in the development of the program. But we didn't stop testing when the program handled regular input, because nasty cases will come up in practice. Getting the easy cases right is seductive; hard cases must be tested too. Automated, systematic testing is the best way to avoid this trap.

All of the testing was mechanized. A shell script generated necessary input data, ran and timed the tests, and printed any anomalous output. The script was configurable so the same tests could be applied to any version of Markov, and every time we made a set of changes to one of the programs, we ran all the tests again to make sure that nothing was broken.

6.9 Summary

The better you write your code originally, the fewer bugs it will have and the more confident you can be that your testing has been thorough. Testing boundary conditions as you write is an effective way to eliminate a lot of silly little bugs. Systematic testing tries to probe at potential trouble spots in an orderly way; again, failures are most commonly found at boundaries, which can be explored by hand or by program. As much as possible, it is desirable to automate testing, since machines don't make mistakes or get tired or fool themselves into thinking that something is working when it isn't. Regression tests check that the program still produces the same answers as it used to. Testing after each small change is a good technique for localizing the source of any problem because new bugs are most likely to occur in new code.

The single most important rule of testing is to *do it*.

Supplementary Reading

One way to learn about testing is to study examples from the best freely available software. Don Knuth's "The Errors of TEX," in *Software—Practice and Experience*, **19**, 7, pp. 607-685, 1989, describes every error found to that point in the TEX formatter, and includes a discussion of Knuth's testing methods. The TRIP test for TEX is an excellent example of a thorough test suite. Perl also comes with an extensive test suite that is meant to verify its correctness after compilation and installation on a new system, and includes modules such as `MakeMaker` and `TestHarness` that aid in the construction of tests for Perl extensions.

Jon Bentley wrote a series of articles in *Communications of the ACM* that were subsequently collected in *Programming Pearls* and *More Programming Pearls*, published by Addison-Wesley in 1986 and 1988 respectively. They often touch on testing, especially frameworks for organizing and mechanizing extensive tests.

7
Performance

His promises were, as he then was, mighty;
But his performance, as he is now, nothing.

Shakespeare, *King Henry VIII*

Long ago, programmers went to great effort to make their programs efficient because computers were slow and expensive. Today, machines are much cheaper and faster, so the need for absolute efficiency is greatly reduced. Is it still worth worrying about performance?

Yes, but only if the problem is important, the program is genuinely too slow, and there is some expectation that it can be made faster while maintaining correctness, robustness, and clarity. A fast program that gets the wrong answer doesn't save any time.

Thus the first principle of optimization is *don't*. Is the program good enough already? Knowing how a program will be used and the environment it runs in, is there any benefit to making it faster? Programs written for assignments in a college class are never used again; speed rarely matters. Nor will speed matter for most personal programs, occasional tools, test frameworks, experiments, and prototypes. The run-time of a commercial product or a central component such as a graphics library can be critically important, however, so we need to understand how to think about performance issues.

When should we try to speed up a program? How can we do so? What can we expect to gain? This chapter discusses how to make programs run faster or use less memory. Speed is usually the most important concern, so that is mostly what we'll talk about. Space (main memory, disk) is less frequently an issue but can be crucial, so we will spend some time and space on that too.

As we observed in Chapter 2, the best strategy is to use the simplest, cleanest algorithms and data structures appropriate for the task. Then measure performance to see if changes are needed; enable compiler options to generate the fastest possible code; assess what changes to the program itself will have the most effect; make changes one at a time and re-assess; and keep the simple versions for testing revisions against.

Measurement is a crucial component of performance improvement since reasoning and intuition are fallible guides and must be supplemented with tools like timing commands and profilers. Performance improvement has much in common with testing, including such techniques as automation, keeping careful records, and using regression tests to make sure that changes preserve correctness and do not undo previous improvements.

If you choose your algorithms wisely and write well originally you may find no need for further speedups. Often minor changes will fix any performance problems in well-designed code, while badly-designed code will require major rewriting.

7.1 A Bottleneck

Let us begin by describing how a bottleneck was removed from a critical program in our local environment.

Our incoming mail funnels through a machine, called a gateway, that connects our internal network with the external Internet. Electronic mail messages from outside—tens of thousands a day for a community of a few thousand people—arrive at the gateway and are transferred to the internal network; this separation isolates our private network from the public Internet and allows us to publish a single machine name (that of the gateway) for everyone in the community.

One of the services of the gateway is to filter out "spam," unsolicited mail that advertises services of dubious merit. After successful early trials of the spam filter, the service was installed as a permanent feature for all users of the mail gateway, and a problem immediately became apparent. The gateway machine, antiquated and already very busy, was overwhelmed because the filtering program was taking so much time—much more time than was required for all the other processing of each message—that the mail queues filled and message delivery was delayed by hours while the system struggled to catch up.

This is an example of a true performance problem: the program was not fast enough to do its job, and people were inconvenienced by the delay. The program simply had to run much faster.

Simplifying quite a bit, the spam filter runs like this. Each incoming message is treated as a single string, and a textual pattern matcher examines that string to see if it contains any phrases from known spam, such as "Make millions in your spare time" or "XXX-rated." Messages tend to recur, so this technique is remarkably effective, and if a spam message is not caught, a phrase is added to the list to catch it next time.

None of the existing string-matching tools, such as grep, had the right combination of performance and packaging, so a special-purpose spam filter was written. The original code was very simple; it looked to see if each message contained any of the phrases (patterns):

```
/* isspam: test mesg for occurrence of any pat */
int isspam(char *mesg)
{
    int i;

    for (i = 0; i < npat; i++)
        if (strstr(mesg, pat[i]) != NULL) {
            printf("spam: match for '%s'\n", pat[i]);
            return 1;
        }
    return 0;
}
```

How could this be made faster? The string must be searched, and the strstr function from the C library is the best way to search: it's standard and efficient.

Using *profiling*, a technique we'll talk about in the next section, it became clear that the implementation of strstr had unfortunate properties when used in a spam filter. By changing the way strstr worked, it could be made more efficient *for this particular problem*.

The existing implementation of strstr looked something like this:

```
/* simple strstr: use strchr to look for first character */
char *strstr(const char *s1, const char *s2)
{
    int n;

    n = strlen(s2);
    for (;;) {
        s1 = strchr(s1, s2[0]);
        if (s1 == NULL)
            return NULL;
        if (strncmp(s1, s2, n) == 0)
            return (char *) s1;
        s1++;
    }
}
```

It had been written with efficiency in mind, and in fact for typical use it was fast because it used highly-optimized library routines to do the work. It called strchr to find the next occurrence of the first character of the pattern, and then called strncmp to see if the rest of the string matched the rest of the pattern. Thus it skipped quickly over most of the message looking for the first character of the pattern, and then did a fast scan to check the rest. Why would this perform badly?

There are several reasons. First, strncmp takes as an argument the length of the pattern, which must be computed with strlen. But the patterns are fixed, so it shouldn't be necessary to recompute their lengths for each message.

Second, strncmp has a complex inner loop. It must not only compare the bytes of the two strings, it must look for the terminating \0 byte on both strings while also counting down the length parameter. Since the lengths of all the strings are known in advance (though not to strncmp), this complexity is unnecessary; we know the counts are right so checking for the \0 wastes time.

Third, strchr is also complex, since it must look for the character and also watch for the \0 byte that terminates the message. For a given call to isspam, the message is fixed, so time spent looking for the \0 is wasted since we know where the message ends.

Finally, although strncmp, strchr, and strlen are all efficient in isolation, the overhead of calling these functions is comparable to the cost of the calculation they will perform. It's more efficient to do all the work in a special, carefully written version of strstr and avoid calling other functions altogether.

These sorts of problems are a common source of performance trouble—a routine or interface works well for the typical case, but performs poorly in an unusual case that happens to be central to the program at issue. The existing strstr was fine when both the pattern and the string were short and changed each call, but when the string is long and fixed, the overhead is prohibitive.

With this in mind, strstr was rewritten to walk the pattern and message strings together looking for matches, without calling subroutines. The resulting implementation has predictable behavior: it is slightly slower in some cases, but much faster in the spam filter and, most important, is never terrible. To verify the new implementation's correctness and performance, a performance test suite was built. This suite included not only simple examples like searching for a word in a sentence, but also pathological cases such as looking for a pattern of a single x in a string of a thousand e's and a pattern of a thousand x's in a string of a single e, both of which can be handled badly by naive implementations. Such extreme cases are a key part of performance evaluation.

The library was updated with the new strstr and the spam filter ran about 30% faster, a good payoff for rewriting a single routine.

Unfortunately, it was still too slow.

When solving problems, it's important to ask the right question. Up to now, we've been asking for the fastest way to search for a textual pattern in a string. But the real problem is to search for a large, fixed set of textual patterns in a long, variable string. Put that way, strstr is not so obviously the right solution.

The most effective way to make a program faster is to use a better algorithm. With a clearer idea of the problem, it's time to think about what algorithm would work best.

The basic loop,

```
for (i = 0; i < npat; i++)
    if (strstr(mesg, pat[i]) != NULL)
        return 1;
```

scans down the message npat independent times; assuming it doesn't find any matches, it examines each byte of the message npat times, for a total of strlen(mesg)*npat comparisons.

A better approach is to invert the loops, scanning the message once in the outer loop while searching for all the patterns in parallel in the inner loop:

```
for (j = 0; mesg[j] != '\0'; j++)
    if (some pattern matches starting at mesg[j])
        return 1;
```

The performance improvement stems from a simple observation. To see if any pattern matches the message at position j, we don't need to look at all patterns, only those that begin with the same character as mesg[j]. Roughly, with 52 upper and lower-case letters we might expect to do only strlen(mesg)*npat/52 comparisons. Since the letters are not evenly distributed—words begin with s much more often than x—we won't see a factor of 52 improvement, but we should see some. In effect, we construct a hash table using the first character of the pattern as the key.

Given some precomputation to construct a table of which patterns begin with each character, isspam is still short:

```
int patlen[NPAT];                    /* length of pattern */
int starting[UCHAR_MAX+1][NSTART];   /* pats starting with char */
int nstarting[UCHAR_MAX+1];          /* number of such patterns */
...
/* isspam: test mesg for occurrence of any pat */
int isspam(char *mesg)
{
    int i, j, k;
    unsigned char c;

    for (j = 0; (c = mesg[j]) != '\0'; j++) {
        for (i = 0; i < nstarting[c]; i++) {
            k = starting[c][i];
            if (memcmp(mesg+j, pat[k], patlen[k]) == 0) {
                printf("spam: match for '%s'\n", pat[k]);
                return 1;
            }
        }
    }
    return 0;
}
```

The two-dimensional array starting[c][] stores, for each character c, the indices of those patterns that begin with that character. Its companion nstarting[c] records how many patterns begin with c. Without these tables, the inner loop would run from 0 to npat, about a thousand; instead it runs from 0 to something like 20. Finally, the array element patlen[k] stores the precomputed result of strlen(pat[k]).

The following figure sketches these data structures for a set of three patterns that begin with the letter b:

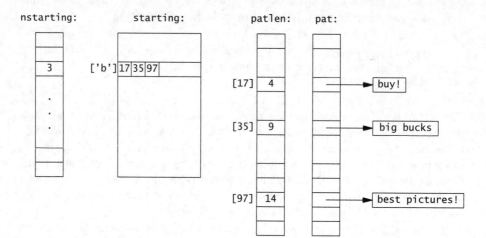

The code to build these tables is easy:

```
int i;
unsigned char c;

for (i = 0; i < npat; i++) {
    c = pat[i][0];
    if (nstarting[c] >= NSTART)
        eprintf("too many patterns (>=%d) begin '%c'",
            NSTART, c);
    starting[c][nstarting[c]++] = i;
    patlen[i] = strlen(pat[i]);
}
```

Depending on the input, the spam filter is now five to ten times faster than it was using the improved strstr, and seven to fifteen times faster than the original implementation. We didn't get a factor of 52, partly because of the non-uniform distribution of letters, partly because the loop is more complicated in the new program, and partly because there are still many failing string comparisons to execute, but the spam filter is no longer the bottleneck for mail delivery. Performance problem solved.

The rest of this chapter will explore the techniques used to discover performance problems, isolate the slow code, and speed it up. Before moving on, though, it's worth looking back at the spam filter to see what lessons it teaches. Most important, make sure performance matters. It wouldn't have been worth all the effort if spam filtering wasn't a bottleneck. Once we knew it was a problem, we used profiling and other techniques to study the behavior and learn where the problem really lay. Then we made sure we were solving the right problem, examining the overall program rather than just focusing on strstr, the obvious but incorrect suspect. Finally, we solved the correct problem using a better algorithm, and checked that it really was faster. Once it was fast enough, we stopped; why over-engineer?

Exercise 7-1. A table that maps a single character to the set of patterns that begin with that character gives an order of magnitude improvement. Implement a version of isspam that uses two characters as the index. How much improvement does that lead to? These are simple special cases of a data structure called a *trie*. Most such data structures are based on trading space for time. □

7.2 Timing and Profiling

Automate timing measurements. Most systems have a command to measure how long a program takes. On Unix, the command is called time:

```
% time slowprogram

real      7.0
user      6.2
sys       0.1
%
```

This runs the command and reports three numbers, all in seconds: "real" time, the elapsed time for the program to complete; "user" CPU time, time spent executing the user's program; and "system" CPU time, time spent within the operating system on the program's behalf. If your system has a similar command, use it; the numbers will be more informative, reliable, and easier to track than time measured with a stop-watch. And keep good notes. As you work on the program, making modifications and measurements, you will accumulate a lot of data that can become confusing a day or two later. (Which version was it that ran 20% faster?) Many of the techniques we discussed in the chapter on testing can be adapted for measuring and improving performance. Use the machine to run and measure your test suites and, most important, use regression testing to make sure your modifications don't break the program.

If your system doesn't have a time command, or if you're timing a function in isolation, it's easy to construct a timing scaffold analogous to a testing scaffold. C and C++ provide a standard routine, clock, that reports how much CPU time the program has consumed so far. It can be called before and after a function to measure CPU usage:

```
#include <time.h>
#include <stdio.h>
    ...
    clock_t before;
    double elapsed;

    before = clock();
    long_running_function();
    elapsed = clock() - before;
    printf("function used %.3f seconds\n",
        elapsed/CLOCKS_PER_SEC);
```

The scaling term, CLOCKS_PER_SEC, records the resolution of the timer as reported by clock. If the function takes only a small fraction of a second, run it in a loop, but be sure to compensate for loop overhead if that is significant:

```
before = clock();
for (i = 0; i < 1000; i++)
    short_running_function();
elapsed = (clock()-before)/(double)i;
```

In Java, functions in the Date class give wall clock time, which is an approximation to CPU time:

```
Date before = new Date();
long_running_function();
Date after = new Date();
long elapsed = after.getTime() - before.getTime();
```

The return value of getTime is in milliseconds.

Use a profiler. Besides a reliable timing method, the most important tool for performance analysis is a system for generating profiles. A *profile* is a measurement of where a program spends its time. Some profiles list each function, the number of times it is called, and the fraction of execution time it consumes. Others show counts of how many times each statement was executed. Statements that are executed frequently contribute more to run-time, while statements that are never executed may indicate useless code or code that is not being tested adequately.

Profiling is an effective tool for finding *hot spots* in a program, the functions or sections of code that consume most of the computing time. Profiles should be interpreted with care, however. Given the sophistication of compilers and the complexity of caching and memory effects, as well as the fact that profiling a program affects its performance, the statistics in a profile can be only approximate.

In the 1971 paper that introduced the term profiling, Don Knuth wrote that "less than 4 per cent of a program generally accounts for more than half of its running time." This indicates that the way to use profiling is to identify the critical time-consuming parts of the program, improve them to the degree possible, and then measure again to see if a new hot spot has surfaced. Eventually, often after only one or two iterations, there is no obvious hot spot left.

Profiling is usually enabled with a special compiler flag or option. The program is run, and then an analysis tool shows the results. On Unix, the flag is usually -p and the tool is called prof:

```
% cc -p spamtest.c -o spamtest
% spamtest
% prof spamtest
```

The following table shows the profile generated by a special version of the spam filter we built to understand its behavior. It uses a fixed message and a fixed set of 217 phrases, which it matches against the message 10,000 times. This run on a 250 MHz

MIPS R10000 used the original implementation of `strstr` that calls other standard functions. The output has been edited and reformatted so it fits the page. Notice how sizes of input (217 phrases) and the number of runs (10,000) show up as consistency checks in the "calls" column, which counts the number of calls of each function.

```
12234768552: Total number of instructions executed
13961810001: Total computed cycles
      55.847: Total computed execution time (secs.)
       1.141: Average cycles / instruction
```

secs	%	cum%	cycles	instructions	calls	function
45.260	81.0%	81.0%	11314990000	9440110000	48350000	strchr
6.081	10.9%	91.9%	1520280000	1566460000	46180000	strncmp
2.592	4.6%	96.6%	648080000	854500000	2170000	strstr
1.825	3.3%	99.8%	456225559	344882213	2170435	strlen
0.088	0.2%	100.0%	21950000	28510000	10000	isspam
0.000	0.0%	100.0%	100025	100028	1	main
0.000	0.0%	100.0%	53677	70268	219	_memccpy
0.000	0.0%	100.0%	48888	46403	217	strcpy
0.000	0.0%	100.0%	17989	19894	219	fgets
0.000	0.0%	100.0%	16798	17547	230	_malloc
0.000	0.0%	100.0%	10305	10900	204	realfree
0.000	0.0%	100.0%	6293	7161	217	estrdup
0.000	0.0%	100.0%	6032	8575	231	cleanfree
0.000	0.0%	100.0%	5932	5729	1	readpat
0.000	0.0%	100.0%	5899	6339	219	getline
0.000	0.0%	100.0%	5500	5720	220	_malloc

It's obvious that `strchr` and `strncmp`, both called by `strstr`, completely dominate the performance. Knuth's guideline is right: a small part of the program consumes most of the run-time. When a program is first profiled, it's common to see the top-running function at 50 percent or more, as it is here, making it easy to decide where to focus attention.

Concentrate on the hot spots. After rewriting `strstr`, we profiled `spamtest` again and found that 99.8% of the time was now spent in `strstr` alone, even though the whole program was considerably faster. When a single function is so overwhelmingly the bottleneck, there are only two ways to go: improve the function to use a better algorithm, or eliminate the function altogether by rewriting the surrounding program.

In this case, we rewrote the program. Here are the first few lines of the profile for `spamtest` using the final, fast implementation of `isspam`. Notice that the overall time is much less, that `memcmp` is now the hot spot, and that `isspam` now consumes a significant fraction of the computation. It is more complex than the version that called `strstr`, but its cost is more than compensated for by eliminating `strlen` and `strchr` from `isspam` and by replacing `strncmp` with `memcmp`, which does less work per byte.

secs	%	cum%	cycles	instructions	calls	function
3.524	56.9%	56.9%	880890000	1027590000	46180000	memcmp
2.662	43.0%	100.0%	665550000	902920000	10000	isspam
0.001	0.0%	100.0%	140304	106043	652	strlen
0.000	0.0%	100.0%	100025	100028	1	main

It's instructive to spend some time comparing the cycle counts and number of calls in the two profiles. Notice that strlen went from a couple of million calls to 652, and that strncmp and memcmp are called the same number of times. Also notice that isspam, which now incorporates the function of strchr, still manages to use far fewer cycles than strchr did before because it examines only the relevant patterns at each step. Many more details of the execution can be discovered by examining the numbers.

A hot spot can often be eliminated, or at least cooled, by much simpler engineering than we undertook for the spam filter. Long ago, a profile of Awk indicated that one function was being called about a million times over the course of a regression test, in this loop:

```
?       for (j = i; j < MAXFLD; j++)
?           clear(j);
```

The loop, which clears fields before each new input line is read, was taking as much as 50 percent of the run-time. The constant MAXFLD, the maximum number of fields permitted in an input line, was 200. But in most uses of Awk, the actual number of fields was only two or three. Thus an enormous amount of time was being wasted clearing fields that had never been set. Replacing the constant by the previous value of the maximum number of fields gave a 25 percent overall speedup. The fix was to change the upper limit of the loop:

```
for (j = i; j < maxfld; j++)
    clear(j);
maxfld = i;
```

Draw a picture. Pictures are especially good for presenting performance measurements. They can convey information about the effects of parameter changes, compare algorithms and data structures, and sometimes point to unexpected behavior. The graphs of chain length counts for several hash multipliers in Chapter 5 showed clearly that some multipliers were better than others.

The following graph shows the effect of the size of the hash table array on run-time for the C version of markov with Psalms as input (42,685 words, 22,482 prefixes). We did two experiments. One set of runs used array sizes that are powers of two from 2 to 16,384; the other used sizes that are the largest prime less than each power of two. We wanted to see if a prime array size made any measurable difference to the performance.

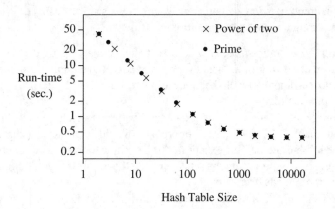

Hash Table Size

The graph shows that run-time for this input is not sensitive to the table size once the size is above 1,000 elements, nor is there a discernible difference between prime and power-of-two table sizes.

Exercise 7-2. Whether or not your system has a `time` command, use `clock` or `getTime` to write a timing facility for your own use. Compare its times to a wall clock. How does other activity on the machine affect the timings? □

Exercise 7-3. In the first profile, `strchr` was called 48,350,000 times and `strncmp` only 46,180,000. Explain the difference. □

7.3 Strategies for Speed

Before changing a program to make it faster, be certain that it really is too slow, and use timing tools and profilers to discover where the time is going. Once you know what's happening, there are a number of strategies to follow. We list a few here in decreasing order of profitability.

Use a better algorithm or data structure. The most important factor in making a program faster is the choice of algorithm and data structure; there can be a huge difference between an algorithm that is efficient and one that is not. Our spam filter saw a change in data structure that was worth a factor of ten; even greater improvement is possible if the new algorithm reduces the order of computation, say from $O(n^2)$ to $O(n\log n)$. We covered this topic in Chapter 2, so we won't dwell on it here.

Be sure that the complexity is really what you expect; if not, there might be a hidden performance bug. This apparently linear algorithm for scanning a string,

```
?      for (i = 0; i < strlen(s); i++)
?          if (s[i] == c)
?              ...
```

is in fact quadratic: if s has *n* characters, each call to `strlen` walks down the *n* characters of the string and the loop is performed *n* times.

Enable compiler optimizations. One zero-cost change that usually produces a reasonable improvement is to turn on whatever optimization the compiler provides. Modern compilers do sufficiently well that they obviate much of the need for small-scale changes by programmers.

By default, most C and C++ compilers do not attempt much optimization. A compiler option enables the *optimizer* (''improver'' would be a more accurate term). It should probably be the default except that the optimizations tend to confuse source-level debuggers, so programmers must enable the optimizer explicitly once they believe the program has been debugged.

Compiler optimization usually improves run-time anywhere from a few percent to a factor of two. Sometimes, though, it slows the program down, so measure the improvement before shipping your product. We compared unoptimized and optimized compilation on a couple of versions of the spam filter. For the test suite using the final version of the matching algorithm, the original run-time was 8.1 seconds, which dropped to 5.9 seconds when optimization was enabled, an improvement of over 25%. On the other hand, the version that used the fixed-up `strstr` showed no improvement under optimization, because `strstr` had already been optimized when it was installed in the library; the optimizer applies only to the source code being compiled now and not to the system libraries. However, some compilers have *global optimizers*, which analyze the entire program for potential improvements. If such a compiler is available on your system, try it; it might squeeze out a few more cycles.

One thing to be aware of is that the more aggressively the compiler optimizes, the more likely it is to introduce bugs into the compiled program. After enabling the optimizer, re-run your regression test suite, as you should for any other modification.

Tune the code. The right choice of algorithm matters if data sizes are big enough. Furthermore, algorithmic improvements work across different machines, compilers and languages. But once the right algorithm is in place, if speed is still an issue the next thing to try is *tuning* the code: adjusting the details of loops and expressions to make things go faster.

The version of `isspam` we showed at the end of Section 7.1 hadn't been tuned. Here, we'll show what further improvements can be achieved by tweaking the loop. As a reminder, this is how we left it:

```
for (j = 0; (c = mesg[j]) != '\0'; j++) {
    for (i = 0; i < nstarting[c]; i++) {
        k = starting[c][i];
        if (memcmp(mesg+j, pat[k], patlen[k]) == 0) {
            printf("spam: match for '%s'\n", pat[k]);
            return 1;
        }
    }
}
```

This initial version takes 6.6 seconds in our test suite when compiled using the optimizer. The inner loop has an array index (`nstarting[c]`) in its loop condition whose value is fixed for each iteration of the outer loop. We can avoid recalculating it by saving the value in a local variable:

```
for (j = 0; (c = mesg[j]) != '\0'; j++) {
    n = nstarting[c];
    for (i = 0; i < n; i++) {
        k = starting[c][i];
        ...
```

This drops the time to 5.9 seconds, about 10% faster, a speedup typical of what tuning can achieve. There's another variable we can pull out: `starting[c]` is also fixed. It seems like pulling that computation out of the loop would also help, but in our tests it made no measurable difference. This, too, is typical of tuning: some things help, some things don't, and one must measure to find out which. And results will vary with different machines or compilers.

There is another change we could make to the spam filter. The inner loop compares the entire pattern against the string, but the algorithm ensures that the first character already matches. We can therefore tune the code to start memcmp one byte further along. We tried this and found it gave about 3% improvement, which is slight but it requires modifying only three lines of the program, one of them in precomputation.

Don't optimize what doesn't matter. Sometimes tuning achieves nothing because it is applied where it makes no difference. Make sure the code you're optimizing is where time is really spent. The following story might be apocryphal, but we'll tell it anyway. An early machine from a now-defunct company was analyzed with a hardware performance monitor and discovered to be spending 50 percent of its time executing the same sequence of several instructions. The engineers built a special instruction to encapsulate the function of the sequence, rebuilt the system, and found it made no difference at all; they had optimized the idle loop of the operating system.

How much effort should you spend making a program run faster? The main criterion is whether the changes will yield enough to be worthwhile. As a guideline, the personal time spent making a program faster should not be more than the time the speedup will recover during the lifetime of the program. By this rule, the algorithmic improvement to isspam was worthwhile: it took a day of work but saved (and continues to save) hours every day. Removing the array index from the inner loop was less dramatic, but still worth doing, since the program provides a service to a large community. Optimizing public services like the spam filter or a library is almost always worthwhile; speeding up test programs is almost never worthwhile. And for a program that runs for a year, squeeze out everything you can. It may be worth restarting if you find a way to make a ten percent improvement even after the program has been running for a month.

Competitive programs—games, compilers, word processors, spreadsheets, database systems—fall into this category as well, since commercial success is often to the swiftest, at least in published benchmark results.

It's important to time programs as changes are being made, to make sure that things are improving. Sometimes two changes that each improve a program will interact, negating their individual effects. It's also the case that timing mechanisms can be so erratic that it's hard to draw firm conclusions about the effect of changes. Even on single-user systems, times can fluctuate unpredictably. If the variability of the internal timer (or at least what is reported back to you) is ten percent, changes that yield improvements of only ten percent are hard to distinguish from noise.

7.4 Tuning the Code

There are many techniques to reduce run-time when a hot spot is found. Here are some suggestions, which should be applied with care, and with regression testing after each to be sure that the code still works. Bear in mind that good compilers will do some of these for you, and in fact you may impede their efforts by complicating the program. Whatever you try, measure its effect to make sure it helps.

Collect common subexpressions. If an expensive computation appears multiple times, do it in only one place and remember the result. For example, in Chapter 1 we showed a macro that computed a distance by calling sqrt twice in a row with the same values; in effect the computation was

```
?       sqrt(dx*dx + dy*dy) + ((sqrt(dx*dx + dy*dy) > 0) ? ...)
```

Compute the square root once and use its value in two places.

If a computation is done within a loop but does not depend on anything that changes within the loop, move the computation outside, as when we replaced

```
        for (i = 0; i < nstarting[c]; i++) {
```

by

```
        n = nstarting[c];
        for (i = 0; i < n; i++) {
```

Replace expensive operations by cheap ones. The term *reduction in strength* refers to optimizations that replace an expensive operation by a cheaper one. In olden times, this used to mean replacing multiplications by additions or shifts, but that rarely buys much now. Division and remainder are much slower than multiplication, however, so there may be improvement if a division can be replaced with multiplication by the inverse, or a remainder by a masking operation if the divisor is a power of two. Replacing array indexing by pointers in C or C++ might speed things up, although most compilers do this automatically. Replacing a function call by a simpler calcula-

tion can still be worthwhile. Distance in the plane is determined by the formula
sqrt(dx*dx+dy*dy), so to decide which of two points is further away would normally involve calculating two square roots. But the same decision can be made by
comparing the squares of the distances;

```
if (dx1*dx1+dy1*dy1 < dx2*dx2+dy2*dy2)
    ...
```

gives the same result as comparing the square roots of the expressions.

Another instance occurs in textual pattern matchers such as our spam filter or
grep. If the pattern begins with a literal character, a quick search is made down the
input text for that character; if no match is found, the more expensive search machin-
ery is not invoked at all.

Unroll or eliminate loops. There is a certain overhead in setting up and running a
loop. If the body of the loop isn't too long and doesn't iterate too many times, it can
be more efficient to write out each iteration in sequence. Thus, for example,

```
for (i = 0; i < 3; i++)
    a[i] = b[i] + c[i];
```

becomes

```
a[0] = b[0] + c[0];
a[1] = b[1] + c[1];
a[2] = b[2] + c[2];
```

This eliminates loop overhead, particularly branching, which can slow modern processors by interrupting the flow of execution.

If the loop is longer, the same kind of transformation can be used to amortize the
overhead over fewer iterations:

```
for (i = 0; i < 3*n; i++)
    a[i] = b[i] + c[i];
```

becomes

```
for (i = 0; i < 3*n; i += 3) {
    a[i+0] = b[i+0] + c[i+0];
    a[i+1] = b[i+1] + c[i+1];
    a[i+2] = b[i+2] + c[i+2];
}
```

Note that this works only if the length is a multiple of the step size; otherwise additional code is needed to fix up the ends, which is a place for mistakes to creep in and
for some of the efficiency to be lost again.

Cache frequently-used values. Cached values don't have to be recomputed. Caching
takes advantage of *locality*, the tendency for programs (and people) to re-use recently
accessed or nearby items in preference to older or distant data. Computing hardware
makes extensive use of caches; indeed, adding cache memory to a computer can make

great improvements in how fast a machine appears. The same is true of software. Web browsers, for instance, cache pages and images to avoid the slow transfer of data over the Internet. In a print preview program we wrote years ago, non-alphabetic special characters like ½ had to be looked up in a table. Measurement showed that much of the use of special characters involved drawing lines with long sequences of the same single character. Caching just the single most recently used character made the program significantly faster on typical inputs.

It's best if the caching operation is invisible from outside, so that it doesn't affect the rest of the program except for making it run faster. Thus in the case of the print previewer, the interface to the character drawing function didn't change; it was always

```
drawchar(c);
```

The original version of drawchar called show(lookup(c)). The cache implementation used internal static variables to remember the previous character and its code:

```
if (c != lastc) { /* update cache */
    lastc = c;
    lastcode = lookup(c);
}
show(lastcode);
```

Write a special-purpose allocator. Often the single hot spot in a program is memory allocation, which manifests itself as lots of calls on malloc or new. When most requests are for blocks of the same size, substantial speedups are possible by replacing calls to the general-purpose allocator by calls to a special-purpose one. The special-purpose allocator makes one call to malloc to fetch a big array of items, then hands them out one at a time as needed, a cheaper operation. Freed items are placed back in a *free list* so they can be reused quickly.

If the requested sizes are similar, you can trade space for time by always allocating enough for the largest request. This can be effective for managing short strings if you use the same size for all strings up to a specified length.

Some algorithms can use stack-based allocation, where a whole sequence of allocations is done, and then the entire set is freed at once. The allocator obtains one big chunk for itself and treats it as a stack, pushing allocated items on as needed and popping them all off in a single operation at the end. Some C libraries offer a function alloca for this kind of allocation, though it is not standard. It uses the local call stack as the source of memory, and frees all the items when the function that calls alloca returns.

Buffer input and output. Buffering batches transactions so that frequent operations are done with as little overhead as possible, and the high-overhead operations are done only when necessary. The cost of an operation is thereby spread over multiple data values. When a C program calls printf, for example, the characters are stored in a buffer but not passed to the operating system until the buffer is full or flushed explicitly. The operating system itself may in turn delay writing the data to disk. The drawback is the need to flush output buffers to make data visible; in the worst case, information still in a buffer will be lost if a program crashes.

Handle special cases separately. By handling same-sized objects in separate code, special-purpose allocators reduce time and space overhead in the general allocator and incidentally reduce fragmentation. In the graphics library for the Inferno system, the basic draw function was written to be as simple and straightforward as possible. With that working, optimizations for a variety of cases (chosen by profiling) were added one at a time; it was always possible to test the optimized version against the simple one. In the end, only a handful of cases were optimized because the dynamic distribution of calls to the drawing function was heavily skewed towards displaying characters; it wasn't worth writing clever code for all the cases.

Precompute results. Sometimes it is possible to make a program run faster by pre-computing values so they are ready when they are needed. We saw this in the spam filter, which precomputed strlen(pat[i]) and stored it in the array at patlen[i]. If a graphics system needs to repeatedly compute a mathematical function like sine but only for a discrete set of values, such as integer degrees, it will be faster to pre-compute a table with 360 entries (or provide it as data) and index into it as needed. This is an example of trading space for time. There are many opportunities to replace code by data or to do computation during compilation, to save time and sometimes space as well. For example, the ctype functions like isdigit are almost always implemented by indexing into a table of bit flags rather than by evaluating a sequence of tests.

Use approximate values. If accuracy isn't an issue, use lower-precision data types. On older or smaller machines, or machines that simulate floating point in software, single-precision floating-point arithmetic is often faster than double-precision, so use float instead of double to save time. Some modern graphics processors use a related trick. The IEEE floating-point standard requires "graceful underflow" as calculations approach the low end of representable values, but this is expensive to compute. For images, the feature is unnecessary, and it is faster and perfectly acceptable to truncate to zero. This not only saves time when the numbers underflow, it can simplify the hardware for all arithmetic. The use of integer sin and cos routines is another example of using approximate values.

Rewrite in a lower-level language. Lower-level languages tend to be more efficient, although at a cost in programmer time. Thus rewriting some critical part of a C++ or Java program in C or replacing an interpreted script by a program in a compiled language may make it run much faster.

Occasionally, one can get significant speedups with machine-dependent code. This is a last resort, not a step to be taken lightly, because it destroys portability and makes future maintenance and modifications much harder. Almost always, operations to be expressed in assembly language are relatively small functions that should be embedded in a library; memset and memmove, or graphics operations, are typical examples. The approach is to write the code as cleanly as possible in a high-level language and make sure it's correct by testing it as we described for memset in Chapter 6. This is your portable version, which will work everywhere, albeit slowly. When you move to a new environment, you can start with a version that is known to work. Now when you write an assembly-language version, test it exhaustively against the portable one. When bugs occur, non-portable code is always suspect; it's comforting to have a comparison implementation.

Exercise 7-4. One way to make a function like memset run faster is to have it write in word-sized chunks instead of byte-sized; this is likely to match the hardware better and might reduce the loop overhead by a factor of four or eight. The downside is that there are now a variety of end effects to deal with if the target is not aligned on a word boundary and if the length is not a multiple of the word size. Write a version of memset that does this optimization. Compare its performance to the existing library version and to a straightforward byte-at-a-time loop. □

Exercise 7-5. Write a memory allocator smalloc for C strings that uses a special-purpose allocator for small strings but calls malloc directly for large ones. You will need to define a struct to represent the strings in either case. How do you decide where to switch from calling smalloc to malloc? □

7.5 Space Efficiency

Memory used to be the most precious computing resource, always in short supply, and much bad programming was done in an attempt to squeeze the most out of what little there was. The infamous "Year 2000 Problem" is frequently cited as an example of this; when memory was truly scarce, even the two bytes needed to store 19 were deemed too expensive. Whether or not space is the true reason for the problem—such code may simply reflect the way people use dates in everyday life, where the century is commonly omitted—it demonstrates the danger inherent in short-sighted optimization.

In any case, times have changed, and both main memory and secondary storage are amazingly cheap. Thus the first approach to optimizing space should be the same as to improving speed: *don't bother*.

There are still situations, however, where space efficiency matters. If a program doesn't fit into the available main memory, parts of it will be paged out, and that will make its performance unacceptable. We see this when new versions of software squander memory; it is a sad reality that software upgrades are often followed by the purchase of more memory.

Save space by using the smallest possible data type. One step to space efficiency is to make minor changes to use existing memory better, for example by using the smallest data type that will work. This might mean replacing `int` with `short` *if* the data will fit; this is a common technique for coordinates in 2-D graphics systems, since 16 bits are likely to handle any expected range of screen coordinates. Or it might mean replacing `double` with `float`; the potential problem is loss of precision, since `float`s usually hold only 6 or 7 decimal digits.

In these cases and analogous ones, other changes may be required as well, notably format specifications in `printf` and especially `scanf` statements.

The logical extension of this approach is to encode information in a byte or even fewer bits, say a single bit where possible. Don't use C or C++ bitfields; they are highly non-portable and tend to generate voluminous and inefficient code. Instead, encapsulate the operations you want in functions that fetch and set individual bits within words or an array of words with shift and mask operations. This function returns a group of contiguous bits from the middle of a word:

```
/* getbits:  get n bits from position p */
/*  bits are numbered from 0 (least significant) up */
unsigned int getbits(unsigned int x, int p, int n)
{
        return (x >> (p+1-n)) & ~(~0 << n);
}
```

If such functions turn out to be too slow, they can be improved with the techniques described earlier in this chapter. In C++, operator overloading can be used to make bit accesses look like regular subscripting.

Don't store what you can easily recompute. Changes like these are minor, however; they are analogous to code tuning. Major improvements are more likely to come from better data structures, perhaps coupled with algorithm changes. Here's an example. Many years ago, one of us was approached by a colleague who was trying to do a computation on a matrix so large that it was necessary to shut down the machine and reload a stripped-down operating system so the matrix would fit. He wanted to know if there was an alternative, since this was an operational nightmare. We asked what the matrix was like, and learned that it contained integer values, *most of which were zero*. In fact, fewer than five percent of the matrix elements were non-zero. This immediately suggested a representation in which only the non-zero elements of the matrix were stored, and each matrix access like `m[i][j]` would be replaced by a function call `m(i,j)`. There are several ways to store the data; the easiest is probably an array of pointers, one for each row, each of which points to a compact array of column numbers and corresponding values. This has higher space overhead per non-zero item but requires much less space overall, and although individual accesses will be slower, they will be noticeably faster than reloading the operating system. To complete the story: the colleague applied the suggestion and went away completely satisfied.

We used a similar approach to solve a modern version of the same problem. A radio design system needed to represent terrain data and radio signal strengths over a very large geographical area (100 to 200 kilometers on a side) to a resolution of 100 meters. Storing this as a large rectangular array exceeded the memory available on the target machine and would have caused unacceptable paging behavior. But over large regions, the terrain and signal strength values are likely to be the same, so a hierarchical representation that coalesces regions of the same value into a single cell makes the problem manageable.

Variations on this theme are frequent, and so are specific representations, but all share the same basic idea: store the common value or values implicitly or in a compact form, and spend more time and space on the remaining values. If the most common values are really common, this is a win.

The program should be organized so that the specific data representation of complex types is hidden in a class or set of functions operating on a private data type. This precaution ensures that the rest of the program will not be affected if the representation changes.

Space efficiency concerns sometimes manifest themselves in the external representation of information as well, both conversion and storage. In general, it is best to store information as text wherever feasible rather than in some binary representation. Text is portable, easy to read, and amenable to processing by all kinds of tools; binary representations have none of these advantages. The argument in favor of binary is usually based on ''speed,'' but this should be treated with some skepticism, since the disparity between text and binary forms may not be all that great.

Space efficiency often comes with a cost in run-time. One application had to transfer a big image from one program to another. Images in a simple format called PPM were typically a megabyte, so we thought it would be much faster to encode them for transfer in the compressed GIF format instead; those files were more like 50K bytes. But the encoding and decoding of GIF took as much time as was saved by transferring a shorter file, so nothing was gained. The code to handle the GIF format is about 500 lines long; the PPM source is about 10 lines. For ease of maintenance, therefore, the GIF encoding was dropped and the application continues to use PPM exclusively. Of course the tradeoff would be different if the file were to be sent across a slow network instead; then a GIF encoding would be much more cost-effective.

7.6 Estimation

It's hard to estimate ahead of time how fast a program will be, and it's doubly hard to estimate the cost of specific language statements or machine instructions. It's easy, though, to create a *cost model* for a language or a system, which will give you at least a rough idea of how long important operations take.

One approach that is often used for conventional programming languages is a program that times representative code sequences. There are operational difficulties, like getting reproducible results and canceling out irrelevant overheads, but it is possible to get useful insights without much effort. For example, we have a C and C++ cost model program that estimates the costs of individual statements by enclosing them in a loop that runs them many millions of times, then computes an average time. On a 250 MHz MIPS R10000, it produces this data, with times in nanoseconds per operation.

```
Int Operations
   i1++                             8
   i1 = i2 + i3                    12
   i1 = i2 - i3                    12
   i1 = i2 * i3                    12
   i1 = i2 / i3                   114
   i1 = i2 % i3                   114

Float Operations
   f1 = f2                          8
   f1 = f2 + f3                    12
   f1 = f2 - f3                    12
   f1 = f2 * f3                    11
   f1 = f2 / f3                    28

Double Operations
   d1 = d2                          8
   d1 = d2 + d3                    12
   d1 = d2 - d3                    12
   d1 = d2 * d3                    11
   d1 = d2 / d3                    58

Numeric Conversions
   i1 = f1                          8
   f1 = i1                          8
```

Integer operations are fast, except for division and modulus. Floating-point operations are as fast or faster, a surprise to people who grew up at a time when floating-point operations were much more expensive than integer operations.

Other basic operations are also quite fast, including function calls, the last three lines of this group:

```
Integer Vector Operations
   v[i] = i                        49
   v[v[i]] = i                     81
   v[v[v[i]]] = i                 100

Control Structures
   if (i == 5) i1++                 4
   if (i != 5) i1++                12
   while (i < 0) i1++               3
   i1 = sum1(i2)                   57
   i1 = sum2(i2, i3)              58
   i1 = sum3(i2, i3, i4)          54
```

But input and output are not so cheap, nor are most other library functions:

```
Input/Output
  fputs(s, fp)                        270
  fgets(s, 9, fp)                     222
  fprintf(fp, "%d\n", i)             1820
  fscanf(fp, "%d", &i1)              2070

Malloc
  free(malloc(8))                     342

String Functions
  strcpy(s, "0123456789")            157
  i1 = strcmp(s, s)                   176
  i1 = strcmp(s, "a123456789")        64

String/Number Conversions
  i1 = atoi("12345")                  402
  sscanf("12345", "%d", &i1)         2376
  sprintf(s, "%d", i)                1492
  f1 = atof("123.45")                4098
  sscanf("123.45", "%f", &f1)        6438
  sprintf(s, "%6.2f", 123.45)        3902
```

The times for malloc and free are probably not indicative of true performance, since freeing immediately after allocating is not a typical pattern.

Finally, math functions:

```
Math Functions
  i1 = rand()                         135
  f1 = log(f2)                        418
  f1 = exp(f2)                        462
  f1 = sin(f2)                        514
  f1 = sqrt(f2)                       112
```

These values would be different on different hardware, of course, but the trends can be used for back-of-the-envelope estimates of how long something might take, or for comparing the relative costs of I/O versus basic operations, or for deciding whether to rewrite an expression or use an inline function.

There are many sources of variability. One is compiler optimization level. Modern compilers can find optimizations that elude most programmers. Furthermore, current CPUs are so complicated that only a good compiler can take advantage of their ability to issue multiple instructions concurrently, pipeline their execution, fetch instructions and data before they are needed, and the like.

Computer architecture itself is another major reason why performance numbers are hard to predict. Memory caches make a great difference in speed, and much cleverness in hardware design goes into hiding the fact that main memory is quite a bit slower than cache memory. Raw processor clock rates like ''400 MHz'' are suggestive but don't tell the whole story; one of our old 200 MHz Pentiums is significantly slower than an even older 100 MHz Pentium because the latter has a big second-level cache and the former has none. And different generations of processor, even for the same instruction set, take different numbers of clock cycles to do a particular operation.

Exercise 7-6. Create a set of tests for estimating the costs of basic operations for computers and compilers near you, and investigate similarities and differences in performance. □

Exercise 7-7. Create a cost model for higher-level operations in C++. Among the features that might be included are construction, copying, and deletion of class objects; member function calls; virtual functions; inline functions; the `iostream` library; the STL. This exercise is open-ended, so concentrate on a small set of representative operations. □

Exercise 7-8. Repeat the previous exercise for Java. □

7.7 Summary

Once you have chosen the right algorithm, performance optimization is generally the last thing to worry about as you write a program. If you must undertake it, however, the basic cycle is to measure, focus on the few places where a change will make the most difference, verify the correctness of your changes, then measure again. Stop as soon as you can, and preserve the simplest version as a baseline for timing and correctness.

When you're trying to improve the speed or space consumption of a program, it's a good idea to make up some benchmark tests and problems so you can estimate and keep track of performance for yourself. If there are already standard benchmarks for your task, use them too. If the program is relatively self-contained, one approach is to find or create a collection of ''typical'' inputs; these might well be part of a test suite as well. This is the genesis of benchmark suites for commercial and academic systems like compilers, computers, and the like. For example, Awk comes with about 20 small programs that together cover most of the commonly-used language features; these programs are run over a very large input file to assure that the same results are computed and that no performance bug has been introduced. We also have a collection of standard large data files that can be used for timing tests. In some cases it might help that such files have easily verified properties, for example a size that is a power of ten or of two.

Benchmarking can be managed with the same kind of scaffolding as we recommended for testing in Chapter 6. Timing tests are run automatically; outputs include enough identification that they can be understood and replicated; records are kept so that trends and significant changes can be observed.

By the way, it's extremely difficult to do good benchmarking, and it is not unknown for companies to tune their products to show up well on benchmarks, so it is wise to take all benchmark results with a grain of salt.

Supplementary Reading

Our discussion of the spam filter is based on work by Bob Flandrena and Ken Thompson. Their filter includes regular expressions for more sophisticated matching and automatically classifies messages (certainly spam, possibly spam, not spam) according to the strings they match.

Knuth's profiling paper, "An Empirical Study of FORTRAN Programs," appeared in *Software—Practice and Experience*, **1**, 2, pp. 105-133, 1971. The core of the paper is a statistical analysis of a set of programs found by rummaging in waste baskets and publicly-visible directories on the computer center's machines.

Jon Bentley's *Programming Pearls* and *More Programming Pearls* (Addison-Wesley, 1986 and 1988) have several fine examples of algorithmic and code-tuning improvements; there are also good essays on scaffolds for performance improvements and the use of profiles.

Inner Loops, by Rick Booth (Addison-Wesley, 1997), is a good reference on tuning PC programs, although processors evolve so fast that specific details age quickly.

John Hennessy and David Patterson's family of books on computer architecture (for example, *Computer Organization and Design: The Hardware/Software Interface*, Morgan Kaufman, 1997) contain thorough discussions of performance considerations for modern computers.

8

Portability

Finally, standardization, like convention, can be another manifestation of the strong order. But unlike convention it has been accepted in Modern architecture as an enriching product of our technology, yet dreaded for its potential domination and brutality.

Robert Venturi, *Complexity and Contradiction in Architecture*

It's hard to write software that runs correctly and efficiently. So once a program works in one environment, you don't want to repeat much of the effort if you move it to a different compiler or processor or operating system. Ideally, it should need no changes whatsoever.

This ideal is called *portability*. In practice, "portability" more often stands for the weaker concept that it will be easier to modify the program as it moves than to rewrite it from scratch. The less revision it needs, the more portable it is.

You may wonder why we worry about portability at all. If software is going to run in only one environment, under specified conditions, why spend time giving it broader applicability? First, any successful program, almost by definition, gets used in unexpected ways and unexpected places. Building software to be more general than its original specification will result in less maintenance and more utility down the road. Second, environments change. When the compiler or operating system or hardware is upgraded, features may change. The less the program depends on special features, the less likely it is to break and the more easily it will adapt to changing circumstances. Finally, and most important, a portable program is a better program. The effort invested to make a program portable also makes it better designed, better constructed, and more thoroughly tested. The techniques of portable programming are closely related to the techniques of good programming in general.

Of course the degree of portability must be tempered by reality. There is no such thing as an absolutely portable program, only a program that hasn't yet been tried in enough environments. But we can keep portability as our goal by aiming towards software that runs without change almost everywhere. Even if this goal isn't met completely, time spent on portability as the program is created will pay off when the software must be updated.

Our message is this: try to write software that works within the intersection of the various standards, interfaces and environments it must accommodate. Don't fix every portability problem by adding special code; instead, adapt the software to work within the new constraints. Use abstraction and encapsulation to restrict and control unavoidable non-portable code. By staying within the intersection of constraints and by localizing system dependencies, your code will become cleaner and more general as it is ported.

8.1 Language

Stick to the standard. The first step to portable code is of course to program in a high-level language, and within the language standard if there is one. Binaries don't port well, but source code does. Even so, the way that a compiler translates a program into machine instructions is not precisely defined, even for standard languages. Few languages in wide use have only a single implementation; there are usually multiple suppliers, or versions for different operating systems, or releases that have evolved over time. How they interpret your source code will vary.

Why isn't a standard a strict definition? Sometimes a standard is incomplete and fails to define the behavior when features interact. Sometimes it's deliberately indefinite; for example, the char type in C and C++ may be signed or unsigned, and need not even have exactly 8 bits. Leaving such issues up to the compiler writer may allow more efficient implementations and avoid restricting the hardware the language will run on, at the risk of making life harder for programmers. Politics and technical compatibility issues may lead to compromises that leave details unspecified. Finally, languages are intricate and compilers are complex; there will be errors in the interpretation and bugs in the implementation.

Sometimes the languages aren't standardized at all. C has an official ANSI/ISO standard issued in 1988, but the ISO C++ standard was ratified only in 1998; at the time we are writing this, not all compilers in use support the official definition. Java is new and still years away from standardization. A language standard is usually developed only after the language has a variety of conflicting implementations to unify, and is in wide enough use to justify the expense of standardization. In the meantime, there are still programs to write and multiple environments to support.

So although reference manuals and standards give the impression of rigorous specification, they never define a language fully, and different implementations may make valid but incompatible interpretations. Sometimes there are even errors. A small illustration showed up while we were first writing this chapter. This external declaration is illegal in C and C++:

```
?      *x[] = {"abc"};
```

A test of a dozen compilers turned up a few that correctly diagnosed the missing char type specifier for x, a fair number that warned of mismatched types (apparently using an old definition of the language to infer incorrectly that x is an array of int pointers), and a couple that compiled the illegal code without a murmur of complaint.

Program in the mainstream. The inability of some compilers to flag this error is unfortunate, but it also indicates an important aspect of portability. Languages have dark corners where practice varies—bitfields in C and C++, for example—and it is prudent to avoid them. Use only those features for which the language definition is unambiguous and well understood. Such features are more likely to be widely available and to behave the same way everywhere. We call this the *mainstream* of the language.

It's hard to know just where the mainstream is, but it's easy to recognize constructions that are well outside it. Brand new features such as // comments and complex in C, or features specific to one architecture such as the keywords near and far, are guaranteed to cause trouble. If a feature is so unusual or unclear that to understand it you need to consult a "language lawyer"—an expert in reading language definitions—don't use it.

In this discussion, we'll focus on C and C++, general-purpose languages commonly used to write portable software. The C standard is more than a decade old and the language is very stable, but a new standard is in the works, so upheaval is coming. Meanwhile, the C++ standard is hot off the press, so not all implementations have had time to converge.

What is the C mainstream? The term usually refers to the established style of use of the language, but sometimes it's better to plan for the future. For example, the original version of C did not require function prototypes. One declared sqrt to be a function by saying

```
?    double sqrt();
```

which defines the type of the return value but not of the parameters. ANSI C added function prototypes, which specify everything:

```
double sqrt(double);
```

ANSI C compilers are required to accept the earlier syntax, but you should nonetheless write prototypes for all your functions. Doing so will guarantee safer code—function calls will be fully type-checked—and if interfaces change, the compiler will catch them. If your code calls

```
func(7, PI);
```

but func has no prototype, the compiler might not verify that func is being called correctly. If the library later changes so that func has three arguments, the need to repair the software might be missed because the old-style syntax disables type checking of function arguments.

C++ is a larger language with a more recent standard, so its mainstream is harder to identify. For example, although we expect the STL to become mainstream, this will not happen immediately, and some current implementations do not support it completely.

Beware of language trouble spots. As we mentioned, standards leave some things intentionally undefined or unspecified, usually to give compiler writers more flexibility. The list of such behaviors is discouragingly long.

Sizes of data types. The sizes of basic data types in C and C++ are not defined; other than the basic rules that

```
sizeof(char) ≤ sizeof(short) ≤ sizeof(int) ≤ sizeof(long)
sizeof(float) ≤ sizeof(double)
```

and that char must have at least 8 bits, short and int at least 16, and long at least 32, there are no guaranteed properties. It's not even required that a pointer value fit in an int.

It's easy enough to find out what the sizes are for a specific compiler:

```
/* sizeof: display sizes of basic types */
int main(void)
{
    printf("char %d, short %d, int %d, long %d,",
        sizeof(char), sizeof(short),
        sizeof(int), sizeof(long));
    printf(" float %d, double %d, void* %d\n",
        sizeof(float), sizeof(double), sizeof(void *));
    return 0;
}
```

The output is the same on most of the machines we use regularly:

```
char 1, short 2, int 4, long 4, float 4, double 8, void* 4
```

but other values are certainly possible. Some 64-bit machines produce this:

```
char 1, short 2, int 4, long 8, float 4, double 8, void* 8
```

and early PC compilers typically produced this:

```
char 1, short 2, int 2, long 4, float 4, double 8, void* 2
```

In the early days of PCs, the hardware supported several kinds of pointers. Coping with this mess caused the invention of pointer modifiers like far and near, neither of which is standard, but whose reserved-word ghosts still haunt current compilers. If your compiler can change the sizes of basic types, or if you have machines with different sizes, try to compile and test your program in these different configurations.

The standard header file stddef.h defines a number of types that can help with portability. The most commonly-used of these is size_t, which is the unsigned integral type returned by the `sizeof` operator. Values of this type are returned by functions like `strlen` and used as arguments by many functions, including `malloc`.

Learning from some of these experiences, Java defines the sizes of all basic data types: `byte` is 8 bits, `char` and `short` are 16, `int` is 32, and `long` is 64.

We will ignore the rich set of potential issues related to floating-point computation since that is a book-sized topic in itself. Fortunately, most modern machines support the IEEE standard for floating-point hardware, and thus the properties of floating-point arithmetic are reasonably well defined.

Order of evaluation. In C and C++, the order of evaluation of operands of expressions, side effects, and function arguments is not defined. For example, in the assignment

```
?    n = (getchar() << 8) | getchar();
```

the second `getchar` could be called first: the way the expression is written is not necessarily the way it executes. In the statement

```
?    ptr[count] = name[++count];
```

`count` might be incremented before or after it is used to index `ptr`, and in

```
?    printf("%c %c\n", getchar(), getchar());
```

the first input character could be printed second instead of first. In

```
?    printf("%f %s\n", log(-1.23), strerror(errno));
```

the value of `errno` may be evaluated before `log` is called.

There are rules for when certain expressions are evaluated. By definition, all side effects and function calls must be completed at each semicolon, or when a function is called. The `&&` and `||` operators execute left to right and only as far as necessary to determine their truth value (including side effects). The condition in a `?:` operator is evaluated (including side effects) and then exactly one of the two expressions that follow is evaluated.

Java has a stricter definition of order of evaluation. It requires that expressions, including side effects, be evaluated left to right, though one authoritative manual advises not writing code that depends "crucially" on this behavior. This is sound advice if there's any chance that Java code will be converted to C or C++, which make no such promises. Converting between languages is an extreme but occasionally reasonable test of portability.

Signedness of char. In C and C++, it is not specified whether the `char` data type is signed or unsigned. This can lead to trouble when combining `char`s and `int`s, such as in code that calls the `int`-valued routine `getchar()`. If you say

```
?    char c;   /* should be int */
?    c = getchar();
```

the value of c will be between 0 and 255 if char is unsigned, and between −128 and 127 if char is signed, for the almost universal configuration of 8-bit characters on a two's complement machine. This has implications if the character is to be used as an array subscript or if it is to be tested against EOF, which usually has value -1 in stdio. For instance, we had developed this code in Section 6.1 after fixing a few boundary conditions in the original version. The comparison s[i] == EOF will always fail if char is unsigned:

```
?       int i;
?       char s[MAX];
?
?       for (i = 0; i < MAX-1; i++)
?           if ((s[i] = getchar()) == '\n' || s[i] == EOF)
?               break;
?       s[i] = '\0';
```

When getchar returns EOF, the value 255 (0xFF, the result of converting -1 to unsigned char) will be stored in s[i]. If s[i] is unsigned, this will remain 255 for the comparison with EOF, which will fail.

Even if char is signed, however, the code isn't correct. The comparison will succeed at EOF, but a valid input byte of 0xFF will look just like EOF and terminate the loop prematurely. So regardless of the sign of char, you must always store the return value of getchar in an int for comparison with EOF. Here is how to write the loop portably:

```
    int c, i;
    char s[MAX];

    for (i = 0; i < MAX-1; i++) {
        if ((c = getchar()) == '\n' || c == EOF)
            break;
        s[i] = c;
    }
    s[i] = '\0';
```

Java has no unsigned qualifier; integral types are signed and the (16-bit) char type is not.

Arithmetic or logical shift. Right shifts of signed quantities with the >> operator may be arithmetic (a copy of the sign bit is propagated during the shift) or logical (zeros fill the vacated bits during the shift). Again, learning from the problems with C and C++, Java reserves >> for arithmetic right shift and provides a separate operator >>> for logical right shift.

Byte order. The byte order within short, int, and long is not defined; the byte with the lowest address may be the most significant byte or the least significant byte. This is a hardware-dependent issue that we'll discuss at length later in this chapter.

Alignment of structure and class members. The alignment of items within structures, classes, and unions is not defined, except that members are laid out in the order of declaration. For example, in this structure,

```
struct X {
    char c;
    int i;
};
```

the address of i could be 2, 4, or 8 bytes from the beginning of the structure. A few machines allow ints to be stored on odd boundaries, but most demand that an n-byte primitive data type be stored at an n-byte boundary, for example that doubles, which are usually 8 bytes long, are stored at addresses that are multiples of 8. On top of this, the compiler writer may make further adjustments, such as forcing alignment for performance reasons.

You should never assume that the elements of a structure occupy contiguous memory. Alignment restrictions introduce "holes"; struct X will have at least one byte of unused space. These holes imply that a structure may be bigger than the sum of its member sizes, and will vary from machine to machine. If you're allocating memory to hold one, you must ask for sizeof(struct X) bytes, not sizeof(char) + sizeof(int).

Bitfields. Bitfields are so machine-dependent that no one should use them.

This long list of perils can be skirted by following a few rules. Don't use side effects except for a very few idiomatic constructions like

```
a[i++] = 0;
c = *p++;
*s++ = *t++;
```

Don't compare a char to EOF. Always use sizeof to compute the size of types and objects. Never right shift a signed value. Make sure the data type is big enough for the range of values you are storing in it.

Try several compilers. It's easy to think that you understand portability, but compilers will see problems that you don't, and different compilers sometimes see your program differently, so you should take advantage of their help. Turn on all compiler warnings. Try multiple compilers on the same machine and on different machines. Try a C++ compiler on a C program.

Since the language accepted by different compilers varies, the fact that your program compiles with one compiler is no guarantee that it is even syntactically correct. If several compilers accept your code, however, the odds improve. We have compiled every C program in this book with three C compilers on three unrelated operating systems (Unix, Plan 9, Windows) and also a couple of C++ compilers. This was a sobering experience, but it caught dozens of portability errors that no amount of human scrutiny would have uncovered. They were all trivial to fix.

Of course, compilers cause portability problems too, by making different choices for unspecified behaviors. But our approach still gives us hope. Rather than writing code in a way that amplifies the differences among systems, environments, and compilers, we strive to create software that behaves independently of the variations. In short, we steer clear of features and properties that are likely to vary.

8.2 Headers and Libraries

Headers and libraries provide services that augment the basic language. Examples include input and output through stdio in C, iostream in C++, and java.io in Java. Strictly speaking, these are not part of the language, but they are defined along with the language itself and are expected to be part of any environment that claims to support it. But because libraries cover a broad spectrum of activities, and must often deal with operating system issues, they can still harbor non-portabilities.

Use standard libraries. The same general advice applies here as for the core language: stick to the standard, and within its older, well-established components. C defines a standard library of functions for input and output, string operations, character class tests, storage allocation, and a variety of other tasks. If you confine your operating system interactions to these functions, there is a good chance that your code will behave the same way and perform well as it moves from system to system. But you must still be careful, because there are many implementations of the library and some of them contain features that are not defined in the standard.

ANSI C does not define the string-copying function strdup, yet most environments provide it, even those that claim to conform to the standard. A seasoned programmer may use strdup out of habit, and not be warned that it is non-standard. Later, the program will fail to compile when ported to an environment that does not provide the function. This sort of problem is the major portability headache introduced by libraries; the only solution is to stick to the standard and test your program in a wide variety of environments.

Header files and package definitions declare the interface to standard functions. One problem is that headers tend to be cluttered because they are trying to cope with several languages in the same file. For example, it is common to find a single header file like stdio.h serving pre-ANSI C, ANSI C, and even C++ compilers. In such cases, the file is littered with conditional compilation directives like #if and #ifdef. Because the preprocessor language is not very flexible, the files are complicated and hard to read, and sometimes contain errors.

This excerpt from a header file on one of our systems is better than most, because it is neatly formatted:

```
?      #ifdef _OLD_C
?         extern int fread();
?         extern int fwrite();
?      #else
?      #  if defined(__STDC__) || defined(__cplusplus)
?            extern size_t fread(void*, size_t, size_t, FILE*);
?            extern size_t fwrite(const void*, size_t, size_t, FILE*);
?      #  else /* not __STDC__ || __cplusplus */
?            extern size_t fread();
?            extern size_t fwrite();
?      #  endif /* else not __STDC__ || __cplusplus */
?      #endif
```

Even though the example is relatively clean, it demonstrates that header files (and programs) structured like this are intricate and hard to maintain. It might be easier to use a different header for each compiler or environment. This would require maintaining separate files, but each would be self-contained and appropriate for a particular system, and would reduce the likelihood of errors like including strdup in a strict ANSI C environment.

Header files also can ''pollute'' the name space by declaring a function with the same name as one in your program. For example, our warning-message function weprintf was originally called wprintf, but we discovered that some environments, in anticipation of the new C standard, define a function with that name in stdio.h. We needed to change the name of our function in order to compile on those systems and be ready for the future. If the problem was an erroneous implementation rather than a legitimate change of specification, we could work around it by redefining the name when including the header:

```
?      /* some versions of stdio use wprintf so define it away: */
?      #define wprintf stdio_wprintf
?      #include <stdio.h>
?      #undef wprintf
?      /* code using our wprintf() follows... */
```

This maps all occurrences of wprintf in the header file to stdio_wprintf so they will not interfere with our version. We can then use our own wprintf without changing its name, at the cost of some clumsiness and the risk that a library we link with will call our wprintf expecting to get the official one. For a single function, it's probably not worth the trouble, but some systems make such a mess of the environment that one must resort to extremes to keep the code clean. Be sure to comment what the construction is doing, and don't make it worse by adding conditional compilation. If some environments define wprintf, assume they all do; then the fix is permanent and you won't have to maintain the #ifdef statements as well. It may be easier to switch than fight and it's certainly safer, so that's what we did when we changed the name to weprintf.

Even if you try to stick to the rules and the environment is clean, it is easy to step outside the limits by implicitly assuming that some favorite property is true everywhere. For instance, ANSI C defines six signals that can be caught with signal; the POSIX standard defines 19; most Unix systems support 32 or more. If you want to use a non-ANSI signal, there is clearly a tradeoff between functionality and portability, and you must decide which matters more.

There are many other standards that are not part of a programming language definition; examples include operating system and network interfaces, graphics interfaces, and the like. Some are meant to carry across more than one system, like POSIX; others are specific to one system, like the various Microsoft Windows APIs. Similar advice holds here as well. Your programs will be more portable if you choose widely used and well-established standards, and if you stick to the most central and commonly used aspects.

8.3 Program Organization

There are two major approaches to portability, which we will call union and intersection. The union approach is to use the best features of each particular system, and make the compilation and installation process conditional on properties of the local environment. The resulting code handles the union of all scenarios, taking advantage of the strengths of each system. The drawbacks include the size and complexity of the installation process and the complexity of code riddled with compile-time conditionals.

Use only features available everywhere. The approach we recommend is intersection: use only those features that exist in all target systems; don't use a feature if it isn't available everywhere. One danger is that the requirement of universal availability of features may limit the range of target systems or the capabilities of the program; another is that performance may suffer in some environments.

To compare these approaches, let's look at a couple of examples that use union code and rethink them using intersection. As you will see, union code is by design unportable, despite its stated goal, while intersection code is not only portable but usually simpler.

This small example attempts to cope with an environment that for some reason doesn't have the standard header file stdlib.h:

```
?       #if defined (STDC_HEADERS) || defined (_LIBC)
?       #include <stdlib.h>
?       #else
?       extern void *malloc(unsigned int);
?       extern void *realloc(void *, unsigned int);
?       #endif
```

This style of defense is acceptable if used occasionally, but not if it appears often. It also begs the question of how many other functions from stdlib will eventually find their way into this or similar conditional code. If one is using malloc and realloc, surely `free` will be needed as well, for instance. What if `unsigned int` is not the same as `size_t`, the proper type of the argument to `malloc` and `realloc`? Moreover, how do we know that `STDC_HEADERS` or `_LIBC` are defined, and defined correctly? How can we be sure that there is no other name that should trigger the substitution in some environment? Any conditional code like this is incomplete—unportable—because eventually a system that doesn't match the condition will come along, and we must edit the `#ifdefs`. If we could solve the problem without conditional compilation, we would eliminate the ongoing maintenance headache.

Still, the problem this example is solving is real, so how can we solve it once and for all? Our preference would be to assume that the standard headers exist; it's someone else's problem if they don't. Failing that, it would be simpler to ship with the software a header file that defines `malloc`, `realloc`, and `free`, exactly as ANSI C defines them. This file can always be included, instead of applying band-aids throughout the code. Then we will always know that the necessary interface is available.

Avoid conditional compilation. Conditional compilation with `#ifdef` and similar preprocessor directives is hard to manage, because information tends to get sprinkled throughout the source.

```
?       #ifdef NATIVE
?           char *astring = "convert ASCII to native character set";
?       #else
?       #ifdef MAC
?           char *astring = "convert to Mac textfile format";
?       #else
?       #ifdef DOS
?           char *astring = "convert to DOS textfile format";
?       #else
?           char *astring = "convert to Unix textfile format";
?       #endif /* ?DOS */
?       #endif /* ?MAC */
?       #endif /* ?NATIVE */
```

This excerpt would have been better with `#elif` after each definition, rather than having `#endif`s pile up at the end. But the real problem is that, despite its intention, this code is highly non-portable because it behaves differently on each system and needs to be updated with a new `#ifdef` for every new environment. A single string with more general wording would be simpler, completely portable, and just as informative:

```
    char *astring = "convert to local text format";
```

This needs no conditional code since it is the same on all systems.

Mixing compile-time control flow (determined by `#ifdef` statements) with runtime control flow is much worse, since it is very difficult to read.

```
?     #ifndef DISKSYS
?          for (i = 1; i <= msg->dbgmsg.msg_total; i++)
?     #endif
?     #ifdef DISKSYS
?          i = dbgmsgno;
?          if (i <= msg->dbgmsg.msg_total)
?     #endif
?          {
?               ...
?               if (msg->dbgmsg.msg_total == i)
?     #ifndef DISKSYS
?                    break; /* no more messages to wait for */
?                    about 30 more lines, with further conditional compilation
?     #endif
?          }
```

Even when apparently innocuous, conditional compilation can frequently be replaced by cleaner methods. For instance, #ifdefs are often used to control debugging code:

```
?     #ifdef DEBUG
?          printf(...);
?     #endif
```

but a regular if statement with a constant condition may work just as well:

```
      enum { DEBUG = 0 };
      ...
      if (DEBUG) {
           printf(...);
      }
```

If DEBUG is zero, most compilers won't generate any code for this, but they will check the syntax of the excluded code. An #ifdef, by contrast, can conceal syntax errors that will prevent compilation if the #ifdef is later enabled.

Sometimes conditional compilation excludes large blocks of code:

```
      #ifdef notdef    /* undefined symbol */
           ...
      #endif
```

or

```
      #if 0
           ...
      #endif
```

but conditional code can often be avoided altogether by using files that are conditionally substituted during compilation. We will return to this topic in the next section.

When you must modify a program to adapt to a new environment, don't begin by making a copy of the entire program. Instead, adapt the existing source. You will probably need to make changes to the main body of the code, and if you edit a copy, before long you will have divergent versions. As much as possible, there should only be a single source for a program; if you find you need to change something to port to a particular environment, find a way to make the change work everywhere. Change internal interfaces if you need to, but keep the code consistent and #ifdef-free. This will make your code more portable over time, rather than more specialized. Narrow the intersection, don't broaden the union.

We have spoken out against conditional compilation and shown some of the problems it causes. But the nastiest problem is one we haven't mentioned: it is almost impossible to test. An #ifdef turns a single program into two separately-compiled programs. It is difficult to know whether all the variant programs have been compiled and tested. If a change is made in one #ifdef block, we may need to make it in others, but the changes can be verified only within the environment that causes those #ifdefs to be enabled. If a similar change needs to be made for other configurations, it cannot be tested. Also, when we add a new #ifdef block, it is hard to isolate the change to determine what other conditions need to be satisfied to get here, and where else this problem might need to be fixed. Finally, if something is in code that is conditionally omitted, the compiler doesn't see it. It could be utter nonsense and we won't know until some unlucky customer tries to compile it in the environment that triggers that condition. This program compiles when _MAC is defined and fails when it is not:

```
#ifdef _MAC
    printf("This is Macintosh\r");
#else
    This will give a syntax error on other systems
#endif
```

So our preference is to use only features that are common to all target environments. We can compile and test all the code. If something is a portability problem, we rewrite to avoid it rather than adding conditional code; this way, portability will steadily increase and the program itself will improve rather than becoming more complicated.

Some large systems are distributed with a configuration script to tailor code to the local environment. At compilation time, the script tests the environment properties—location of header files and libraries, byte order within words, size of types, implementations known to be broken (surprisingly common), and so on—and generates configuration parameters or makefiles that will give the right configuration settings for that situation. These scripts can be large and intricate, a significant fraction of a software distribution, and require continual maintenance to keep them working. Sometimes such techniques are necessary but the more portable and #ifdef-free the code is, the simpler and more reliable the configuration and installation will be.

Exercise 8-1. Investigate how your compiler handles code contained within a conditional block like

```
const int DEBUG = 0;
/* or enum { DEBUG = 0 }; */
/* or final boolean DEBUG = false; */

if (DEBUG) {
    ...
}
```

Under what circumstances does it check syntax? When does it generate code? If you have access to more than one compiler, how do the results compare? □

8.4 Isolation

Although we would like to have a single source that compiles without change on all systems, that may be unrealistic. But it is a mistake to have non-portable code scattered throughout a program; that is one of the problems that conditional compilation creates.

Localize system dependencies in separate files. When different code is needed for different systems, the differences should be localized in separate files, one file for each system. For example, the text editor Sam runs on Unix, Windows, and several other operating systems. The system interfaces for these environments vary widely, but most of the code for Sam is identical everywhere. A single file captures the system variations for a particular environment; `unix.c` provides the interface code for Unix systems, and `windows.c` for the Windows environment. These files implement a portable interface to the operating system and hide the differences. Sam is, in effect, written to its own virtual operating system, which is ported to various real systems by writing a couple of hundred lines of C to implement half a dozen small but non-portable operations using locally available system calls.

The graphics environments of these operating systems are almost unrelated. Sam copes by having a portable library for its graphics. Although it's a lot more work to build such a library than to hack the code to adapt to a given system—the code to interface to the X Window system, for example, is about half as big as the rest of Sam put together—the cumulative effort is less in the long run. And as a side benefit, the graphics library is itself valuable, and has been used separately to make a number of other programs portable, too.

Sam is an old program; today, portable graphics environments such as OpenGL, Tcl/Tk and Java are available for a variety of platforms. Writing your code with these rather than a proprietary graphics library will give your program wider utility.

Hide system dependencies behind interfaces. Abstraction is a powerful technique for creating boundaries between portable and non-portable parts of a program. The I/O libraries that accompany most programming languages provide a good example: they present an abstraction of secondary storage in terms of files to be opened and closed, read and written, without any reference to their physical location or structure. Programs that adhere to the interface will run on any system that implements it.

The implementation of Sam provides another example of abstraction. An interface is defined for the file system and graphics operations and the program uses only features of the interface. The interface itself uses whatever facilities are available in the underlying system. That might require significantly different implementations on different systems, but the program that uses the interface is independent of that and should require no changes as it is moved.

The Java approach to portability is a good example of how far this can be carried. A Java program is translated into operations in a "virtual machine," that is, a simulated computer that can be implemented to run on any real machine. Java libraries provide uniform access to features of the underlying system, including graphics, user interface, networking, and the like; the libraries map into whatever the local system provides. In theory, it should be possible to run the same Java program (even after translation) everywhere without change.

8.5 Data Exchange

Textual data moves readily from one system to another and is the simplest portable way to exchange arbitrary information between systems.

Use text for data exchange. Text is easy to manipulate with other tools and to process in unexpected ways. For example, if the output of one program isn't quite right as input for another, an Awk or Perl script can be used to adjust it; grep can be used to select or discard lines; your favorite editor can be used to make more complicated changes. Text files are also much easier to document and may not even need much documentation, since people can read them. A comment in a text file can indicate what version of software is needed to process the data; the first line of a PostScript file, for instance, identifies the encoding:

```
%!PS-Adobe-2.0
```

By contrast, binary files need specialized tools and rarely can be used together even on the same machine. A variety of widely-used programs convert arbitrary binary data into text so it can be shipped with less chance of corruption; these include binhex for Macintosh systems, uuencode and uudecode for Unix, and various tools that use MIME encoding for transferring binary data in mail messages. In Chapter 9, we show a family of pack and unpack routines to encode binary data portably for transmission. The sheer variety of such tools speaks to the problems of binary formats.

There is one continuing irritation with exchanging text: PC systems use a carriage return '\r' and a newline or line-feed '\n' to terminate each line, while Unix systems use only newline. The carriage return is an artifact of an ancient device called a

Teletype that had a carriage-return (CR) operation to return the typing mechanism to the beginning of a line, and a separate line-feed operation (LF) to advance it to the next line.

Even though today's computers have no carriages to return, PC software for the most part continues to expect the combination (familiarly known as CRLF, pronounced "curliff") on each line. If there are no carriage returns, a file may be interpreted as one giant line. Line and character counts can be wrong or change unexpectedly. Some software adapts gracefully, but much does not. PCs are not the only culprits; thanks to a sequence of incremental compatibilities, some modern networking standards such as HTTP also use CRLF to delimit lines.

Our advice is to use standard interfaces, which will treat CRLF consistently on any given system, either (on PCs) by removing \r on input and adding it back on output, or (on Unix) by always using \n rather than CRLF to delimit lines in files. For files that must be moved back and forth, a program to convert files from each format to the other is a necessity.

Exercise 8-2. Write a program to remove spurious carriage returns from a file. Write a second program to add them by replacing each newline with a carriage return and newline. How would you test these programs? □

8.6 Byte Order

Despite the disadvantages discussed above, binary data is sometimes necessary. It can be significantly more compact and faster to decode, factors that make it essential for many problems in computer networking. But binary data has severe portability problems.

At least one issue is decided: all modern machines have 8-bit bytes. Different machines have different representations of any object larger than a byte, however, so relying on specific properties is a mistake. A short integer (typically 16 bits, or two bytes) may have its low-order byte stored at a lower address than the high-order byte (little-endian), or at a higher address (big-endian). The choice is arbitrary, and some machines even support both modes.

Therefore, although big- and little-endian machines see memory as a sequence of words in the same order, they interpret the bytes within a word in the opposite order. In this diagram, the four bytes starting at location 0 will represent the hexadecimal integer 0x11223344 on a big-endian machine and 0x44332211 on a little-endian.

```
       0   1   2   3   4   5   6   7   8
     +---+---+---+---+---+---+---+---+---+---
     |11 |22 |33 |44 |   |   |   |   |   |
     +---+---+---+---+---+---+---+---+---+---
```

To see byte order in action, try this program:

```
/* byteorder: display bytes of a long */
int main(void)
{
    unsigned long x;
    unsigned char *p;
    int i;
    /* 11 22 33 44 => big-endian */
    /* 44 33 22 11 => little-endian */
    /* x = 0x1122334455667788UL; for 64-bit long */
    x = 0x11223344UL;
    p = (unsigned char *) &x;
    for (i = 0; i < sizeof(long); i++)
        printf("%x ", *p++);
    printf("\n");
    return 0;
}
```

On a 32-bit big-endian machine, the output is

```
11 22 33 44
```

but on a little-endian machine, it is

```
44 33 22 11
```

and on the PDP-11 (a vintage 16-bit machine still found in embedded systems), it is

```
22 11 44 33
```

On machines with 64-bit longs, we can make the constant bigger and see similar behaviors.

This may seem like a silly program, but if we wish to send an integer down a byte-wide interface such as a network connection, we need to choose which byte to send first, and that choice is in essence the big-endian/little-endian decision. In other words, this program is doing explicitly what

```
fwrite(&x, sizeof(x), 1, stdout);
```

does implicitly. It is not safe to write an int (or short or long) from one computer and read it as an int on another computer.

For example, if the source computer writes with

```
unsigned short x;
fwrite(&x, sizeof(x), 1, stdout);
```

and the receiving computer reads with

```
unsigned short x;
fread(&x, sizeof(x), 1, stdin);
```

the value of x will not be preserved if the machines have different byte orders. If x starts as 0x1000 it may arrive as 0x0010.

This problem is frequently solved using conditional compilation and ''byte swapping,'' something like this:

```
?      short x;
?      fread(&x, sizeof(x), 1, stdin);
?      #ifdef BIG_ENDIAN
?      /* swap bytes */
?      x = ((x&0xFF) << 8) | ((x>>8) & 0xFF);
?      #endif
```

This approach becomes unwieldy when many two- and four-byte integers are being exchanged. In practice, the bytes end up being swapped more than once as they pass from place to place.

If the situation is bad for short, it's worse for longer data types, because there are more ways to permute the bytes. Add in the variable padding between structure members, alignment restrictions, and the mysterious byte orders of older machines, and the problem looks intractable.

Use a fixed byte order for data exchange. There is a solution. Write the bytes in a canonical order using portable code:

```
unsigned short x;
putchar(x >> 8);       /* write high-order byte */
putchar(x & 0xFF);     /* write low-order byte */
```

then read it back a byte at a time and reassemble it:

```
unsigned short x;
x = getchar() << 8;        /* read high-order byte */
x |= getchar() & 0xFF;     /* read low-order byte */
```

The approach generalizes to structures if you write the values of the structure members in a defined sequence, a byte at a time, without padding. It doesn't matter what byte order you pick; anything consistent will do. The only requirement is that sender and receiver agree on the byte order in transmission and on the number of bytes in each object. In the next chapter we show a pair of routines to wrap up the packing and unpacking of general data.

Byte-at-a-time processing may seem expensive, but relative to the I/O that makes the packing and unpacking necessary, the penalty is minute. Consider the X Window system, in which the client writes data in its native byte order and the server must unpack whatever the client sends. This may save a few instructions on the client end, but the server is made larger and more complicated by the necessity of handling multiple byte orders at the same time—it may well have concurrent big-endian and little-endian clients—and the cost in complexity and code is much more significant. Besides, this is a graphics environment where the overhead to pack bytes will be swamped by the execution of the graphical operation it encodes.

The X Window system negotiates a byte order for the client and requires the server to be capable of both. By contrast, the Plan 9 operating system defines a byte order for messages to the file server (or the graphics server) and data is packed and unpacked with portable code, as above. In practice the run-time effect is not detectable; compared to I/O, the cost of packing the data is insignificant.

Java is a higher-level language than C or C++ and hides byte order completely. The libraries provide a `Serializable` interface that defines how data items are packed for exchange.

If you're working in C or C++, however, you must do the work yourself. The key point about the byte-at-a-time approach is that it solves the problem, without `#ifdefs`, for any machines that have 8-bit bytes. We'll discuss this further in the next chapter.

Still, the best solution is often to convert information to text format, which (except for the CRLF problem) is completely portable; there is no ambiguity about representation. It's not always the right answer, though. Time or space can be critical, and some data, particularly floating point, can lose precision due to roundoff when passed through `printf` and `scanf`. If you must exchange floating-point values accurately, make sure you have a good formatted I/O library; such libraries exist, but may not be part of your existing environment. It's especially hard to represent floating-point values portably in binary, but with care, text will do the job.

There is one subtle portability issue in using standard functions to handle binary files—it is necessary to open such files in binary mode:

```
FILE *fin;

fin = fopen(binary_file, "rb");
c = getc(fin);
```

If the 'b' is omitted, it typically makes no difference at all on Unix systems, but on Windows systems the first control-Z byte (octal 032, hex 1A) of input will terminate reading (we saw this happen to the `strings` program in Chapter 5). On the other hand, using binary mode to read text files will cause \r to be preserved on input, and not generated on output.

8.7 Portability and Upgrade

One of the most frustrating sources of portability problems is system software that changes during its lifetime. These changes can happen at any interface in the system, causing gratuitous incompatibilities between existing versions of programs.

Change the name if you change the specification. Our favorite (if that is the word) example is the changing properties of the Unix `echo` command, whose initial design was just to echo its arguments:

```
% echo hello, world
hello, world
%
```

However, echo became a key part of many shell scripts, and the need to generate formatted output became important. So echo was changed to *interpret* its arguments, somewhat like printf:

```
% echo 'hello\nworld'
hello
world
%
```

This new feature is useful, but causes portability problems for any shell script that depends on the echo command to do nothing more than echo. The behavior of

```
% echo $PATH
```

now depends on which version of echo we have. If the variable happens by accident to contain a backslash, as may happen on DOS or Windows, it may be interpreted by echo. The difference is similar to that between the output from printf(str) and printf("%s", str) if the string str contains a percent sign.

We've told only a fraction of the full echo story, but it illustrates the basic problem: changes to systems can generate different versions of software that *intentionally* behave differently, leading to *unintentional* portability problems. And the problems are very hard to work around. It would have caused much less trouble had the new version of echo been given a distinct name.

As a more direct example, consider the Unix command sum, which prints the size and a checksum of a file. It was written to verify that a transfer of information was successful:

```
% sum file
52313 2 file
%
% copy file to other machine
%
% telnet othermachine
$
$ sum file
52313 2 file
$
```

The checksum is the same after the transfer, so we can be reasonably confident that the old and new copies are identical.

Then systems proliferated, versions mutated, and someone observed that the checksum algorithm wasn't perfect, so sum was modified to use a better algorithm. Someone else made the same observation and gave sum a different better algorithm. And so on, so that today there are multiple versions of sum, each giving a different answer. We copied one file to nearby machines to see what sum computed:

```
% sum file
52313 2 file
%
% copy file to machine 2
% copy file to machine 3
% telnet machine2
$
$ sum file
eaa0d468     713      file
$ telnet machine3
>
> sum file
62992    1 file
>
```

Is the file corrupted, or do we just have different versions of sum? Maybe both.

Thus sum is the perfect portability disaster: a program intended to aid in the copying of software from one machine to another has different incompatible versions that render it useless for its original purpose.

For its simple task, the original sum was fine; its low-tech checksum algorithm was adequate. ''Fixing'' it may have made it a better program, but not by much, and certainly not enough to make the incompatibility worthwhile. The problem is not the enhancements but that incompatible programs have the same name. The change introduced a versioning problem that will plague us for years.

Maintain compatibility with existing programs and data. When a new version of software such as a word processor is shipped, it's common for it to read files produced by the old version. That's what one would expect: as unanticipated features are added, the format must evolve. But new versions sometimes fail to provide a way to *write* the previous file format. Users of the new version, even if they don't use the new features, cannot share their files with people using the older software and everyone is forced to upgrade. Whether an engineering oversight or a marketing strategy, this design is most regrettable.

Backwards compatibility is the ability of a program to meet its older specification. If you're going to change a program, make sure you don't break old software and data that depend on it. Document the changes well, and provide ways to recover the original behavior. Most important, consider whether the change you're proposing is a genuine improvement when weighed against the cost of any non-portability you will introduce.

8.8 Internationalization

If one lives in the United States, it's easy to forget that English is not the only language, ASCII is not the only character set, $ is not the only currency symbol, dates can be written with the day first, times can be based on a 24-hour clock, and so on. So another aspect of portability, taken broadly, deals with making programs portable across language and cultural boundaries. This is potentially a very big topic, but we have space to point out only a few basic concerns.

Internationalization is the term for making a program run without assumptions about its cultural environment. The problems are many, ranging from character sets to the interpretation of icons in interfaces.

Don't assume ASCII. Character sets are richer than ASCII in most parts of the world. The standard character-testing functions in `ctype.h` generally hide these differences:

```
if (isalpha(c)) ...
```

is independent of the specific encoding of characters, and in addition will work correctly in locales where there are more or fewer letters than those from *a* to *z* if the program is compiled in that locale. Of course, even the name `isalpha` speaks to its origins; some languages don't have alphabets at all.

Most European countries augment the ASCII encoding, which defines values only up to `0x7F` (7 bits), with extra characters to represent the letters of their language. The Latin-1 encoding, commonly used throughout Western Europe, is an ASCII superset that specifies byte values from 80 to FF for symbols and accented characters; E7, for instance, represents the accented letter ç. The English word boy is represented in ASCII (or Latin-1) by three bytes with hexadecimal values 62 6F 79, while the French word garçon is represented in Latin-1 by the bytes 67 61 72 E7 6F 6E. Other languages define other symbols, but they can't all fit in the 128 values left unused by ASCII, so there are a variety of conflicting standards for the characters assigned to bytes 80 through FF.

Some languages don't fit in 8 bits at all; there are thousands of characters in the major Asian languages. The encodings used in China, Japan, and Korea all have 16 bits per character. As a result, to read a document written in one language on a computer set up for another is a major portability problem. Assuming the characters arrive intact, to read a Chinese document on an American computer involves, at a minimum, special software and fonts. If we want to use Chinese, English, and Russian together, the obstacles are formidable.

The Unicode character set is an attempt to ameliorate this situation by providing a single encoding for all languages throughout the world. Unicode, which is compatible with the 16-bit subset of the ISO 10646 standard, uses 16 bits per character, with values 00FF and below corresponding to Latin-1. Thus the word garçon is represented by the 16-bit values 0067 0061 0072 00E7 006F 006E, while the Cyrillic alphabet occupies values 0401 through 04FF, and the ideographic languages occupy a large block starting at 3000. All well-known languages, and many not so well-known, are represented in Unicode, so it is the encoding of choice for transferring documents between countries or for storing multilingual text. Unicode is becoming popular on the Internet and some systems even support it as a standard format; Java, for example, uses Unicode as its native character set for strings. The Plan 9 and Inferno operating systems use Unicode throughout, even for the names of files and users. Microsoft

Windows supports the Unicode character set, but does not mandate it; most Windows applications still work best in ASCII but practice is rapidly evolving towards Unicode.

Unicode introduces a problem, though: characters no longer fit in a byte, so Unicode text suffers from the byte-order confusion. To avoid this, Unicode documents are usually translated into a byte-stream encoding called UTF-8 before being sent between programs or over a network. Each 16-bit character is encoded as a sequence of 1, 2, or 3 bytes for transmission. The ASCII character set uses values 00 through 7F, all of which fit in a single byte using UTF-8, so UTF-8 is backwards compatible with ASCII. Values between 80 and 7FF are represented in two bytes, and values 800 and above are represented in three bytes. The word garçon appears in UTF-8 as the bytes 67 61 72 C3 A7 6F 6E; Unicode value E7, the ç character, is represented as the two bytes C3 A7 in UTF-8.

The backwards compatibility of UTF-8 and ASCII is a boon, since it permits programs that treat text as an uninterpreted byte stream to work with Unicode text in any language. We tried the Markov programs from Chapter 3 on UTF-8 encoded text in Russian, Greek, Japanese, and Chinese, and they ran without problems. For the European languages, whose words are separated by ASCII space, tab, or newline, the output was reasonable nonsense. For the others, it would be necessary to change the word-breaking rules to get output closer in spirit to the intent of the program.

C and C++ support ''wide characters,'' which are 16-bit or larger integers and some accompanying functions that can be used to process characters in Unicode or other large character sets. Wide character string literals are written as L"...", but they introduce further portability problems: a program with wide character constants can only be understood when examined on a display that uses that character set. Since characters must be converted into byte streams such as UTF-8 for portable transmission between machines, C provides functions to convert wide characters to and from bytes. But which conversion do we use? The interpretation of the character set and the definition of the byte-stream encoding are hidden in the libraries and difficult to extract; the situation is unsatisfactory at best. It is possible that in some rosy future everyone will agree on which character set to use but a likelier scenario will be confusion reminiscent of the byte-order problems that still pester us.

Don't assume English. Creators of interfaces must keep in mind that different languages often take significantly different numbers of characters to say the same thing, so there must be enough room on the screen and in arrays.

What about error messages? At the very least, they should be free of jargon and slang that will be meaningful only among a selected population; writing them in simple language is a good start. One common technique is to collect the text of all messages in one spot so that they can be replaced easily by translations into other languages.

There are plenty of cultural dependencies, like the mm/dd/yy date format that is used only in North America. If there is any prospect that software will be used in another country, this kind of dependency should be avoided or minimized. Icons in graphical interfaces are often culture-dependent; many icons are inscrutable to natives of the intended environment, let alone people from other backgrounds.

8.9 Summary

Portable code is an ideal that is well worth striving for, since so much time is wasted making changes to move a program from one system to another or to keep it running as it evolves and the systems it runs on changes. Portability doesn't come for free, however. It requires care in implementation and knowledge of portability issues in all the potential target systems.

We have dubbed the two approaches to portability union and intersection. The union approach amounts to writing versions that work on each target, merging the code as much as possible with mechanisms like conditional compilation. The drawbacks are many: it takes more code and often more complicated code, it's hard to keep up to date, and it's hard to test.

The intersection approach is to write as much of the code as possible in a form that will work without change on each system. Inescapable system dependencies are encapsulated in single source files that act as an interface between the program and the underlying system. The intersection approach has drawbacks too, including potential loss of efficiency and even of features, but in the long run, the benefits outweigh the costs.

Supplementary Reading

There are many descriptions of programming languages, but few are precise enough to serve as definitive references. The authors admit to a personal bias towards *The C Programming Language* by Brian Kernighan and Dennis Ritchie (Prentice Hall, 1988), but it is not a replacement for the standard. Sam Harbison and Guy Steele's *C: A Reference Manual* (Prentice Hall, 1994), now in its fourth edition, has good advice on C portability. The official C and C++ standards are available from ISO, the International Organization for Standardization. The closest thing to an official standard for Java is *The Java Language Specification*, by James Gosling, Bill Joy, and Guy Steele (Addison-Wesley, 1996).

Rich Stevens's *Advanced Programming in the Unix Environment* (Addison-Wesley, 1992) is an excellent resource for Unix programmers, and provides thorough coverage of portability issues among Unix variants.

POSIX, the Portable Operating System Interface, is an international standard defining commands and libraries based on Unix. It provides a standard environment, source code portability for applications, and a uniform interface to I/O, file systems and processes. It is described in a series of books published by the IEEE.

The term "big-endian" was coined by Jonathan Swift in 1726. The article by Danny Cohen, "On holy wars and a plea for peace," *IEEE Computer*, October 1981, is a wonderful fable about byte order that introduced the "endian" terms to computing.

The Plan 9 system developed at Bell Labs has made portability a central priority. The system compiles from the same #ifdef-free source on a variety of processors and uses the Unicode character set throughout. Recent versions of Sam (first described in "The Text Editor sam," *Software—Practice and Experience*, **17**, 11, pp. 813-845, 1987) use Unicode, but run on a wide variety of systems. The problems of dealing with 16-bit character sets like Unicode are discussed in the paper by Rob Pike and Ken Thompson, "Hello World or Καλημέρα κόσμε or こんにちは世界," *Proceedings of the Winter 1993 USENIX Conference*, San Diego, 1993, pp. 43-50. The UTF-8 encoding made its first appearance in this paper. This paper is also available at the Plan 9 web site at Bell Labs, as is the current version of Sam.

The Inferno system, which is based on the Plan 9 experience, is somewhat analogous to Java, in that it defines a virtual machine that can be implemented on any real machine, provides a language (Limbo) that is translated into instructions for this virtual machine, and uses Unicode as its native character set. It also includes a virtual operating system that provides a portable interface to a variety of commercial systems. It is described in "The Inferno Operating System," by Sean Dorward, Rob Pike, David Leo Presotto, Dennis M. Ritchie, Howard W. Trickey, and Philip Winterbottom, *Bell Labs Technical Journal*, **2**, 1, Winter, 1997.

9

$$\overline{}$$

Notation

Perhaps of all the creations of man
language is the most astonishing.

Giles Lytton Strachey, *Words and Poetry*

The right language can make all the difference in how easy it is to write a program. This is why a practicing programmer's arsenal holds not only general-purpose languages like C and its relatives, but also programmable shells, scripting languages, and lots of application-specific languages.

The power of good notation reaches beyond traditional programming into specialized problem domains. Regular expressions let us write compact (if occasionally cryptic) definitions of classes of strings; HTML lets us define the layout of interactive documents, often using embedded programs in other languages such as JavaScript; PostScript expresses an entire document—this book, for example—as a stylized program. Spreadsheets and word processors often include programming languages like Visual Basic to evaluate expressions, access information, or control layout.

If you find yourself writing too much code to do a mundane job, or if you have trouble expressing the process comfortably, maybe you're using the wrong language. If the right language doesn't yet exist, that might be an opportunity to create it yourself. Inventing a language doesn't necessarily mean building the successor to Java; often a thorny problem can be cleared up by a change of notation. Consider the format strings in the `printf` family, which are a compact and expressive way to control the display of printed values.

In this chapter, we'll talk about how notation can solve problems, and demonstrate some of the techniques you can use to implement your own special-purpose languages. We'll even explore the possibilities of having one program write another program, an apparently extreme use of notation that happens more often, and is far easier to do, than many programmers realize.

9.1 Formatting Data

There is always a gap between what we want to say to the computer (''solve my problem'') and what we are required to say to get a job done. The narrower this gap, the better. Good notation makes it easier to say what we want and harder to say the wrong thing by mistake. Sometimes, good notation can provide new insight, allowing us to solve problems that seemed too difficult, or even lead us to new discoveries.

Little languages are specialized notations for narrow domains. They not only provide a good interface but also help organize the program that implements them. The printf control sequences are a good example:

```
printf("%d %6.2f %-10.10s\n", i, f, s);
```

Each % in the format string signals a place to interpolate the value of the next printf argument; after some optional flags and field widths, the terminating letter says what kind of parameter to expect. This notation is compact, intuitive, and easy to write, and the implementation is straightforward. The alternatives in C++ (iostream) and Java (java.io) seem more awkward since they don't provide special notation, although they extend to user-defined types and offer type-checking.

Some non-standard implementations of printf let you add your own conversions to the built-in set. This is convenient if you have other data types that need output conversion. For example, a compiler might use %L for line number and file name; a graphics system might use %P for a point and %R for a rectangle. The cryptic string of letters and numbers for retrieving stock quotes that we saw in Chapter 4 was in the same spirit, a compact notation for arranging combinations of stock data.

We can synthesize similar examples in C and C++. Suppose we want to send packets containing various combinations of data types from one system to another. As we saw in Chapter 8, the cleanest solution may be to convert to a textual representation. For a standard network protocol, though, the format is likely to be binary for reasons of efficiency or size. How can we write the packet-handling code to be portable, efficient, and easy to use?

To make this discussion concrete, imagine that we plan to send packets of 8-bit, 16-bit, and 32-bit data items from system to system. ANSI C says that we can always store at least 8 bits in a char, 16 bits in a short, and 32 bits in a long, so we will use these data types to represent our values. There will be many types of packets; packet type 1 might have a 1-byte type specifier, a 2-byte count, a 1-byte value and a 4-byte data item:

0x01	cnt_1	cnt_0	val	$data_3$	$data_2$	$data_1$	$data_0$

Packet type 2 might contain a short and two long data words:

0x02	cnt_1	cnt_0	$dw1_3$	$dw1_2$	$dw1_1$	$dw1_0$	$dw2_3$	$dw2_2$	$dw2_1$	$dw2_0$

One approach is to write pack and unpack functions for each possible packet type:

```
int pack_type1(unsigned char *buf, unsigned short count,
        unsigned char val, unsigned long data)
{
    unsigned char *bp;

    bp = buf;
    *bp++ = 0x01;
    *bp++ = count >> 8;
    *bp++ = count;
    *bp++ = val;
    *bp++ = data >> 24;
    *bp++ = data >> 16;
    *bp++ = data >> 8;
    *bp++ = data;
    return bp - buf;
}
```

For a realistic protocol, there will be dozens of such routines, all variations on a theme. The routines could be simplified by using macros or functions to handle the basic data types (short, long, and so on), but even so, such repetitive code is easy to get wrong, hard to read, and hard to maintain.

The inherent repetitiveness of the code is a clue that notation can help. Borrowing the idea from printf, we can define a tiny specification language in which each packet is described by a brief string that captures the packet layout. Successive elements of the packet are encoded with c for an 8-bit character, s for a 16-bit short integer, and l for a 32-bit long integer. Thus, for example, the packet type 1 built by our example above, including the initial type byte, might be described by the format string cscl. Then we can use a single pack function to create packets of any type; this packet would be created with

```
pack(buf, "cscl", 0x01, count, val, data);
```

Because our format string contains only data definitions, there's no need for the % characters used by printf.

In practice, information at the beginning of the packet might tell the recipient how to decode the rest, but we'll assume the first byte of the packet can be used to determine the layout. The sender encodes the data in this format and ships it; the receiver reads the packet, picks off the first byte, and uses that to decode what follows.

Here is an implementation of pack, which fills buf with the encoded representation of its arguments as determined by the format. We make all values unsigned, including the bytes in the packet buffer, to avoid sign-extension problems. We also use some conventional typedefs to keep the declarations short:

```
typedef unsigned char  uchar;
typedef unsigned short ushort;
typedef unsigned long  ulong;
```

Like sprintf, strcpy, and similar functions, pack assumes that the buffer is big enough to hold the result; it is the caller's responsibility to ensure this. There is also no attempt to detect mismatches between the format and the argument list.

```c
#include <stdarg.h>

/* pack: pack binary items into buf, return length */
int pack(uchar *buf, char *fmt, ...)
{
    va_list args;
    char *p;
    uchar *bp;
    ushort s;
    ulong l;

    bp = buf;
    va_start(args, fmt);
    for (p = fmt; *p != '\0'; p++) {
        switch (*p) {
        case 'c':   /* char */
            *bp++ = va_arg(args, int);
            break;
        case 's':   /* short */
            s = va_arg(args, int);
            *bp++ = s >> 8;
            *bp++ = s;
            break;
        case 'l':   /* long */
            l = va_arg(args, ulong);
            *bp++ = l >> 24;
            *bp++ = l >> 16;
            *bp++ = l >> 8;
            *bp++ = l;
            break;
        default:    /* illegal type character */
            va_end(args);
            return -1;
        }
    }
    va_end(args);
    return bp - buf;
}
```

The pack routine uses the stdarg.h header more extensively than eprintf did in Chapter 4. The successive arguments are extracted using the macro va_arg, with first operand the variable of type va_list set up by calling va_start and second operand the *type* of the argument (this is why va_arg is a macro, not a function). When processing is done, va_end must be called. Although the arguments for 'c' and 's' represent char and short values, they must be extracted as ints because C promotes char and short arguments to int when they are represented by an ellipsis ... parameter.

Each `pack_type` routine will now be one line long, marshaling its arguments into a call of pack:

```
/* pack_type1: pack format 1 packet */
int pack_type1(uchar *buf, ushort count, uchar val, ulong data)
{
    return pack(buf, "cscl", 0x01, count, val, data);
}
```

To unpack, we can do the same thing: rather than write separate code to crack each packet format, we call a single unpack with a format string. This centralizes the conversion in one place:

```
/* unpack: unpack packed items from buf, return length */
int unpack(uchar *buf, char *fmt, ...)
{
    va_list args;
    char *p;
    uchar *bp, *pc;
    ushort *ps;
    ulong *pl;

    bp = buf;
    va_start(args, fmt);
    for (p = fmt; *p != '\0'; p++) {
        switch (*p) {
        case 'c':    /* char */
            pc = va_arg(args, uchar*);
            *pc = *bp++;
            break;
        case 's':    /* short */
            ps = va_arg(args, ushort*);
            *ps  = *bp++ << 8;
            *ps |= *bp++;
            break;
        case 'l':    /* long */
            pl = va_arg(args, ulong*);
            *pl  = *bp++ << 24;
            *pl |= *bp++ << 16;
            *pl |= *bp++ << 8;
            *pl |= *bp++;
            break;
        default:     /* illegal type character */
            va_end(args);
            return -1;
        }
    }
    va_end(args);
    return bp - buf;
}
```

Like scanf, unpack must return multiple values to its caller, so its arguments are pointers to the variables where the results are to be stored. Its function value is the number of bytes in the packet, which can be used for error checking.

Because the values are unsigned and because we stayed within the sizes that ANSI C defines for the data types, this code transfers data portably even between machines with different sizes for short and long. Provided the program that uses pack does not try to send as a long (for example) a value that cannot be represented in 32 bits, the value will be received correctly. In effect, we transfer the low 32 bits of the value. If we need to send larger values, we could define another format.

The type-specific unpacking routines that call unpack are easy:

```
/* unpack_type2: unpack and process type 2 packet */
int unpack_type2(int n, uchar *buf)
{
    uchar c;
    ushort count;
    ulong dw1, dw2;

    if (unpack(buf, "csll", &c, &count, &dw1, &dw2) != n)
        return -1;
    assert(c == 0x02);
    return process_type2(count, dw1, dw2);
}
```

To call unpack_type2, we must first recognize that we have a type 2 packet, which implies a receiver loop something like this:

```
while ((n = readpacket(network, buf, BUFSIZ)) > 0) {
    switch (buf[0]) {
    default:
        eprintf("bad packet type 0x%x", buf[0]);
        break;
    case 1:
        unpack_type1(n, buf);
        break;
    case 2:
        unpack_type2(n, buf);
        break;
    ...
    }
}
```

This style of programming can get long-winded. A more compact method is to define a table of function pointers whose entries are the unpacking routines indexed by type:

```
int (*unpackfn[])(int, uchar *) = {
    unpack_type0,
    unpack_type1,
    unpack_type2,
};
```

Each function in the table parses a packet, checks the result, and initiates further processing for that packet. The table makes the recipient's job straightforward:

```
/* receive: read packets from network, process them */
void receive(int network)
{
    uchar type, buf[BUFSIZ];
    int n;

    while ((n = readpacket(network, buf, BUFSIZ)) > 0) {
        type = buf[0];
        if (type >= NELEMS(unpackfn))
            eprintf("bad packet type 0x%x", type);
        if ((*unpackfn[type])(n, buf) < 0)
            eprintf("protocol error, type %x length %d",
                type, n);
    }
}
```

Each packet's handling code is compact, in a single place, and easy to maintain. The receiver is largely independent of the protocol itself; it's clean and fast, too.

This example is based on some real code for a commercial networking protocol. Once the author realized this approach could work, a few thousand repetitive, error-prone lines of code shrunk to a few hundred lines that are easily maintained. Notation reduced the mess enormously.

Exercise 9-1. Modify pack and unpack to transmit signed values correctly, even between machines with different sizes for short and long. How should you modify the format strings to specify a signed data item? How can you test the code to check, for example, that it correctly transfers a -1 from a computer with 32-bit longs to one with 64-bit longs? □

Exercise 9-2. Extend pack and unpack to handle strings; one possibility is to include the length of the string in the format string. Extend them to handle repeated items with a count. How does this interact with the encoding of strings? □

Exercise 9-3. The table of function pointers in the C program above is at the heart of C++'s virtual function mechanism. Rewrite pack and unpack and receive in C++ to take advantage of this notational convenience. □

Exercise 9-4. Write a command-line version of printf that prints its second and subsequent arguments in the format given by its first argument. Some shells already provide this as a built-in. □

Exercise 9-5. Write a function that implements the format specifications found in spreadsheet programs or in Java's DecimalFormat class, which display numbers according to patterns that indicate mandatory and optional digits, location of decimal points and commas, and so on. To illustrate, the format

```
##,##0.00
```

specifies a number with two decimal places, at least one digit to the left of the decimal point, a comma after the thousands digit, and blank-filling up to the ten-thousands place. It would represent 12345.67 as 12,345.67 and .4 as _____0.40 (using underscores to stand for blanks). For a full specification, look at the definition of DecimalFormat or a spreadsheet program. □

9.2 Regular Expressions

The format specifiers for pack and unpack are a very simple notation for defining the layout of packets. Our next topic is a slightly more complicated but much more expressive notation, *regular expressions*, which specify patterns of text. We've used regular expressions occasionally throughout the book without defining them precisely; they are familiar enough to be understood without much explanation. Although regular expressions are pervasive in the Unix programming environment, they are not as widely used in other systems, so in this section we'll demonstrate some of their power. In case you don't have a regular expression library handy, we'll also show a rudimentary implementation.

There are several flavors of regular expressions, but in spirit they are all the same, a way to describe patterns of literal characters, along with repetitions, alternatives, and shorthands for classes of characters like digits or letters. One familiar example is the so-called ''wildcards'' used in command-line processors or shells to match patterns of file names. Typically * is taken to mean ''any string of characters'' so, for example, a command like

```
C:\> del *.exe
```

uses a pattern that matches all files whose names consist of any string ending in ''.exe''. As is often the case, details differ from system to system, and even from program to program.

Although the vagaries of different programs may suggest that regular expressions are an *ad hoc* mechanism, in fact they are a language with a formal grammar and a precise meaning for each utterance in the language. Furthermore, the right implementation can run very fast; a combination of theory and engineering practice makes a lot of difference, an example of the benefit of specialized algorithms that we alluded to in Chapter 2.

A regular expression is a sequence of characters that defines a set of matching strings. Most characters simply match themselves, so the regular expression abc will match that string of letters wherever it occurs. In addition a few *metacharacters* indicate repetition or grouping or positioning. In conventional Unix regular expressions, ^ stands for the beginning of a string and $ for the end, so ^x matches an x only at the beginning of a string, x$ matches an x only at the end, ^x$ matches x only if it is the sole character of the string, and ^$ matches the empty string.

The character "." matches any character, so x.y matches xay, x2y and so on, but not xy or xaby, and ^.$ matches a string with a single arbitrary character.

A set of characters inside brackets [] matches any one of the enclosed characters, so [0123456789] matches a single digit; it may be abbreviated [0-9].

These building blocks are combined with parentheses for grouping, | for alternatives, * for zero or more occurrences, + for one or more occurrences, and ? for zero or one occurrences. Finally, \ is used as a prefix to quote a metacharacter and turn off its special meaning; * is a literal * and \\ is a literal backslash.

The best-known regular expression tool is the program grep that we've mentioned several times. The program is a marvelous example of the value of notation. It applies a regular expression to each line of its input files and prints those lines that contain matching strings. This simple specification, plus the power of regular expressions, lets it solve many day-to-day tasks. In the following examples, note that the regular expression syntax used in the argument to grep is different from the wildcards used to specify a set of file names; this difference reflects the different uses.

Which source file uses class Regexp?

```
% grep Regexp *.java
```

Which implements it?

```
% grep 'class.*Regexp' *.java
```

Where did I save that mail from Bob?

```
% grep '^From:.* bob@' mail/*
```

How many non-blank source lines are there in this program?

```
% grep '.' *.c++ | wc
```

With flags to print line numbers of matched lines, count matches, do case-insensitive matching, invert the sense (select lines that don't match the pattern), and perform other variations of the basic idea, grep is so widely used that it has become the classic example of tool-based programming.

Unfortunately, not every system comes with grep or an equivalent. Some systems include a regular expression library, usually called regex or regexp, that you can use to write a version of grep. If neither option is available, it's easy to implement a modest subset of the full regular expression language. Here we present an implementation of regular expressions, and grep to go along with it; for simplicity, the only metacharacters are ^ $. and *, with * specifying a repetition of the single previous period or literal character. This subset provides a large fraction of the power with a tiny fraction of the programming complexity of general expressions.

Let's start with the match function itself. Its job is to determine whether a text string matches a regular expression:

```
/* match: search for regexp anywhere in text */
int match(char *regexp, char *text)
{
    if (regexp[0] == '^')
        return matchhere(regexp+1, text);
    do {    /* must look even if string is empty */
        if (matchhere(regexp, text))
            return 1;
    } while (*text++ != '\0');
    return 0;
}
```

If the regular expression begins with ∧, the text must begin with a match of the remainder of the expression. Otherwise, we walk along the text, using `matchhere` to see if the text matches at any position. As soon as we find a match, we're done. Note the use of a do-while: expressions can match the empty string (for example, $ matches the empty string at the end of a line and .* matches any number of characters, including zero), so we must call `matchhere` even if the text is empty.

The recursive function `matchhere` does most of the work:

```
/* matchhere: search for regexp at beginning of text */
int matchhere(char *regexp, char *text)
{
    if (regexp[0] == '\0')
        return 1;
    if (regexp[1] == '*')
        return matchstar(regexp[0], regexp+2, text);
    if (regexp[0] == '$' && regexp[1] == '\0')
        return *text == '\0';
    if (*text!='\0' && (regexp[0]=='.' || regexp[0]==*text))
        return matchhere(regexp+1, text+1);
    return 0;
}
```

If the regular expression is empty, we have reached the end and thus have found a match. If the expression ends with $, it matches only if the text is also at the end. If the expression begins with a period, that matches any character. Otherwise the expression begins with a plain character that matches itself in the text. A ∧ or $ that appears in the middle of a regular expression is thus taken as a literal character, not a metacharacter.

Notice that `matchhere` calls itself after matching one character of pattern and string, so the depth of recursion can be as much as the length of the pattern.

The one tricky case occurs when the expression begins with a starred character, for example x*. Then we call `matchstar`, with first argument the operand of the star (x) and subsequent arguments the pattern after the star and the text.

```
/* matchstar; search for c*regexp at beginning of text */
int matchstar(int c, char *regexp, char *text)
{
    do {    /* a * matches zero or more instances */
        if (matchhere(regexp, text))
            return 1;
    } while (*text != '\0' && (*text++ == c || c == '.'));
    return 0;
}
```

Here is another do-while, again triggered by the requirement that the regular expression x* can match zero characters. The loop checks whether the text matches the remaining expression, trying at each position of the text as long as the first character matches the operand of the star.

This is an admittedly unsophisticated implementation, but it works, and at fewer than 30 lines of code, it shows that regular expressions don't need advanced techniques to be put to use.

We'll soon present some ideas for extending the code. For now, though, let's write a version of grep that uses match. Here is the main routine:

```
/* grep main: search for regexp in files */
int main(int argc, char *argv[])
{
    int i, nmatch;
    FILE *f;

    setprogname("grep");
    if (argc < 2)
        eprintf("usage: grep regexp [file ...]");
    nmatch = 0;
    if (argc == 2) {
        if (grep(argv[1], stdin, NULL))
            nmatch++;
    } else {
        for (i = 2; i < argc; i++) {
            f = fopen(argv[i], "r");
            if (f == NULL) {
                weprintf("can't open %s:", argv[i]);
                continue;
            }
            if (grep(argv[1], f, argc>3 ? argv[i] : NULL) > 0)
                nmatch++;
            fclose(f);
        }
    }
    return nmatch == 0;
}
```

It is conventional that C programs return 0 for success and non-zero values for various failures. Our grep, like the Unix version, defines success as finding a matching line, so it returns 0 if there were any matches, 1 if there were none, and 2 (via `eprintf`) if an error occurred. These status values can be tested by other programs like a shell.

The function `grep` scans a single file, calling `match` on each line:

```
/* grep: search for regexp in file */
int grep(char *regexp, FILE *f, char *name)
{
    int n, nmatch;
    char buf[BUFSIZ];

    nmatch = 0;
    while (fgets(buf, sizeof buf, f) != NULL) {
        n = strlen(buf);
        if (n > 0 && buf[n-1] == '\n')
            buf[n-1] = '\0';
        if (match(regexp, buf)) {
            nmatch++;
            if (name != NULL)
                printf("%s:", name);
            printf("%s\n", buf);
        }
    }
    return nmatch;
}
```

The main routine doesn't quit if it fails to open a file. This design was chosen because it's common to say something like

```
% grep herpolhode *.*
```

and find that one of the files in the directory can't be read. It's better for `grep` to keep going after reporting the problem, rather than to give up and force the user to type the file list manually to avoid the problem file. Also, notice that `grep` prints the file name and the matching line, but suppresses the name if it is reading standard input or a single file. This may seem an odd design, but it reflects an idiomatic style of use based on experience. When given only one input, `grep`'s task is usually selection, and the file name would clutter the output. But if it is asked to search through many files, the task is most often to find all occurrences of something, and the names are informative. Compare

```
% strings markov.exe | grep 'DOS mode'
```

with

```
% grep grammer chapter*.txt
```

These touches are part of what makes `grep` so popular, and demonstrate that notation must be packaged with human engineering to build a natural, effective tool.

Our implementation of `match` returns as soon as it finds a match. For `grep`, that is a fine default. But for implementing a substitution (search-and-replace) operator in a text editor the *leftmost longest* match is more suitable. For example, given the text "aaaaa" the pattern a* matches the null string at the beginning of the text, but it seems more natural to match all five a's. To cause match to find the leftmost longest string, matchstar must be rewritten to be *greedy*: rather than looking at each character of the text from left to right, it should skip over the longest string that matches the starred operand, then back up if the rest of the string doesn't match the rest of the pattern. In other words, it should run from right to left. Here is a version of matchstar that does leftmost longest matching:

```
/* matchstar: leftmost longest search for c*regexp */
int matchstar(int c, char *regexp, char *text)
{
    char *t;

    for (t = text; *t != '\0' && (*t == c || c == '.'); t++)
        ;
    do {    /* * matches zero or more */
        if (matchhere(regexp, t))
            return 1;
    } while (t-- > text);
    return 0;
}
```

It doesn't matter which match grep finds, since it is just checking for the presence of any match and printing the whole line. So since leftmost longest matching does extra work, it's not necessary for grep, but for a substitution operator, it is essential.

Our grep is competitive with system-supplied versions, regardless of the regular expression. There are pathological expressions that can cause exponential behavior, such as a*a*a*a*b when given the input aaaaaaaaac, but the exponential behavior is present in some commercial implementations too. A grep variant available on Unix, called egrep, uses a more sophisticated matching algorithm that guarantees linear performance by avoiding backtracking when a partial match fails.

What about making match handle full regular expressions? These would include character classes like [a-zA-Z] to match an alphabetic character, the ability to quote a metacharacter (for example to search for a literal period), parentheses for grouping, and alternatives (abc or def). The first step is to help match by compiling the pattern into a representation that is easier to scan. It is expensive to parse a character class every time we compare it against a character; a pre-computed representation based on bit vectors could make character classes much more efficient. For full regular expressions, with parentheses and alternatives, the implementation must be more sophisticated, but can use some of the techniques we'll talk about later in this chapter.

Exercise 9-6. How does the performance of match compare to strstr when searching for plain text? □

Exercise 9-7. Write a non-recursive version of matchhere and compare its performance to the recursive version. □

Exercise 9-8. Add some options to grep. Popular ones include -v to invert the sense of the match, -i to do case-insensitive matching of alphabetics, and -n to include line numbers in the output. How should the line numbers be printed? Should they be printed on the same line as the matching text? □

Exercise 9-9. Add the + (one or more) and ? (zero or one) operators to match. The pattern a+bb? matches one or more a's followed by one or two b's. □

Exercise 9-10. The current implementation of match turns off the special meaning of ∧ and $ if they don't begin or end the expression, and of * if it doesn't immediately follow a literal character or a period. A more conventional design is to quote a metacharacter by preceding it with a backslash. Fix match to handle backslashes this way. □

Exercise 9-11. Add character classes to match. Character classes specify a match for any one of the characters in the brackets. They can be made more convenient by adding ranges, for example [a-z] to match any lower-case letter, and inverting the sense, for example [∧0-9] to match any character *except* a digit. □

Exercise 9-12. Change match to use the leftmost-longest version of matchstar, and modify it to return the character positions of the beginning and end of the matched text. Use that to build a program gres that is like grep but prints every input line after substituting new text for text that matches the pattern, as in

```
% gres 'homoiousian' 'homoousian' mission.stmt
```

□

Exercise 9-13. Modify match and grep to work with UTF-8 strings of Unicode characters. Because UTF-8 and Unicode are a superset of ASCII, this change is upwardly compatible. Regular expressions, as well as the searched text, will also need to work properly with UTF-8. How should character classes be implemented? □

Exercise 9-14. Write an automatic tester for regular expressions that generates test expressions and test strings to search. If you can, use an existing library as a reference implementation; perhaps you will find bugs in it too. □

9.3 Programmable Tools

Many tools are structured around a special-purpose language. The grep program is just one of a family of tools that use regular expressions or other languages to solve programming problems.

One of the first examples was the command interpreter or job control language. It was realized early that common sequences of commands could be placed in a file, and an instance of the command interpreter or *shell* could be executed with that file as input. From there it was a short step to adding parameters, conditionals, loops, variables, and all the other trappings of a conventional programming language. The main difference was that there was only one data type—strings—and the operators in shell programs tended to be entire programs that did interesting computations. Although shell programming has fallen out of favor, often giving ground to alternatives like Perl in command environments and to pushing buttons in graphical user interfaces, it is still an effective way to build up complex operations out of simpler pieces.

Awk is another programmable tool, a small, specialized pattern-action language that focuses on selection and transformation of an input stream. As we saw in Chapter 3, Awk automatically reads input files and splits each line into fields called $1 through $NF, where NF is the number of fields on the line. By providing default behavior for many common tasks, it makes useful one-line programs possible. For example, this complete Awk program,

```
# split.awk: split input into one word per line
{ for (i = 1; i <= NF; i++) print $i }
```

prints the "words" of each input line one word per line. To go in the other direction, here is an implementation of fmt, which fills each output line with words, up to at most 60 characters; a blank line causes a paragraph break.

```
# fmt.awk: format into 60-character lines
/./  { for (i = 1; i <= NF; i++) addword($i) } # nonblank line
/^$/ { printline(); print "" }                 # blank line
END  { printline() }

function addword(w) {
    if (length(line) + 1 + length(w) > 60)
        printline()
    if (length(line) == 0)
        line = w
    else
        line = line " " w
}
function printline() {
    if (length(line) > 0) {
        print line
        line = ""
    }
}
```

We often use fmt to re-paragraph mail messages and other short documents; we also use it to format the output of Chapter 3's Markov programs.

Programmable tools often originate in little languages designed for natural expression of solutions to problems within a narrow domain. One nice example is the Unix tool eqn, which typesets mathematical formulas. Its input language is close to what a mathematician might say when reading equations aloud: $\frac{\pi}{2}$ is written pi over 2.

TEX follows the same approach; its notation for this formula is \pi \over 2. If there is a natural or familiar notation for the problem you're solving, use it or adapt it; don't start from scratch.

Awk was inspired by a program that used regular expressions to identify anomalous data in telephone traffic records, but Awk includes variables, expressions, loops, and so on, to make it a real programming language. Perl and Tcl were designed from the beginning to combine the convenience and expressiveness of little languages with the power of big ones. They are true general-purpose languages, although they are most often used for processing text.

The generic term for such tools is *scripting languages* because they evolved from early command interpreters whose programmability was limited to executing canned ''scripts'' of programs. Scripting languages permit creative use of regular expressions, not only for pattern matching—recognizing that a particular pattern occurs—but also for identifying regions of text to be transformed. This occurs in the two regsub (regular expression substitution) commands in the following Tcl program. The program is a slight generalization of the program we showed in Chapter 4 that retrieves stock quotes; this one fetches the URL given by its first argument. The first substitution removes the string http:// if it is present; the second replaces the first / by a blank, thereby splitting the argument into two fields. The lindex command retrieves fields from a string (starting with index 0). Text enclosed in [] is executed as a Tcl command and replaced by the resulting text; $x is replaced by the value of the variable x.

```
# geturl.tcl: retrieve document from URL
# input has form [http://]abc.def.com[/whatever...]

regsub "http://" $argv "" argv     ;# remove http:// if present
regsub "/" $argv " " argv          ;# replace leading / with blank

set so [socket [lindex $argv 0] 80] ;# make network connection
set q "/[lindex $argv 1]"

puts $so "GET $q HTTP/1.0\n\n"      ;# send request
flush $so
while {[gets $so line] >= 0 && $line != ""} {} ;# skip header
puts [read $so]                    ;# read and print entire reply
```

This script typically produces voluminous output, much of which is HTML tags bracketed by < and >. Perl is good at text substitution, so our next tool is a Perl script that uses regular expressions and substitutions to discard the tags:

```
# unhtml.pl: delete HTML tags

while (<>) {              # collect all input into single string
    $str .= $_;          # by concatenating input lines
}

$str =~ s/<[^>]*>//g;    # delete <...>
$str =~ s/ / /g;    # replace   by blank
$str =~ s/\s+/\n/g;      # compress white space
print $str;
```

This example is cryptic if one does not speak Perl. The construction

```
$str =~ s/regexp/repl/g
```

substitutes the string `repl` for the text in `str` that matches (leftmost longest) the regular expression `regexp`; the trailing `g`, for "global," means to do so for all matches in the string rather than just the first. The metacharacter sequence \s is shorthand for a white space character (blank, tab, newline, and the like); \n is a newline. The string "` `" is an HTML character, like those in Chapter 2, that defines a non-breakable space character.

Putting all this together, here is a moronic but functional web browser, implemented as a one-line shell script:

```
# web: retrieve web page and format its text, ignoring HTML
geturl.tcl $1 | unhtml.pl | fmt.awk
```

This retrieves the web page, discards all the control and formatting information, and formats the text by its own rules. It's a fast way to grab a page of text from the web.

Notice the variety of languages we cascade together, each suited to a particular task: Tcl, Perl, Awk and, within each of those, regular expressions. The power of notation comes from having a good one for each problem. Tcl is particularly good for grabbing text over the network; Perl and Awk are good at editing and formatting text; and of course regular expressions are good at specifying pieces of text for searching and modifying. These languages together are more powerful than any one of them in isolation. It's worth breaking the job into pieces if it enables you to profit from the right notation.

9.4 Interpreters, Compilers, and Virtual Machines

How does a program get from its source-code form into execution? If the language is simple enough, as in `printf` or our simplest regular expressions, we can execute straight from the source. This is easy and has very fast startup.

There is a tradeoff between setup time and execution speed. If the language is more complicated, it is generally desirable to convert the source code into a convenient and efficient internal representation for execution. It takes some time to process the source originally but this is repaid in faster execution. Programs that combine the conversion and execution into a single program that reads the source text, converts it, and runs it are called *interpreters*. Awk and Perl interpret, as do many other scripting and special-purpose languages.

A third possibility is to generate instructions for the specific kind of computer the program is meant to run on, as compilers do. This requires the most up-front effort and time but yields the fastest subsequent execution.

Other combinations exist. One that we will study in this section is compiling a program into instructions for a made-up computer (a *virtual machine*) that can be simulated on any real computer. A virtual machine combines many of the advantages of conventional interpretation and compilation.

If a language is simple, it doesn't take much processing to infer the program structure and convert it to an internal form. If, however, the language has some complexity—declarations, nested structures, recursively-defined statements or expressions, operators with precedence, and the like—it is more complicated to parse the input to determine the structure.

Parsers are often written with the aid of an automatic parser generator, also called a compiler-compiler, such as yacc or bison. Such programs translate a description of the language, called its *grammar*, into (typically) a C or C++ program that, once compiled, will translate statements in the language into an internal representation. Of course, generating a parser directly from a grammar is another demonstration of the power of good notation.

The representation produced by a parser is usually a tree, with internal nodes containing operators and leaves containing operands. A statement such as

```
a = max(b, c/2);
```

might produce this parse (or syntax) tree:

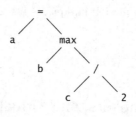

Many of the tree algorithms described in Chapter 2 can be used to build and process parse trees.

Once the tree is built, there are a variety of ways to proceed. The most direct, used in Awk, is to walk the tree directly, evaluating the nodes as we go. A simplified version of such an evaluation routine for an integer-based expression language might involve a post-order traversal like this:

```
typedef struct Symbol Symbol;
typedef struct Tree Tree;

struct Symbol {
    int     value;
    char    *name;
};
```

```
struct Tree {
    int     op;          /* operation code */
    int     value;       /* value if number */
    Symbol  *symbol;     /* Symbol entry if variable */
    Tree    *left;
    Tree    *right;
};

/* eval: version 1: evaluate tree expression */
int eval(Tree *t)
{
    int left, right;

    switch (t->op) {
    case NUMBER:
        return t->value;
    case VARIABLE:
        return t->symbol->value;
    case ADD:
        return eval(t->left) + eval(t->right);
    case DIVIDE:
        left = eval(t->left);
        right = eval(t->right);
        if (right == 0)
            eprintf("divide %d by zero", left);
        return left / right;
    case MAX:
        left = eval(t->left);
        right = eval(t->right);
        return left>right ? left : right;
    case ASSIGN:
        t->left->symbol->value = eval(t->right);
        return t->left->symbol->value;
    /* ... */
    }
}
```

The first few cases evaluate simple expressions like constants and values; later ones evaluate arithmetic expressions, and others might do special processing, conditionals, and loops. To implement control structures, the tree will need extra information, not shown here, that represents the control flow.

As in pack and unpack, we can replace the explicit switch with a table of function pointers. Individual operators are much the same as in the switch statement:

```
/* addop: return sum of two tree expressions */
int addop(Tree *t)
{
    return eval(t->left) + eval(t->right);
}
```

The table of function pointers relates operators to the functions that perform the operations:

```
enum {  /* operation codes, Tree.op */
    NUMBER,
    VARIABLE,
    ADD,
    DIVIDE,
    /* ... */
};

/* optab: operator function table */
int (*optab[])(Tree *) = {
    pushop,       /* NUMBER */
    pushsymop,    /* VARIABLE */
    addop,        /* ADD */
    divop,        /* DIVIDE */
    /* ... */
};
```

Evaluation uses the operator to index into the table of function pointers to call the right functions; this version will invoke other functions recursively.

```
/* eval: version 2: evaluate tree from operator table */
int eval(Tree *t)
{
    return (*optab[t->op])(t);
}
```

Both these versions of eval are recursive. There are ways of eliminating recursion, including a clever technique called *threaded code* that flattens the call stack completely. The neatest method is to do away with the recursion altogether by storing the functions in an array that is then traversed sequentially to execute the program. This array becomes a sequence of instructions to be executed by a little special-purpose machine.

We still need a stack to represent the partially evaluated values in the computation, so the form of the functions changes, but the transformation is easy to see. In effect, we invent a *stack machine* in which the instructions are tiny functions and the operands are stored on a separate operand stack. It's not a real machine but we can program it as if it were, and we can implement it easily as an interpreter.

Instead of walking the tree to evaluate it, we walk it to generate the array of functions to execute the program. The array will also contain data values that the instructions use, such as constants and variables (symbols), so the type of the elements of the array should be a union:

```
typedef union Code Code;
union Code {
    void    (*op)(void); /* function if operator */
    int     value;       /* value if number */
    Symbol  *symbol;     /* Symbol entry if variable */
};
```

Here is the routine to generate the function pointers and place them in an array, code, of these items. The return value of generate is not the value of the expression—that will be computed when the generated code is executed—but the index in code of the next operation to be generated:

```
/* generate: generate instructions by walking tree */
int generate(int codep, Tree *t)
{
    switch (t->op) {
    case NUMBER:
        code[codep++].op = pushop;
        code[codep++].value = t->value;
        return codep;
    case VARIABLE:
        code[codep++].op = pushsymop;
        code[codep++].symbol = t->symbol;
        return codep;
    case ADD:
        codep = generate(codep, t->left);
        codep = generate(codep, t->right);
        code[codep++].op = addop;
        return codep;
    case DIVIDE:
        codep = generate(codep, t->left);
        codep = generate(codep, t->right);
        code[codep++].op = divop;
        return codep;
    case MAX:
        /* ... */
    }
}
```

For the statement a = max(b, c/2) the generated code would look like this:

```
pushsymop
b
pushsymop
c
pushop
2
divop
maxop
storesymop
a
```

The operator functions manipulate the stack, popping operands and pushing results.

The interpreter is a loop that walks a program counter along the array of function pointers:

```
Code code[NCODE];
int stack[NSTACK];
int stackp;
int pc; /* program counter */

/* eval: version 3: evaluate expression from generated code */
int eval(Tree *t)
{
    pc = generate(0, t);
    code[pc].op = NULL;

    stackp = 0;
    pc = 0;
    while (code[pc].op != NULL)
        (*code[pc++].op)();
    return stack[0];
}
```

This loop simulates in software on our invented stack machine what happens in hardware on a real machine. Here are a couple of representative operators:

```
/* pushop: push number; value is next word in code stream */
void pushop(void)
{
    stack[stackp++] = code[pc++].value;
}

/* divop: compute ratio of two expressions */
void divop(void)
{
    int left, right;

    right = stack[--stackp];
    left = stack[--stackp];
    if (right == 0)
        eprintf("divide %d by zero\n", left);
    stack[stackp++] = left / right;
}
```

Notice that the check for zero divisors appears in divop, not generate.

Conditional execution, branches, and loops operate by modifying the program counter within an operator function, performing a branch to a different point in the array of functions. For example a goto operator always sets the value of the pc variable, while a conditional branch sets pc only if the condition is true.

The code array is internal to the interpreter, of course, but imagine we wanted to save the generated program in a file. If we wrote out the function addresses, the result would be unportable and fragile. But we could instead write out constants that represented the functions, say 1000 for addop, 1001 for pushop, and so on, and translate these back into the function pointers when we read the program in for interpretation.

If we examine a file this procedure produces, it looks like an instruction stream for a virtual machine whose instructions implement the basic operators of our little language, and the `generate` function is really a compiler that translates the language into the virtual machine. Virtual machines are a lovely old idea, recently made fashionable again by Java and the Java Virtual Machine (JVM); they give an easy way to produce portable, efficient representations of programs written in a high-level language.

9.5 Programs that Write Programs

Perhaps the most remarkable thing about the `generate` function is that it is a program that writes a program: its output is an executable instruction stream for another (virtual) machine. Compilers do this all the time, translating source code into machine instructions, so the idea is certainly familiar. In fact, programs that write programs appear in many forms.

One common example is the dynamic generation of HTML for web pages. HTML is a language, however limited, and it can contain JavaScript code as well. Web pages are often generated on the fly by Perl or C programs, with specific contents (for example, search results and targeted advertising) determined by incoming requests. We used specialized languages for the graphs, pictures, tables, mathematical expressions, and index in this book. As another example, PostScript is a programming language that is generated by word processors, drawing programs, and a variety of other sources; at the final stage of processing, this whole book is represented as a 57,000 line PostScript program.

A document is a static program, but the idea of using a programming language as notation for any problem domain is extremely powerful. Many years ago, programmers dreamt of having computers write all their programs for them. That will probably never be more than a dream, but today computers routinely write programs for us, often to represent things we would not previously have considered programs at all.

The most common program-writing program is a compiler that translates high-level language into machine code. It's often useful, though, to translate code *into* a mainstream programming language. In the previous section, we mentioned that parser generators convert a definition of a language's grammar into a C program that parses the language. C is often used in this way, as a kind of "high level assembly language." Modula-3 and C++ are among the general-purpose languages whose first compilers created C code, which was then compiled by a standard C compiler. The approach has several advantages, including efficiency—because programs can in principle run as fast as C programs—and portability—because compilers can be carried to any system that has a C compiler. This greatly helped the early spread of these languages.

As another example, Visual Basic's graphical interface generates a set of Visual Basic assignment statements to initialize objects that the user has selected from menus and positioned on the screen with a mouse. A variety of other languages have "visual" development systems and "wizards" that synthesize user-interface code out of mouse clicks.

In spite of the power of program generators, and in spite of the existence of many good examples, the notion is not appreciated as much as it should be and is infrequently used by individual programmers. But there are plenty of small-scale opportunities for creating code by a program, so that you can get some of the advantages for yourself. Here are several examples that generate C or C++ code.

The Plan 9 operating system generates error messages from a header file that contains names and comments; the comments are converted mechanically into quoted strings in an array that can be indexed by the enumerated value. This fragment shows the structure of the header file:

```
/* errors.h: standard error messages */

enum {
    Eperm,      /* Permission denied */
    Eio,        /* I/O error */
    Efile,      /* File does not exist */
    Emem,       /* Memory limit reached */
    Espace,     /* Out of file space */
    Egreg       /* It's all Greg's fault */
};
```

Given this input, a simple program can produce the following set of declarations for the error messages:

```
/* machine-generated; do not edit. */

char *errs[] = {
    "Permission denied", /* Eperm */
    "I/O error", /* Eio */
    "File does not exist", /* Efile */
    "Memory limit reached", /* Emem */
    "Out of file space", /* Espace */
    "It's all Greg's fault", /* Egreg */
};
```

There are a couple of benefits to this approach. First, the relationship between the enum values and the strings they represent is literally self-documenting and easy to make natural-language independent. Also, the information appears only once, a "single point of truth" from which other code is generated, so there is only one place to keep information up to date. If instead there are multiple places, it is inevitable that they will get out of sync sometime. Finally, it's easy to arrange that the .c file will be recreated and recompiled whenever the header file is changed. When an error message must be changed, all that is needed is to modify the header file and compile the operating system. The messages are automatically updated.

The generator program can be written in any language. A string processing language like Perl makes it easy:

```
# enum.pl: generate error strings from enum+comments
print "/* machine-generated; do not edit. */\n\n";
print "char *errs[] = {\n";
while (<>) {
    chop;                            # remove newline
    if (/^\s*(E[a-z0-9]+),?/) {      # first word is E...
        $name = $1;                  # save name
        s/.*\/\* *//;                # remove up to /*
        s/ *\*\///;                  # remove */
        print "\t\"$_\", /* $name */\n";
    }
}
print "};\n";
```

Regular expressions are in action again. Lines whose first fields look like identifiers followed by a comma are selected. The first substitution deletes everything up to the first non-blank character of the comment, while the second removes the comment terminator and any blanks that precede it.

As part of a compiler-testing effort, Andy Koenig developed a convenient way to write C++ code to check that the compiler caught program errors. Code fragments that should cause a compiler diagnostic are decorated with magic comments to describe the expected messages. Each line has a comment that begins with /// (to distinguish it from ordinary comments) and a regular expression that matches the diagnostics from that line. Thus, for example, the following two code fragments should generate diagnostics:

```
int f() {}
    /// warning.* non-void function .* should return a value

void g() {return 1;}
    /// error.* void function may not return a value
```

If we run the second test through our C++ compiler, it prints the expected message, which matches the regular expression:

```
% CC x.c
"x.c", line 1: error(321): void function may not return a value
```

Each such code fragment is given to the compiler, and the output is compared against the expected diagnostics, a process that is managed by a combination of shell and Awk programs. Failures indicate a test where the compiler output differed from what was expected. Because the comments are regular expressions there is some latitude in the output; they can be made more or less forgiving, depending on what is needed.

The idea of comments with semantics is not new. They appear in PostScript, where regular comments begin with %. Comments that begin with %% by convention may carry extra information about page numbers, bounding boxes, font names, and the like:

```
%%PageBoundingBox: 126 307 492 768
%%Pages: 14
%%DocumentFonts: Helvetica Times-Italic Times-Roman
              LucidaSans-Typewriter
```

In Java, comments that begin with /** and end with */ are used to create documentation for the class definition that follows. The large-scale version of self-documenting code is *literate programming*, which integrates a program and its documentation so one process prints it in a natural order for reading, and another arranges it in the right order for compilation.

In all of the examples above, it is important to observe the role of notation, the mixture of languages, and the use of tools. The combination magnifies the power of the individual components.

Exercise 9-15. One of the old chestnuts of computing is to write a program that when executed will reproduce itself exactly, in source form. This is a neat special case of a program that writes a program. Give it a try in some of your favorite languages. □

9.6 Using Macros to Generate Code

Descending a couple of levels, it's possible to have macros write code at compile time. Throughout this book, we've cautioned against using macros and conditional compilation; they encourage a style of programming that is full of problems. But they do have their place; sometimes textual substitution is exactly the right answer to a problem. One example is using the C/C++ macro preprocessor to assemble pieces of a stylized, repetitive program.

For instance, the program that estimated the speed of elementary language constructs for Chapter 7 uses the C preprocessor to assemble the tests by wrapping them in boilerplate code. The essence of the test is to encapsulate a code fragment in a loop that starts a timer, runs the fragment many times, stops the timer, and reports the results. All of the repeated code is captured in a couple of macros, and the code to be timed is passed in as an argument. The primary macro takes this form:

```
#define LOOP(CODE) {                              \
    t0 = clock();                                 \
    for (i = 0; i < n; i++) { CODE; }             \
    printf("%7d ", clock() - t0);                 \
}
```

The backslashes allow the macro body to span multiple lines. This macro is used in "statements" that typically look like this:

```
LOOP(f1 = f2)
LOOP(f1 = f2 + f3)
LOOP(f1 = f2 - f3)
```

There are sometimes other statements for initialization, but the basic timing part is represented in these single-argument fragments that expand to a significant amount of code.

Macro processing can be used to generate production code, too. Bart Locanthi once wrote an efficient version of a two-dimensional graphics operator. The operator, called `bitblt` or `rasterop`, is hard to make fast because there are many arguments that combine in complicated ways. Through careful case analysis, Locanthi reduced the combinations to individual loops that could be separately optimized. Each case was then constructed by macro substitution, analogous to the performance-testing example, with all the variants laid out in a single big switch statement. The original source code was a few hundred lines; the result of macro processing was several thousand. The macro-expanded code was not optimal but, considering the difficulty of the problem, it was practical and very easy to produce. Also, as high-performance code goes, it was relatively portable.

Exercise 9-16. Exercise 7-7 involved writing a program to measure the cost of various operations in C++. Use the ideas of this section to create another version of the program. □

Exercise 9-17. Exercise 7-8 involved doing a cost model for Java, which has no macro capability. Solve the problem by writing another program, in whatever language (or languages) you choose, that writes the Java version and automates the timing runs. □

9.7 Compiling on the Fly

In the previous section, we talked about programs that write programs. In each of the examples, the generated program was in source form; it still needed to be compiled or interpreted to run. But it is possible to generate code that is ready to run immediately by producing machine instructions rather than source. This is known as compiling "on the fly" or "just in time"; the first term is older but the latter, including its acronym, JIT, is more popular.

Although compiled code is necessarily non-portable—it will run only on a single type of processor—it can be extremely fast. Consider the expression

```
max(b, c/2)
```

The calculation must evaluate c, divide it by two, compare the result to b, and choose the larger. If we evaluate the expression using the virtual machine we sketched earlier in the chapter, we could eliminate the check for division by zero in `divop`. Since 2 is never zero, the check is pointless. But given any of the designs we laid out for implementing the virtual machine, there is no way to eliminate the check; every implementation of the divide operation compares the divisor to zero.

This is where generating code dynamically can help. If we build the code for the expression directly, rather than just by stringing out predefined operations, we can avoid the zero-divide check for divisors that are known to be non-zero. In fact, we can go even further; if the entire expression is constant, such as max(3*3, 4/2), we can evaluate it once when we generate the code, and replace it by the constant value 9. If the expression appears in a loop, we save time each trip around the loop, and if the loop runs enough times, we will win back the overhead it took to study the expression and generate code for it.

The key idea is that the notation gives us a general way to express a problem, but the compiler for the notation can customize the code for the details of the specific calculation. For example, in a virtual machine for regular expressions, we would likely have an operator to match a literal character:

```
int matchchar(int literal, char *text)
{
    return *text == literal;
}
```

When we generate code for a particular pattern, however, the value of a given literal is fixed, say 'x', so we could instead use an operator like this:

```
int matchx(char *text)
{
    return *text == 'x';
}
```

And then, rather than predefining a special operator for each literal character value, we make things simpler by generating the code for the operators we really need for the current expression. Generalizing the idea for the full set of operations, we can write an on-the-fly compiler that translates the current regular expression into special code optimized for that expression.

Ken Thompson did exactly this for an implementation of regular expressions on the IBM 7094 in 1967. His version generated little blocks of binary 7094 instructions for the various operations in the expression, threaded them together, and then ran the resulting program by calling it, just like a regular function. Similar techniques can be applied to creating specific instruction sequences for screen updates in graphics systems, where there are so many special cases that it is more efficient to create dynamic code for each one that arises than to write them all out ahead of time or to include conditional tests in more general code.

To demonstrate what is involved in building a real on-the-fly compiler would take us much too far into the details of a particular instruction set, but it is worth spending some time to show how such a system works. The rest of this section should be read for ideas and insight but not for implementation details.

Recall that we left our virtual machine with a structure like this:

```
Code code[NCODE];
int stack[NSTACK];
int stackp;
int pc; /* program counter */
    ...
    Tree *t;

    t = parse();
    pc = generate(0, t);
    code[pc].op = NULL;

    stackp = 0;
    pc = 0;
    while (code[pc].op != NULL)
        (*code[pc++].op)();
    return stack[0];
```

To adapt this code to on-the-fly compilation, we must make some changes. First, the code array is no longer an array of function pointers, but an array of executable instructions. Whether the instructions will be of type char, int, or long will depend on the processor we're compiling for; we'll assume int. After the code is generated, we call it as a function. There will be no virtual program counter because the processor's own execution cycle will walk along the code for us; once the calculation is done, it will return, like a regular function. Also, we can choose to maintain a separate operand stack for the machine or use the processor's own stack. Each approach has advantages, but we've chosen to stick with a separate stack and concentrate on the details of the code itself. The implementation now looks like this:

```
typedef int Code;
Code code[NCODE];
int codep;
int stack[NSTACK];
int stackp;
    ...
    Tree *t;
    void (*fn)(void);
    int pc;

    t = parse();
    pc = generate(0, t);
    genreturn(pc);          /* generate function return sequence */
    stackp = 0;
    flushcaches();          /* synchronize memory with processor */
    fn = (void(*)(void)) code;  /* cast array to ptr to func */
    (*fn)();                /* call function */
    return stack[0];
```

After generate finishes, genreturn lays down the instructions that make the generated code return control to eval.

The function flushcaches stands for the steps needed to prepare the processor for running freshly generated code. Modern machines run fast in part because they have caches for instructions and data, and internal *pipelines* that overlap the execution of many successive instructions. These caches and pipelines expect the instruction stream to be static; if we generate code just before execution, the processor can become confused. The CPU needs to drain its pipeline and flush its caches before it can execute newly generated instructions. These are highly machine-dependent operations; the implementation of flushcaches will be different on each particular type of computer.

The remarkable expression (void(*)(void)) code is a cast that converts the address of the array containing the generated instructions into a function pointer that can be used to call the code as a function.

Technically, it's not too hard to generate the code itself, though there is a fair amount of engineering to do so efficiently. We start with some building blocks. As before, a code array and an index into it are maintained during compilation. For simplicity, we'll make them both global, as we did earlier. Then we can write a function to lay down instructions:

```
/* emit: append instruction to code stream */
void emit(Code inst)
{
    code[codep++] = inst;
}
```

The instructions themselves can be defined by processor-dependent macros or tiny functions that assemble the instructions by filling in the fields of the instruction word. Hypothetically, we might have a function called popreg that generates code to pop a value off the stack and store it in a processor register, and another called pushreg that generates code to take the value stored in a register and push it onto the stack. Our revised addop function would use them like this, given some defined constants that describe the instructions (like ADDINST) and their layout (the various SHIFT positions that define the format):

```
/* addop: generate ADD instruction */
void addop(void)
{
    Code inst;

    popreg(2);        /* pop stack into register 2 */
    popreg(1);        /* pop stack into register 1 */
    inst = ADDINST << INSTSHIFT;
    inst |= (R1) << OP1SHIFT;
    inst |= (R2) << OP2SHIFT;
    emit(inst);       /* emit ADD R1, R2 */
    pushreg(2);       /* push val of register 2 onto stack */
}
```

This is only a starting point. If we were writing an on-the-fly compiler for real, we would employ optimizations. If we're adding a constant, we don't need to push the constant on the stack, pop it off, and add it; we can just add it directly. Similar thinking can eliminate more of the overhead. Even as written, however, addop will run much faster than the versions we wrote earlier because the various operators are not threaded together by function calls. Instead, the code to execute them is laid out in memory as a single block of instructions, with the real processor's program counter doing all the threading for us.

The generate function looks pretty much as it did for the virtual machine implementation. But this time, it lays out real machine instructions instead of pointers to predefined functions. And to generate efficient code, it should spend some effort looking for constants to eliminate and other optimizations.

Our whirlwind tour of code generation has shown only glimpses of some of the techniques used by real compilers and entirely missed many more. It has also sidestepped many of the issues raised by the complexities of modern CPUs. But it does illustrate how a program can analyze the description of a problem to produce special purpose code for solving it efficiently. You can use these ideas to write a blazing fast version of grep, to implement a little language of your own devising, to design and build a virtual machine optimized for special-purpose calculation, or even, with a little help, to write a compiler for an interesting language.

A regular expression is a long way from a C++ program, but both are just notations for solving problems. With the right notation, many problems become easier. And designing and implementing the notation can be a lot of fun.

Exercise 9-18. The on-the-fly compiler generates faster code if it can replace expressions that contain only constants, such as max(3*3, 4/2), by their value. Once it has recognized such an expression, how should it compute its value? □

Exercise 9-19. How would you test an on-the-fly compiler? □

Supplementary Reading

The Unix Programming Environment, by Brian Kernighan and Rob Pike (Prentice Hall, 1984), contains an extended discussion of the tool-based approach to computing that Unix supports so well. Chapter 8 of that book presents a complete implementation, from yacc grammar to executable code, of a simple programming language.

TEX: The Program, by Don Knuth (Addison-Wesley, 1986), describes a complex document formatter by presenting the entire program, about 13,000 lines of Pascal, in a "literate programming" style that combines explanation with program text and uses programs to format documentation and extract compilable code. *A Retargetable C Compiler: Design and Implementation* by Chris Fraser and David Hanson (Addison-Wesley, 1995) does the same for an ANSI C compiler.

The Java virtual machine is described in *The Java Virtual Machine Specification, 2nd Edition*, by Tim Lindholm and Frank Yellin (Addison-Wesley, 1999).

Ken Thompson's algorithm (one of the earliest software patents) was described in "Regular Expression Search Algorithm," *Communications of the ACM*, **11**, 6, pp. 419-422, 1968. Jeffrey E. F. Friedl's *Mastering Regular Expressions* (O'Reilly, 1997) is an extensive treatment of the subject.

An on-the-fly compiler for two-dimensional graphics operations is described in "Hardware/Software Tradeoffs for Bitmap Graphics on the Blit," by Rob Pike, Bart Locanthi, and John Reiser, *Software—Practice and Experience*, **15**, 2, pp. 131-152, February 1985.

Epilogue

If men could learn from history, what lessons it might teach us! But passion and party blind our eyes, and the light which experience gives is a lantern on the stern, which shines only on the waves behind us!

Samuel Taylor Coleridge, *Recollections*

The world of computing changes all the time, and the pace seems to accelerate. Programmers must cope with new languages, new tools, new systems, and of course incompatible changes to old ones. Programs are bigger, interfaces are more complicated, deadlines are shorter.

But there are some constants, some points of stability, where lessons and insight from the past can help with the future. The underlying themes in this book are based on these lasting concepts.

Simplicity and **clarity** are first and most important, since almost everything else follows from them. Do the simplest thing that works. Choose the simplest algorithm that is likely to be fast enough, and the simplest data structure that will do the job; combine them with clean, clear code. Don't complicate them unless performance measurements show that more engineering is necessary. Interfaces should be lean and spare, at least until there is compelling evidence that the benefits outweigh the added complexity.

Generality often goes hand in hand with simplicity, for it may make possible solving a problem once and for all rather than over and over again for individual cases. It is often the right approach to portability as well: find the single general solution that works on each system instead of magnifying the differences between systems.

Evolution comes next. It is not possible to create a perfect program the first time. The insight necessary to find the right solution comes only with a combination of thought and experience; pure introspection will not produce a good system, nor will pure hacking. Reactions from users count heavily here; a cycle of prototyping, experiment, user feedback, and further refinement is most effective. Programs we build for

247

ourselves often do not evolve enough; big programs that we buy from others change too fast without necessarily improving.

Interfaces are a large part of the battle in programming, and interface issues appear in many places. Libraries present the most obvious cases, but there are also interfaces between programs and between users and programs. The desire for simplicity and generality applies especially strongly to the design of interfaces. Make interfaces consistent and easy to learn and use; adhere to them scrupulously. Abstraction is an effective technique: imagine a perfect component or library or program; make the interface match that ideal as closely as possible; hide implementation details behind the boundary, out of harm's way.

Automation is under-appreciated. It is much more effective to have a computer do your work than to do it by hand. We saw examples in testing, in debugging, in performance analysis, and notably in writing code, where for the right problem domain, programs can create programs that would be hard for people to write.

Notation is also under-appreciated, and not only as the way that programmers tell computers what to do. It provides an organizing framework for implementing a wide range of tools and also guides the structure of the programs that write programs. We are all comfortable in the large general-purpose languages that serve for the bulk of our programming. But as tasks become so focused and well understood that programming them feels almost mechanical, it may be time to create a notation that naturally expresses the tasks and a language that implements it. Regular expressions are one of our favorite examples, but there are countless opportunities to create little languages for specialized applications. They do not have to be sophisticated to reap benefits.

As individual programmers, it's easy to feel like small cogs in a big machine, using languages and systems and tools imposed upon us, doing tasks that should be done for us. But in the long run, what counts is how well we work with what we have. By applying some of the ideas in this book, you should find that your code is easier to work with, your debugging sessions are less painful, and your programming is more confident. We hope that this book has given you something that will make your computing more productive and more rewarding.

Appendix: Collected Rules

Each truth that I discovered became a rule that served me afterwards in the discovery of others.

René Descartes, *Le Discours de la Méthode*

Several chapters contain rules or guidelines that summarize a discussion. The rules are collected here for easy reference. Bear in mind that each was presented in a context that explains its purpose and applicability.

Style

Use descriptive names for globals, short names for locals.
Be consistent.
Use active names for functions.
Be accurate.
Indent to show structure.
Use the natural form for expressions.
Parenthesize to resolve ambiguity.
Break up complex expressions.
Be clear.
Be careful with side effects.
Use a consistent indentation and brace style.
Use idioms for consistency.
Use else-ifs for multi-way decisions.
Avoid function macros.
Parenthesize the macro body and arguments.
Give names to magic numbers.
Define numbers as constants, not macros.
Use character constants, not integers.
Use the language to calculate the size of an object.
Don't belabor the obvious.

Comment functions and global data.
Don't comment bad code, rewrite it.
Don't contradict the code.
Clarify, don't confuse.

Interfaces

Hide implementation details.
Choose a small orthogonal set of primitives.
Don't reach behind the user's back.
Do the same thing the same way everywhere.
Free a resource in the same layer that allocated it.
Detect errors at a low level, handle them at a high level.
Use exceptions only for exceptional situations.

Debugging

Look for familiar patterns.
Examine the most recent change.
Don't make the same mistake twice.
Debug it now, not later.
Get a stack trace.
Read before typing.
Explain your code to someone else.
Make the bug reproducible.
Divide and conquer.
Study the numerology of failures.
Display output to localize your search.
Write self-checking code.
Write a log file.
Draw a picture.
Use tools.
Keep records.

Testing

Test code at its boundaries.
Test pre- and post-conditions.
Use assertions.
Program defensively.
Check error returns.
Test incrementally.
Test simple parts first.
Know what output to expect.
Verify conservation properties.
Compare independent implementations.

Measure test coverage.
Automate regression testing.
Create self-contained tests.

Performance

Automate timing measurements.
Use a profiler.
Concentrate on the hot spots.
Draw a picture.
Use a better algorithm or data structure.
Enable compiler optimizations.
Tune the code.
Don't optimize what doesn't matter.
Collect common subexpressions.
Replace expensive operations by cheap ones.
Unroll or eliminate loops.
Cache frequently-used values.
Write a special-purpose allocator.
Buffer input and output.
Handle special cases separately.
Precompute results.
Use approximate values.
Rewrite in a lower-level language.
Save space by using the smallest possible data type.
Don't store what you can easily recompute.

Portability

Stick to the standard.
Program in the mainstream.
Beware of language trouble spots.
Try several compilers.
Use standard libraries.
Use only features available everywhere.
Avoid conditional compilation.
Localize system dependencies in separate files.
Hide system dependencies behind interfaces.
Use text for data exchange.
Use a fixed byte order for data exchange.
Change the name if you change the specification.
Maintain compatibility with existing programs and data.
Don't assume ASCII.
Don't assume English.

Index

Woman: Is my Aunt Minnie in here?

Driftwood: Well, you can come in and prowl around if you want to. If she isn't in here, you can probably find somebody just as good.

The Marx Brothers, *A Night at the Opera*

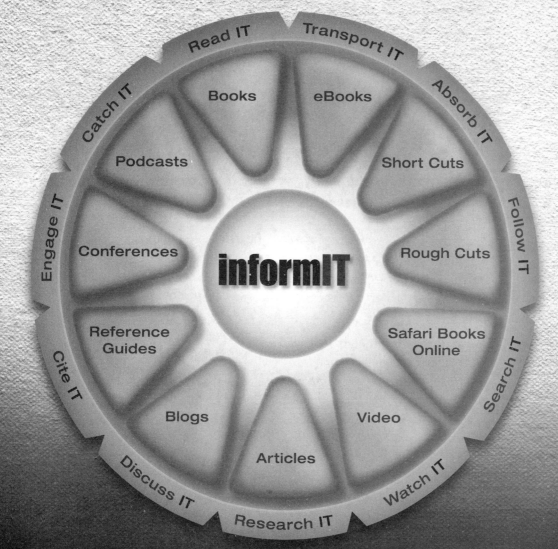